VICE CAPADES

VICE

CAPADES

Sex, Drugs, and Bowling from
the Pilgrims to the Present

Mark Stein

Potomac Books

An imprint of the University of Nebraska Press

∞

Library of Congress Cataloging-in-Publication Data
Names: Stein, Mark, 1951-, author.
Title: Vice capades: sex, drugs, and bowling from the
pilgrims to the present / Mark Stein.
Description: Lincoln: Potomac Books, 2017. | Includes
bibliographical references and index.
Identifiers: LCCN 2016049880
ISBN 9781612348940 (hardback: alk. paper)
ISBN 9781612349275 (epub)
ISBN 9781612349282 (mobi)
ISBN 9781612349299 (pdf)
Subjects: LCSH: Vice—United States. | BISAC: HISTORY
/ United States / General. | PHILOSOPHY / Ethics &
Moral Philosophy. | POLITICAL SCIENCE / Public Pol-
icy / Cultural Policy.
Classification: LCC BJ1534 .S74 2017 | DDC
379/.80973—dc23
LC record available at https://lccn.loc
.gov/2016049880

Set in Lyon Text by John Klopping.

Contents

Illustrations

Acknowledgments

For providing information and insights into aspects of vice, I am indebted to and wish to thank Daniel Aherne; Eğlence Atasever-Arda, MD; Debra Bruno; Christopher Ehrman; Marian Fox; Daniel L. Goldberg; Tom Jabine; Nancy Lisagore; Prof. Marianne Noble; Roberta Redfern; Amy Ujiji Swift; and Debby Vivari.

Any viewpoint or image in this book does not necessarily reflect the views of the Department of Health and Human Services (HHS) and/or the Centers for Disease Control (CDC), nor imply an endorsement by HHS and/or the CDC of any particular organization or product. If that sounds like I'm reciting something I was told to say, it's because I am—but am happily doing so, as data and publications provided to the public by the CDC were of invaluable help in writing this book.

I particularly want to thank my editor, Tom Swanson (assisted by Emily Wendell); my wonderfully sharp-eyed copyeditor Mary M. Hill; and the entire team at the University of Nebraska Press for all their work and for, each of them, truly being a joy to work with.

In the category of Above and Beyond, my agent, Alec Shane, performed exceptional obstetrical service in bringing this book into the world. Emerging from his comments, questions, and thought-provoking wisecracks in our talks and emails, the view in this book took shape regarding why views of vice vary among people and why they often change over time.

Also in the realm of Above and Beyond, I am indebted to Arlene Balkansky at the Library of Congress Serial and Government Publications Division for helping me obtain the public domain illustrations in this book from the extraordinary collections of the Library of Congress and from its Chronicling America database. I am also grateful to her for information, in the form of stern warnings, regarding copyright intricacies of digitized images and something called posthumous rights of noncopyright holders. And I am grateful to her for marrying me thirty-nine years ago.

VICE CAPADES

Introduction

Americans have a love-hate relationship with vice. We indulge in it while combating it, often by enacting laws that, just as often, we later unenact—or double down by increasing their penalties. Plus, over the span of American history, that which we view as punishable vice has changed—sometimes slowly, sometimes rapidly (as seen recently with views of those who are lesbian, gay, bisexual, transgender, or what is sometimes referred to as queer or questioning). Indeed, a number of views of vice have changed not only in the span of history but also sometimes within our individual lives.

But what caused these views to change?

Also, of course, our views differ. But there, too, what's behind those differences? Be it sex, drugs, violence, gambling, dancing, shuffleboard, juggling . . . Yes, once upon a time in America, shuffleboard and juggling were punishable vices. What's the deal with what we view as punishable vice?

Let's take some quick peeks at what, over the past two thousand years or so, people considered to be vice, keeping an eye out for a common denominator that can and (no surprise to say) will be explored more closely in this book regarding punishable vices in American history.

Aristotle said vice consisted of those acts that lead to infamy. For instance, we view the Marlboro Man as infamous, that cigarette-smoking modern cowboy who, for over twenty years, was the television and print advertising symbol for Marlboro cigarettes. Except he was not viewed as infamous during those years—quite the contrary: many people smoked cigarettes in emulation of his allure. Aristotle also said vice included that which appears to be "base." In the nineteenth century, many Americans considered Mormon leader

Brigham Young base for having fifty-five wives—but his wives did not consider him base. Or did they? We know of one who expressed her reverence for him in her private writings and another who thought him so depraved she fled and expressed her disgust.[1]

Clearly, vice is in the eye of the beholder. The underlying question is: What's it doing there? Why, for instance, do many people view certain vices as punishable when engaged in on Sunday but not on the other days of the week? Selling alcohol tops this list. Why, however, did the list formerly include many more businesses prohibited from being open on Sundays? Why, at one time, were the federal penalties for marijuana equivalent to those of heroin, while lesser penalties were stipulated for cocaine? Why is whistling at women now something that might get you fired when previously it was widely acceptable? Clearly, these views were then, as now, serving the powers-that-be, which, though sinister sounding, are not necessarily nefarious. Just as clearly, those included among those sources of power have shifted.

But what about Rock Hudson? This movie star from the 1950s and 1960s—who was gay, albeit secretly—stated in 1962 that the Motion Picture Production Code should never have been changed in regard to homosexuality. "It's all right to let the bars down for a man like [director] William Wyler," he told Hollywood columnist Hedda Hopper. "When he does a touchy subject, you know it will be done with great taste. But it leaves the way open for the boys who want to make a quick buck by turning out dirty pictures."[2] Did Rock Hudson consider his own sexuality a vice? Or might he have been expressing such views to hide it? Suppose we ask it this way: What power was he seeking to maintain through this view of vice? The power that accompanies stardom, I suspect. And if so, suppose we ask: What group(s) in 1962 had the power to bestow stardom?

Groups and power also figure into the director Hudson mentioned. William Wyler's much-lauded films included *Mrs. Miniver* (1942), *The Best Years of Our Lives* (1946), *Ben-Hur* (1959), and, the year before Hudson's remark, *The Children's Hour*, based on Lillian Hellman's play by the same name, which depicted the shattering impact of a rumor that two teachers were lesbians. In fact, Wyler directed *two* films based on this 1934 Broadway play. The first, released in 1936, changed the title to *These Three* and changed the rumor to being one of the teachers having slept with the other's fiancé. In the 1930s, references to a long-term, monogamous, same-sex relationship were evidently viewed as acceptable to the groups that predominated in a Broadway audience but not to the groups that predominated in a movie audience. Yet those very same references were acceptable in movies by the 1960s, which Hollywood recognized (to Rock's consternation) by altering that aspect of its Motion Picture Production Code.

Which brings us back to Aristotle, who addressed vice in entertainment. He emphasized that, in comedy, vice is depicted for laughs, and, he noted, that's a good use of vice in entertainment, since it ridicules vice. In tragedy, he pointed out, vice is not presented for laughs but as the cause of our concern, and we witness the damage it does. Also a good thing to do, said he. And said the Motion Picture Production Code for many years by prohibiting films in which crime or vice was not punished.

But not everyone is sure of all that today. Regarding both unpunished violence in entertainment and cartoon violence, one of its most outspoken opponents is herself a cartoon, Marge Simpson, from the longest-running television series, *The Simpsons*. In one episode, Marge crusaded against the graphic violence in *The Itchy and Scratchy Show*, a cat-and-mouse cartoon show her children, Bart and Lisa, frequently watch. Stepping out of Marge's TV world and into our own, we find that many Americans agree with Marge that cartoon violence is a vice. In 1991 a fourteen-year-old viewer wrote a letter to the editor of the *New York Times* complaining about an episode of *The Simpsons* in which "Maggie, the baby, seeing a mouse hit a cat over the head with a mallet . . . then hit Homer Simpson, the father, over the head with a mallet."[3]

Setting aside for the moment this idea of views of vice serving the interests of those who hold power, let's ask (as this book will continue to ask) a very important question: Does vice lead to crime? Or to put it more specifically for this instance: Do depictions of violence, even cartoon violence, engender violence? The same year that the fourteen-year-old girl wrote her letter to the *New York Times*, syndicated columnist Ray Richmond told readers,

> You probably haven't heard the story of a certain vile individual in New York City who actually put a lit firecracker inside the mouth of a kitten and blew up the poor animal. We bring this up on the TV page because at least one woman is convinced that this horrendous, unfathomable act was perpetrated by someone imitating the actions of Itchy and Scratchy, the cat and mouse cartoon characters on "The Simpsons." . . . Their actions inspired the viewer to charge in her letter to WNYW-TV . . . that Itchy and Scratchy send a dangerous message of violence.[4]

Maybe that viewer was overreacting to an isolated psycho. On the other hand, Chicago's highly respected reviewer Richard Christiansen wrote in 1993, "Sociological and psychological studies are demonstrating with regularity that youngsters are indeed influenced by the violence they see in so-called television programming, a disturbing condition that is treated satirically in 'The Simpsons,' where cartoon kiddies, Bart and Lisa Simpson, sit entranced in front of the TV set while they watch the bloody cartoons of 'The Itchy and Scratchy Show.' What to do? What to do? The issue has perplexed many a lawmaker, including Sen. Paul Simon (D-IL), a man of conscience, who has suggested setting up an industry monitoring panel."[5]

What to do indeed. Combating vice has long proven to be akin to playing Whac-A-Mole, the arcade game in which one tries to bop unsightly fuzzy-wuzzies that keep popping up. Often adding to the difficulty has been getting others to agree on what should be bopped. Supreme Court Justice Potter Stewart spoke directly to this Whac-A-Mole element when he wrote in a 1964 ruling, "Recently this Court put its hand to the task of defining 'obscenity' in *Roth v. United States* . . . . Yet obscenity cases continue to come to this Court." Bottom line, Justice Stewart stated, he would not try to define the vice of obscenity. He simply concluded, "I know it when I see it."[6]

The same can be said in regard to all vice. We all sense it, we all know it when we see it—but what is it that we see? And why doesn't everyone see it the same way? Think about power and think about this: In 1929 a jury convicted Mary Ware Dennett of sending obscene material through the mail. The dirty book, titled *Sex Side of Life, or Advice to the Young,* contained information and illustrations on the human reproductive system.[7] Mary Ware Dennett was a prominent women's rights advocate and did not view her book as vice.

Or think about power and think about this: In 1775 lawyer William Kendrick lamented, "The licentiousness of married women of the present day . . . [threatens] dreadful consequences to society." What particularly bugged him was female adultery, which, he declared, "distinguishes the present from any former era."[8] Hard to believe there were more moms on the make in the late 1700s than ever before, but equally intriguing is what Kendrick didn't say. Adultery by men went unmentioned, let alone condemned. Perhaps it wasn't even on their radar in 1775—or maybe just not on the printed page. After all, would you want to explain condemning married men diddling around to nobles and kings whose mistresses were legion? As we shall see, moral reformers have often opted to zip their lips rather than some- one else's pants. The key question is: Whose pants get zipped by law?

Regarding the power of what's behind those zippers, until the late twentieth century, spanking one's wife was not viewed as punishable vice—if, indeed, as vice at all. As authoritative (arguably, perhaps) as Supreme Court Justice Stewart, this nation's preeminent television attorney, Perry Mason, stood by silently in one 1961 episode in which a beautiful young wife complained of her husband, "When the steak fell in the fire [at a barbecue they were hosting], he spanked me in front of everyone!" Unclear is whether her anger was more at being spanked (did she mean he actually plopped down in a lawn chair and threw her over his knee?) or at this happening in front of their guests. No one in the scene or at any point in the episode voiced criticism of this act by her husband. In fact, after the wife's exit, Mason, the hero of this popular, long-running show, referred to himself as the hus- band's "old friend." Stepping outside the TV screen again, inscriptions inside women's wedding rings from the eighteenth and nineteenth centuries often read, "I kiss the rod from thee and God."[9]

While these examples all suggest we've made progress, many Americans today would view as retrogressive a 2003 news report that former senator and presidential aspirant Rick Santorum "believes the state has the right to determine whether a husband and wife can use contraceptive devices."[10] Quoting Santorum, it continued, "'All of those things are antithetical to a healthy, stable, traditional family, and that's sort of where we are in today's world, unfortunately. It all comes from, I would argue, this right to privacy that doesn't exist, in my opinion, in the United States Constitution.'"

Rick Santorum and social conservatives are not alone in present-day efforts to combat what they consider vice. One contemporary website has voiced a concern shared by many Americans across the political spectrum: violence in video games. Distinguishing this form of violence in entertainment from that in movies and TV, the website notes, "In order to play and win, the player has to be the aggressor. Rather than watching violence, as he might do on television, he's committing the violent acts. . . . [T]his kind of active participation affects a person's thought patterns."[11]

This book does not seek to dismiss concern over vice. I confess to being influenced by the (not necessarily nefarious) powers-that-be in my life when I say I believe stable families are preferable to unstable families; violence is not good, even when necessary; and health is better than illness. This book does not seek to mock moral reformers. (Well, it may not *seek* to, but it does take quite a few swats at them.) It will also explore the fact that, despite the continued prevalence of substance abuse, hanky-panky, and violence in entertainment, there have been successes in combating vice. In 1965, for example (and we will see others), 42 percent of Americans smoked cigarettes; in 2011 the figure was 17 percent.

By stepping back far enough to survey America's war on vice from the beginnings of British settlement to the present, all those years and all those vices join to provide us with a view unlike any other. Not only does it bring into focus who held power when, but it also enables us to see shifts in power taking place by witnessing the widening and narrowing of gaps between laws against the various vices and adherence to those laws.

It also turns out that the focus achieved by viewing all those vices over all that time provides a view into each of us today.

1

Inheritance

In the 1606 charter for Virginia, the first of the thirteen British colonies that later became the United States, James I urged its settlers to "bring the Infidels and Savages living in those parts to human Civility."[1] For their part, Native Americans offered the newcomers tobacco. And America's tail-chasing war on vice began.

Tobacco smoking is the only vice that originated in the New World. It would be hardly surprising to say that it was not considered a vice back then, as its harmful effects were unknown—but that would be wrong. There were Europeans who knew of its dangers even before Virginia's 1606 charter. Spaniards, who preceded the British in colonizing the New World, had already come home puffing pipes and selling weed—"sot weed," seventeenth-century slang for tobacco. When Sir Walter Raleigh returned to England in 1584 with tobacco from present-day North Carolina and urged its American cultivation, some in England started viewing smoking as a vice. Foremost among them was the king, James I, who also—perhaps not coincidentally, in terms of power and views of vice—despised Raleigh, that dashing and wildly popular explorer/author/soldier, with his feathered hat and that pipe in his mouth.[2]

But James I didn't bad-mouth Raleigh (whom he later beheaded) in his 1604 tract titled *A Counter-Blaste to Tobacco*; much of his reasoning had to do with health. Nor was he the first to write about those dangers. His views amplified (by virtue of being the king) a 1602 antismoking pamphlet that had appeared in England written by someone calling himself Philaretes.[3] Back then and up into the nineteenth century, pamphleteers and the like often cloaked their identity in togas. They thought it made their arguments more powerful, much as we today think robes endow judges with the power of wisdom. Clothing and the ways we "clothe" our views have been perennially connected to views of virtue and vice.

The accuracy of many of the reasons not to smoke presented by Philaretes suggests he was a physician, and a brilliant one at that. Like James I, however, Philaretes had other issues with smoking that had more to do with those he hated than with health. He warned England's smokers that the first Europeans to take up the habit were "the Devil's Priests [Spanish Catholics] . . . and therefore not to be used of us Christians."[4]

When James I wrote his antismoking tract, he too employed a mix of medical and social reasons. In terms of health, despite many medical misconceptions in his day, the king revealed the considerable insight that existed regarding smoking when he wrote, "Oftentimes in the inward parts of men, soiling and infecting them . . . an unctuous and oily kind of soot . . . hath been found in some great tobacco takers that, after their death, were opened." He also noted that "many in this kingdom have had such a continual use of taking this unsavory smoke as now they are not able to forebear the same, no more than an old drunkard can abide to be long sober." Smoking, he and others already knew, was addictive. But he also wrote, "What honour or policy can move us to imitate the barbarous and beastly manners of the wild, godless, and slavish Indians, especially in so vile and stinking a custom?" Most notably, James viewed this vice as pertaining only to those over whom he sought to impose power, vindicating it among those upon whom he had to rely when he asserted that tobacco was being excessively used by "persons of so base and contemptible a condition," in contrast to its use by "persons of good calling and quality."[5] James further sought to discourage the use of tobacco by imposing a high tax on its importation—much as, in the United States today, the federal government imposes a high excise tax on cigarettes. When that didn't work, he imposed stiffer penalties on those found smuggling tobacco and officials who accepted bribes not to enforce the tax.

But then the king changed his approach. Increasingly, the British government benefited—indeed needed—the revenue it collected from its punitive tobacco tax. To maximize that revenue, James *lowered* the tax in order to make smuggling and bribery less worth the risk. He also stopped carping about his mid-Atlantic colonies in America relying so heavily on tobacco for trade, since without their crop, the rapidly growing worldwide market for tobacco would be dominated by tobacco that was grown in colonies controlled by England's rival, Spain.[6] Power prevailed in forming his view of this vice.

But how was it viewed in America? In Massachusetts—later at the forefront for independence and the end of royalty—class distinctions still prevailed. Its laws against "idleness" cited "tobacco takers" as subject to arrest, along with "common coasters" (guys who fish for their dinner, as opposed to commercial fishermen) and "unprofitable fowlers" (bird hunters who aren't very good at it). Smoking was also prohibited in any inn, except in a private room, suggesting that, even then, many found secondhand smoke offensive. In the adjacent Plymouth Colony, which later merged with Massachusetts, lawmakers asserted that God took a dim view of this vice when they enacted a law that anyone caught smoking on Sunday would be fined.[7] These laws against vice provide a peek behind the curtain, giving us a glimpse of who ran the show at the time: religious leaders and those with dough.

A similarly based but different view prevailed in the tobacco-growing colonies farther south. It can be seen by comparing Virginia's laws against loafers with those of Massachusetts. Virginia's list of illegal idleness included beggars, gamblers, fortune tellers, and jugglers but made no mention of smokers.[8]

On the other hand, what's with jugglers? Why was juggling deemed a vice, particularly since Virginia wasn't the only colony that outlawed it? For most antijuggling colonists, the answer can be found in news items from the time telling of itinerants who turned out to be con artists or, particularly if they displayed some fascinating skill, seducers of bedazzled females.[9] But some viewed juggling, in particular, as a gateway to witchcraft. Magicians and fortune tellers, as one might expect, were viewed as hustlers for Satan, but jugglers?

This view entailed, ironically, verbal juggling. Joseph Glanvil, a prominent British Puritan, demonstrated his skill at tossing into the air Deuteronomy 18:10–11 ("There shall not be found among you any one that maketh his son or his daughter to pass through the fire, or that useth divination, or an observer of times, or an enchanter, or a witch, or a charmer, or a consulter with familiar spirits, or a wizard, or a necromancer" [King James version]) and catching every word in a way that now read No Juggling Allowed:

> The [original Hebrew] word . . . which throughout English translation renders, "an observer of Times," should rather be a Declarer of the Seasonableness of the Time, or Unseasonableness of the Time, or Unseasonableness as to Success—a thing which is enquired into from Witches, yet the usual sense, rendered by the learned in language, is Prestidigitator. . . . Prestidigitator, in that sense, we translate in English, Juggler, or an Hocus-Pocus, [and] is so fond a conceit that no man of any depth of wit can endure it—as if a merry juggler that plays tricks of legerdemain at a fair or market, were such an abomination . . . or as if an Hocus-Pocus were so wise a wight [person] as to be consulted as an oracle. . . . Wherefore here is evidently a second name of a witch.[10]

Ta da!

Not everyone was impressed. Even in Puritan Massachusetts, even its most eminent minister, Cotton Mather, declared, "I abhor to see the Scripture so ridiculously trifled with as it is by the legerdemain of those nonsensical commentators."[11] Even among the Puritans, nothing was pure about morals, for the powers that influence one person's life are not necessarily the same in others' lives.

Despite Puritan misgivings about the royally proclaimed religion of England, Cotton Mather echoed James I when he warned, "We have too far degenerated into Indian vices. . . . They are very lazy wretches, and . . . there is no family government among them. We have shamefully Indianized in all those abominable things."[12] Ascribing vice to a group he sought to overpower, calling them lazy and prone to immorality that weakens families, echoes to this day in views voiced by those who say the same about African Americans. Efforts to combat vice can genuinely seek to curb behaviors damaging to health. But they can also be efforts to maintain or obtain dominance over others.

Seemingly blowing smoke into this theory is the fact that the tobacco-growing colonies did not view smoking as a prosecutable vice for a group it viewed as the lowest of the low: enslaved African Americans. And just as they feared attacks from Indians, they feared uprisings from slaves. On the other hand, did slaves smoke? It's not the image one has of that horrific history—and indeed slaves would have had precious little time to do so. In what leisure time they may have had, however, some did smoke. Spain and Portugal had been selling tobacco in Africa well before the large-scale slave trade. One colonial era traveler to Guinea, a center of the slave trade, wrote, "Both the male and the female of the Negroes are so very fond of this tobacco that they will part with the very last penny which should buy them bread, and suffer hunger rather than be without it."[13] Even setting aside the statement's condescension and exaggeration, African smokers appear to have become as addicted as their European and white American counterparts. But laws against smoking by slaves were unnecessary, since slave owners imposed their own laws.

As for this country's original tobacco smokers, Native Americans, its use was viewed as a spiritual experience. But it was not entirely confined to tribal rituals. One thing known is that by 1756 there were Native Americans addicted to nicotine. In that year, a colonist who had been abducted by two members of the Lenape tribe reported, "They sat up eating bread and cheese and dried peaches, and smoking tobacco, which they got at Hicks's, having had no tobacco, as they told us, four or five days, and were in great want of it."[14] Significantly, perhaps, the leader of these two Lenape spoke fluent English and identified himself as Captain Jacobs; his associate went by the name Jim. If nicotine addiction did not exist or was rare among Native Americans prior to the arrival of Europeans, then this incident provides insight into efforts to combat vice. As later examples will demonstrate, the more homogeneous a society—which is to say, the fewer groups there are competing for power—the more successful it can be in maintaining adherence to virtue as perceived by its leaders. With

Native Americans, the arrival and subsequent rise in power of Europeans altered that equation.

First Americans "Under the Influence"

Then as now, where there's smoke from tobacco, there's often firewater too. In colonial America, liquor was often linked with smoking, as evidenced by the laws restricting smoking in taverns and inns. Cotton Mather lamented that "Drinking Houses have been a most undoing stumbling block of iniquity in the midst of us." Court records reveal that so many Puritans got plastered they fell off the pages of our public school textbooks, thus leaving generations of future Americans thinking the Puritans really were pure. One Bostonian, in a 1726 letter to the editor of the *New England Courant*, complained in a nauseating (though rather poetic) description: "There is a considerable branch of the River of Death, and does not the stench of rum, flip [a beer and liquor cocktail] and tobacco, with the sight of sots and tipplers reeling and spewing on either side, offend your senses as you pass?" The letter went on to identify many of these booze and tobacco pukers as "our Young Sparks [who] drink and game and revel for whole nights together."[15]

Then as now, news reports reveal that damage and death caused by drunkenness are both angering and heartbreaking. In 1766 the *Providence Gazette* told readers,

> It appeared to the coroner's inquest, by the evidence of a little son of the deceased, about six years old, that the night before, she went out for half a pint of rum and when she returned, being very drunk, fell backwards down the cellar steps to the floor; that finding she did not get up, the child went and waked his father, who was in bed, and likewise very drunk, but at last got up and went to his wife and shook her, but finding she did not rise, he left her, went again to bed, and next morning remembered nothing of the matter.[16]

While all the colonies had restrictions on alcohol, only one had a total prohibition: Georgia. Its principal founder, James Oglethorpe, sought to provide an outlet and opportunity for England's over-crowded debtors' prisons. He believed that a place where booze was banned would help England's ne'er-do-wells acquire a work ethic. As it turned out, banning booze *did* enhance the work ethic—of neighboring South Carolinians. Profits to be made by smuggling the stuff into Georgia motivated many with an entrepreneurial spirit. Also to promote a work ethic, Oglethorpe prohibited slavery in Georgia. Since smuggling slaves into the colony and keeping them hidden was not possible, that genuinely noble moral reform succeeded. But because of the society surrounding Georgia, Oglethorpe's dream for this colony failed. Georgia was unable to produce crops as cheaply as its slave-holding neighbors. Indeed, these two moral reforms collided when back-breaking work and hopeless poverty rendered many a Georgian in need of a drink. Both prohibitions were soon rescinded.

Among Native Americans, the role of alcohol is more complex than many realize. It is overly simplistic, for example, to state that Europeans introduced alcohol to Indians. Also overly simplistic is the view that colonial leaders turned a blind eye to (if not abetted) Indian drunkenness to sabotage the rank-and-file of these adversaries to colonial expansion. The people who lived throughout the Americas were well aware of various fermented concoctions long before Columbus (or Amerigo Vespucci or, five hundred years earlier, Leif Eriksson) ever stepped ashore and said, "We come in peace; care for a snort?" The colonists, too, were susceptible to overly simplistic perceptions of Indians and alcohol. In 1680 a Dutch settler wrote that a group of drunken Lenape in present-day Brooklyn, "raving, shouting, jumping, fighting each other, and foaming at the mouth like raging beasts . . . conjured the devil." Years later, anthropologists recognized that he was describing, albeit unknowingly, a Lenape healing ceremony that had been adapted by using alcohol to help transport the participants to that spiritual realm.[17]

It is absolutely true, however, that alcoholism became devastatingly widespread among Native Americans after the arrival of European settlers and equally true that this alcohol was provided by those colonial settlers. Was it just for show, then, that within five years of its founding in 1628, the Massachusetts Bay Colony banned the sale of alcohol (or any other form of its distribution) to Indians? Similar prohibitions were enacted in each of the thirteen colonies. Dutch and French authorities also forbade their colonists to sell or trade liquor with the Indians. Clearly not a public relations stunt was a New Jersey law voiding any land sale to a colonist by a Native American in which liquor was part of the transaction.

That this legislation was not just for show is evidenced by the number of indictments of colonists for providing alcohol to Indians. Nevertheless, it is unlikely that such legislation was enacted solely out of concern for Native Americans. While some of these English, Dutch, and French authorities may have felt compassion for these people, all colonial leaders sought to avoid disorder and violence, which often occurred when inebriated Indians mixed with colonists. "The trading houses where the Indians of the east had so much of their drink," Cotton Mather wrote, ". . . [in] every one of them the sword has been drunk with the blood of the English at the hands of those very Indians which have been so often drunk among them."[18] Mather's denunciation of those who provided alcohol to Native Americans suggests quite the opposite of alcohol as a weapon to weaken the Indians. The fear was that it emboldened them. For the same reason, colonial lawmakers prohibited the sale of alcohol to slaves. The predominant concern on the part of whites about drunkenness among nonwhites wasn't that it could be self-destructive to the user; the destruction most whites feared was of themselves.

As New England's population of free African Americans grew, a greater percentage of their drunks appear to have received harsher sentences than white drunks.[19] While obviously attributable to racism, one element that contributed to that racism was fear of rebellious acts by blacks—especially inebriated blacks. Uprisings by enslaved and free African Americans were not uncommon by the latter decades of the colonial era. In 1741 a rebellion by Manhattan's African Americans spread like wildfire into Brooklyn, Queens, and nearby areas of New Jersey.

Many resentments led to such rage among New York's African Americans, but we need look no further than that colony's laws on vice. In 1769 New York rewrote its statute against drunkenness to stipulate a fine of three shillings and four hours in the stocks for whites—but for blacks, as many as forty lashes could be added on.[20] Even with this disparity in sentencing to maintain power over blacks, their punishment often *exceeded* the law. "Mr. Montanny's Negro Man," the *New York Journal* told readers on May 7, 1772, "who had misbehaved and was a remarkable drunkard, was sent to Bridewell [prison] and underwent the usual discipline of the house for such offences, viz., a plentiful dose of warm water and salt to operate as an emetic, and of lamp oil as a purge." What made this incident newsworthy was that the saltwater and oil Mr. Montanny's "Negro Man" was forced to swallow "operated very powerfully," in the news report's words. His body convulsed so much that he died.

Two details tucked into this report reveal even more about how we arrive at our views of vice. The first is that the reporter did not regard as newsworthy the name of Mr. Montanny's "Negro Man." In the prevailing view of vice at that time and place, it was far more worrisome that a "Negro Man" got drunk than that [whatever this man's name was] got drunk. Also significant by its absence in the report is that no law stipulated and no medical research suggested the "discipline of the house" for drunkenness blandly cited in the article: inducing vomiting and diarrhea. It was solely an imposition of power by jailers upon jailed—most frequently upon the least empowered of their prisoners: African Americans.[21]

Then as now, gaps existed in the enforcement of vice laws. To find out why, the best place to start is by following the yellow (as in the color of gold) brick road. Since British, French, and Dutch colonists competed with each other—most intensely in the lucrative market for furs provided by Indians—colonial leaders found that prohibiting giving Indians alcohol put their traders at a disadvantage. Consequently, their political leaders were conflicted. Moreover, these leaders were not necessarily more powerful than their era's bootleggers. New York colonist Johan Jost Herkimer, for example, amassed great wealth in the mid-1700s from the sale of booze to the Iroquois. While Herkimer was not exactly a colonial Al Capone (Herkimer also made money in legitimate businesses and didn't kill his competitors), these illegal transactions were so well known that Gen. Horatio Gates complained about them in a letter to the military commander in that region of New York. The commander, who assured Gates he would investigate the matter, turned out to be a silent partner with Herkimer in this lucrative business.[22]

In 1763 a confederation began to coalesce among Native American tribes seeking to resist incursions of white culture and power. Known as Pontiac's Rebellion after the Ottawa leader who was among its core advocates, it quickly spread through areas of present-day Ohio and Illinois and the western reaches of West Virginia, Maryland, Pennsylvania, and New York. Notably, it was accompanied by a spiritual revival movement that encouraged a return to tribal rituals and lifestyles and the abandonment of customs adopted from whites, particularly alcohol consumption. With sobriety now viewed as a patriotic act for one's tribe, this effort to combat alcohol abuse resulted in considerable success. But then it failed, following the failure of Pontiac's Rebellion.[23]

Regulating Joy

The colony whose leaders included the fewest party animals was Puritan Massachusetts. But its pinched-lipped leaders turned out to have some surprises in their pockets. True, their laws generally "shalted not" at the sight of fun. Not only was gambling illegal, but so too were any card games, whether betting was involved or not, and don't even think about darts or dice.[24]

Also verboten was bowling.

And shuffleboard.

Cards, darts, and dice: one can make some sense out of those prohibitions, but what was their beef with bowling? And shuffleboard, that proverbial diversion for old folks? Back then, however, shuffleboard was played indoors, and the doors inside which it was played were those of taverns. Bowling was originally played outdoors, in some ways similar to pick-up basketball games today. Even if money wasn't on the line (and often it was), egos were. Such games often led to our nation's forefathers going face-to-face, then fist-to-gut or knee-to-groin and down to the ground to work out their differences.

Today bowling provides not only hours of family fun but also a window into power participating in forming views of vice. In only one of the colonies that prohibited games was bowling absent from its Do Not Play list: New York. Originally, what we now call New York was a Dutch colony, and it was the Dutch who brought bowling to America. Though the British ousted the Dutch authorities, they did not oust the Dutch, of whom there were many, and many of them were wealthy and well connected, and they liked to bowl. England even left intact what is today New York City's oldest park, Bowling Green, at the southern end of Manhattan.

But all this folderol over games wasn't simply because they were viewed as gateways to gambling and fights, since there were laws against gambling and assault. So why not let colonial era folks have fun? The reason slipped out in New York's restrictions on games, a law other colonies likely thought talked too much. It referred to its list of forbidden games as "vitiating the manners of many of the people of the said colony and encouraging them to idleness." Playing games was viewed by those rich enough to hire others for grunt work as sapping their energy (vitiating) and using time these employers wanted them using as employees.[25] Making games illegal made it easier to corral workers. Plus there was an added bonus. By making available a larger supply of labor, these laws enabled employers to offer lower wages.

Race also formed views of vice in regard to idleness. Pennsylvania's colonial legislature declared, "If any free Negro, fit and able to work, shall neglect to do so, and loiter and misspend his or her time . . . [magistrates are] required to bind out to service such Negro, from year to year, as to them shall seem meet."[26]

Employers, however, were not as influential as they would later become. Religious leaders so outranked them that they were able to have idleness viewed as a *virtue*. On Sundays. Enforced by law.

With some variation, all of the colonies prohibited any form of work on Sundays.

The power of the clergy also resulted in laws that sought to stop what, for some, is both fun and, at times, of much relief: cursing. Here, however, there was a particularly wide gap between the law and adherence to it, revealing, as such gaps do, a conflicting source of power: typically the power of anger or pain. That colonists continued to say whatever the #*!% they felt can be seen in a 1696 law in Virginia that began, "Whereas there are several and many laws now in force for the suppression of the sins of swearing, cursing, profaning God's holy Name ..." The new law enacted stricter penalties. Apparently that didn't work either, since in 1746 a Virginia publisher reissued *The Whole Duty of Man*, a tract that wagged its finger at cursing in eight separate instances.[27] A different tack was taken by Rhode Island. Founded specifically for freedom of religion, its clergy were less powerful—evidenced in part by its legislature not enacting laws prohibiting profanity. No evidence indicates that colonial Rhode Islanders were any more foulmouthed than the other men and women to whom the United States owes its existence.

More fun for some than cursing was its physical equivalent: fighting. As a form of entertainment, it too was an inheritance from England. A February 13, 1749, *Boston Evening Post* news report from England told readers, "A boxing match for a sum of money was fought in College-Green between a sailor, a short sized man, and a soldier, a lusty man, when the latter was beat in so violent a manner that he was carried off the Green almost for dead. The little sailor had a pretty deal of money given him by the gentlemen present." As in England, only rarely did the authorities enforce laws against assault in regard to boxing, since it was viewed as *consensual* violence. While many, then and now, have viewed boxing as a vice, it has generally been vindicated due less to the fact that the power to fight is power in the raw than to its being a power widely valued by a particularly powerful group: men.[28]

Just as boxing is consensual violence, so too is dueling. Or is it?

Consider the most famous duel in American history, which took place shortly after the colonial era. In 1804 Vice President Aaron

Burr, feeling he had been insulted by Secretary of Treasury Alexander Hamilton, challenged him to retract his remarks or settle the matter by seeing which of the two could kill each other first under the time-honored *code duello*. Hamilton accepted. The night before the duel, Hamilton wrote, "Those who, with me, [abhor] the practice of dueling may think that I ought on no account to have added [to] the number of bad examples. . . . All the considerations which constitute what men of the world denominate honor, impressed on me a peculiar necessity not to decline the call."[29]

Did Hamilton freely consent to the duel, or did he feel overpowered by the fear that, if he did not agree to the duel, he'd be called (in more Founding Fatherly terms) chicken? Or was this note, as some contend, disingenuous—written to disgrace Burr in the event that Hamilton lost? Whatever the intention of his words, it turned out Hamilton did die on the field of so-called honor and Burr did subsequently face disgrace. The questions regarding Hamilton's motive in writing those words reveal that in dueling—and, as we shall see, other vices—consent is often questionable. For that reason, dueling tips the societal scale more toward crime than vice, which is why dueling was illegal in every colony and later in every state.[30]

So what about all those duels where the victor, having won fair and square, looks unflinchingly at observers, holsters his sidearm, and strides into the saloon amid fear and admiration?

Myth.

Moral myths of duels in the olden days have long been purveyed to convey the importance of honor. In point of fact, only those who were very powerful, or important members of powerful groups, got away with it. Aaron Burr, for example, was charged with murder, but the indictment was eventually quashed. Sam Houston killed a man in a duel in Kentucky, then fled to Tennessee, where, being the governor of that state, he refused a request from Kentucky to extradite himself to stand trial. To the extent that dueling has been a vindicated vice, it has been viewed through the lens of the powers-that-be.

The same principle applied to Native Americans, who, even before the arrival of Europeans, also occasionally engaged in duels. Typically, the disputants would shoot arrows (later, guns) at each other—from protected positions, in some tribal traditions; from open positions, in others. Among some tribes, any scar from a wound received by the surviving duelist was a badge of honor. In other tribes, the tradition called for the losing duelist's kin to kill the winner.[31] Though Native Americans considered dueling to be a tragic tradition, it was not always proscribed by tribal leaders. Similar to boxing in white culture, the extent to which some tribes vindicated dueling reflected the extent to which physical power—in this case, the ability to kill in the face of grave danger—was highly valued.

Since power among African Americans was feared by those in power, dueling would have been strictly prohibited, if any blacks ever inherited this deadly tradition. The various dueling traditions in Africa were nonviolent.[32]

Of course, for most folks the most fun was sex, which is also humanity's most regulated joy. All the colonies had laws against sex between anyone other than a husband and his wife. In the colony formed for moral purposes, Massachusetts, the death penalty could be imposed for rape, homosexual acts, incest, and bestiality.

And for adultery.

And for having sex with a virgin and keeping it secret until after her marriage to someone else.

And for "pollution of a woman known to be in her flowers [menstruating]."[33]

Enforcement of these laws, however, turned out to be something other than forceful. Massachusetts minister and judge John Raynor had no problem with the death penalty for gays, since Leviticus 20:13 says they should be put to death. Three lines up, however, Leviticus says the same for adulterers. That made this Puritan jurist flinch. "It is not so manifest that the same acts were to be punished with death . . . which yet by the law of God were capital crimes," he wrote. "Besides other reasons, because sodomy . . . is more against the light of nature than some other capital crimes." Raynor wasn't the only Puritan for whom the lens of self-interest in other men's wives blurred the lines in Leviticus. In colonial Massachusetts, adultery was not a capital crime *for the man* if he was unmarried, but if an unmarried *woman* had sex with someone's husband, to the gallows she went.[34] Here again, views of vice reveal whose hands held the societal reins.

Among those holding the reins was the power of sex, so much so that a considerable gap existed between these Massachusetts laws stipulating the biblically based death sentence and the imposition of that sentence. Records reveal it was very rarely imposed. In 1731, for example, the punishment meted out to an adulterous Boston couple was that they were to be carted to the gallows with ropes around their necks, made to sit there for an hour, and then get whipped. Not all convicted adulterers got off so easily; another such couple in Massachusetts were further required to wear a two-inch-high "A" on their upper garments for the rest of their lives.[35]

Absent from colonial legal codes was prostitution, raising the question: Where were their heads? In this instance, they were in their law books. Proving prostitution in court requires proof that a fee was paid for sex, and obtaining evidence of that transactional moment is difficult to obtain. Colonial laws, however, did not need to specify prostitution, since other laws prohibited fornication. Even these laws were not easy to enforce. A 1643 statute in Virginia created a system of local wardens to report fornicators to the authorities—but the indictments that followed were mostly against the wardens for failing to do their duty.[36] Apparently, even then being a Peeping Tom was viewed as worse than extramarital sex, the reason being that adultery is consensual; being peeped at is not. And the ability to consent, as we shall repeatedly see, is far more powerful than one might expect.

The main way colonial lawmakers sought to quash prostitution was with regulations inherited from England prohibiting "disorderly houses." The burden of proof required to prosecute the goings-on in such suspected bonky-tonks was much lower, since laws against gaming, drinking, and smoking were sufficient to convict the individuals, along with the owner or manager of the joint. When, for example, a woman named Jane Robinson was sentenced to be whipped in 1639 "for disorder in her house, drunkenness, and light behavior," or in 1640 one Margery Rugs was sentenced to be whipped for acts deemed "enticing and alluring," it was probably a safe bet that these women weren't averse to getting a buck for a bang.[37]

Further employing views of vice to impose power, lopsided laws were enacted regarding whites having sex with blacks. In Virginia, any white female who gave birth to "a bastard child by a Negro or Mulatto" was obligated to pay £15 to make provision for the child, who was taken from her and sold off to be raised as an indentured servant until age thirty-one. If the white woman wasn't classy enough to have the cash, Virginia got the money by selling the woman into indentured servitude—or, if she was already an indentured servant, adding five years to her stint. Interracial marriage was, needless to say, forbidden. If a bride and groom selected mismatched skin colors, they honeymooned in jail for six months. If they'd gone so far as to produce a baby, it was sold off for servitude. As for any minister who joined them in wedlock, he was fined ten thousand pounds of tobacco (coin of the realm for large sums in colonial Virginia).[38] On the other hand, no law prohibited a white man from having sex—consensual or not—with a black woman.

But that was Virginia. What about in the North, where there were far fewer slaves, since geographic conditions made slavery less cost-effective? The laws were harsher. In Massachusetts, any interracial couple convicted of having sex was whipped, and the black partner, if he was a free man, was exiled by being sold into slavery in some other colony.[39] In the North, vice laws pinch-hit for slavery.

So what could colonial guys and gals do for fun? Not dance, if they happened to live in New England; that was also illegal, no matter the occasion. In statements that could as well have been uttered in the 1950s against Elvis Presley and the dancing connected with rock and roll, the prominent Puritan minister Increase Mather (Cotton's father) condemned what he called "Gynecandrical Dancing." Its "unchaste touches and gesticulations," he warned, "... have a palpable tendency to that which is evil."[40]

Not surprisingly, any colony that would pass laws prohibiting dancing to fend off gynecandrical vice would pass laws barring gynecandrical clothing as well. (Full disclosure: gynecandrical does not refer to vaginas. It simply means that which brings men and women together.) Along with dancing, colonial Massachusetts banned fashions in clothing designed to attract the opposite sex. Lace, with its enticing see-through quality, was prohibited. Dresses and blouses were limited to one slit in each sleeve and one in the back of the garment for purposes of ventilation in warm weather. But in a Puritan version of Whacketh-Ye-Mole, women eluded the letter of the law by wearing short sleeves. Fashion accessories further reveal views of vice being employed to enhance the grip of those who hold power. Laws in colonial Massachusetts kiboshed gold or silver thread, buttons, or buckles—*unless the household was worth £200 or more.*[41]

One might conclude from all these laws that Puritans viewed joy as a vice. Which brings us to their surprise. Their leaders loved orgasms. True, their laws limited that blast to husband and wife, but those laws did not restrict the big O solely for purposes of procreation—nor was this joy reserved for men. "Procreation of children be one end of marriage, yet is not the only end," one Puritan jurist wrote when ruling that female infertility was not sufficient grounds for divorce, whereas a man's inability to satisfy his wife sexually *was* grounds for divorce. Court records from colonial Massachusetts reveal that one in six divorces were granted to wives on that basis.[42]

Why, then, years later, did we call "puritanical" those Americans responsible for Hollywood not showing husbands and wives having double beds? If they were not driven by fear of straying from our Puritan moral foundations, what was steering them?

Myth again.

For those in control, or those seeking to be, myths often play a vital role in forming views of vice. In 1753, for example, when the *Boston Gazette* reported that a woman named Hannah Dilley had been indicted on charges that she "made entertainments for lechery and fornication, and permitted men . . . to lie with whores, which the said Hannah then and there procured for them," the article concluded by saying, "As this is the first instance of any person thus indicted and convicted, so far as we can learn, in this Province, we truly wish and hope it may be the last."[43]

Really? The first time in anyone's recollection? The statement reveals how quickly moral myths can arise. Only forty years earlier, Cotton Mather recorded in his diary, "I am informed of several houses in this town where there are young women of a very debauched character . . . unto whom there is a very great resort of young men."[44] While Mather's diary was not yet public, the court records for Boston were. They brimmed with references to Alice Thomas, the town's preeminent madam of her day.[45]

One of the most potent myths that became increasingly prevalent after America's colonial era was that our founders all thought alike. They didn't. The best example of two New Englanders with differing views of vice—and of those views being used to project power by the one and to acquire it by the other—involved William Bradford and Thomas Morton. Bradford was governor of the Plymouth Colony in 1628 when Morton cofounded a settlement in what is now part of Quincy, Massachusetts. The settlement, called Mount Wollaston after Morton's cofounding partner, was predominantly male, as was often the case among those first to arrive and break ground. Also as was often the case, the first winter took its toll, with several members of the settlement dying from starvation. Richard Wollaston opted to head for warmer climes in Virginia. According to Governor Bradford, "After this they fell to great licentiousness and led a dissolute life. . . . Morton became Lord of Misrule." Bradford expressed shock that "they also set up a May-pole, drinking and dancing about it many days together, inviting the Indian women for their consorts, dancing and frisking together." And if frisking around an erected pole wasn't scandalous enough, he went on to blush, "They changed also the name of their place, and instead of calling it Mount Wollaston, they call it Merrie-mount."[46] If you're wondering about the pun, the answer is yes.[47]

Morton also wrote poetry, and that too drove Bradford up a tree—or, in this case, a pole. He brandished as an example of Morton's "rhymes and verses . . . which he affixed to this idle, or idol, May-pole a stanza addressed to Indian women":

Lasses in beaver coats, come away,
Ye shall be welcome to us night and day.
Drink and be merry, merry, merry boys,
Let all your delight be in hymen's joys.[48]

Thomas Morton, for his part, had a few things to say about Bradford and his pals. "These are the men that come prepared to rid the land of all pollution," he began, later adding, "Charity is said to be the darling of religion, and it is indeed the mark of a good Christian." Then, delivering the dagger, he subtly reminded those who ruled the home country that the Puritans had separated from England's official church when he wrote, "But I cannot perceive that the Separatists do allow of helping our poor"—a dig twisted in by the fact that the Puritans in Boston and Plymouth showed little, if any, compassion during the hardship and starvation his settlement suffered during its first winter. Morton then recounted his legal battles with Governor Bradford, culminating with his arrest and trial. Referring to himself in the third person, he wrote, "There they all with one assent put him to silence, crying out: Hear the Governor . . . who gave this sentence: That he shall be first put in the billbowes [iron shackles for feet], his goods should be all confiscated, his plantation should be burned down to [the] ground, because the habitation of the wicked should be no more."[49]

As for his own behavior, Morton did not deny he was a fun-loving fellow. But in matters of morals, when push came to shove, Morton did not shove. Native American women, he wrote, "have as much modesty as civilized people, and deserve to be applauded for it." In contrast to prevailing perceptions among the colonists of Native Americans, Morton asserted, "These people are not, as some have thought, a dull or slender witted people, but very ingenious, and very subtle. . . . They are not altogether without the knowledge of God, historically, for they have it amongst them by tradition that God made one man and one woman, and had them live together and get children." Adding an indirect dig about the lack of aid from the Puritans during the starvation that first winter, Morton wrote of the local Indians, "They are willing that anyone shall eat with them," and further on took a swipe at Puritan views of vice by describing Indian joys: "They exercise themselves in gaming and playing of juggling tricks and all manner of revels."[50]

Clearly, Thomas Morton was not your textbook American colonist. Indeed, his behavior was viewed by colonists in Plymouth and Boston as a threat, even though his settlement was some ten miles from Boston and more than thirty from Plymouth. But the threat it presented wasn't merry mounting; it was money—though often, in views of vice, the two go hand in hand. Morton's uninhibited views and open-minded outlook contributed to his settlement getting the best furs from Native Americans. Not only did his settlement get back on its feet, but its profits skyrocketed.[51]

Morton's modern-day legacy reveals that prudes are not the only ones who employ moral myths to enhance their influence. In the 1960s many free-love advocates (moral reformers in their own way) idealized Thomas Morton as a colonial era hippie and his settlement as something of a free-love commune. This view, however, overlooked the very unhippie primary quest of Morton's settlement: making money.

Beyond this rather unusual difference in views of vice serving two local powers, more widespread shifts among the powers-that-be culminated with the American Revolution. Here, too, an indication of the growing fracture in the status quo can be found in a conflicting view of vice being used for purposes of power. "Though I am a churchman, I am an American churchman," one colonist wrote in a 1768 letter to the editor of the *New York Gazette* regarding the "rights of the church of England in England, which Episcopalians in America cannot, as friends to this country, wish to see introduced." The letter writer was referring to the fact that in England secular courts presided over civil crimes, but ecclesiastical courts ruled on religious crimes, including vices such as violations of the Sabbath, cursing, or making heretical statements. "I would limit the power of the church and clergy to mere excommunication, or denial of the sacrament of the Lord's Supper, and give the further punishment of the offences triable in England in the spiritual court to the judges of the court of common law."[52]

By 1768 efforts to change the status quo between England and its colonies in America were no secret, as this letter to the editor explicitly demonstrates. Insight into how far back that effort began can be found implicitly expressed in gaps in adherence or enforcement of laws seeking to combat vice. Ecclesiastical courts never took hold in the American colonies, though not for lack of trying by British religious officials. In 1690 Virginia's governor and House of Burgesses responded to such efforts by expressing support for such courts, then never got around to enacting legislation to create them.[53] Even Massachusetts, created for religious purposes, never set up such courts. Its founders, having been persecuted for their Puritan beliefs in England's ecclesiastical courts, placed all judicial authority in civil courts. By the 1760s, when American discontents were starting to approach the boiling point, church officials in England revived their efforts to get such courts set up in America, leading to responses such as the letter to the editor just cited. A fight was brewing. And views of vice were now out in the open as one of the weapons.

So were other views of vice, such as gambling. In a sense, what is now the United States was founded on a bet. As a means of financing England's first American colony, the Crown permitted the Virginia Company to amass funds by sponsoring lotteries. Later, however, the Crown prohibited its American colonies from using lotteries to amass capital for various endeavors.[54] Why the flip-flop? Because those large endeavors—mostly roads, bridges, and colleges—would ultimately add wealth to the by then increasingly wealthy colonies. And wealth is power. Likewise, even in that most officially moral colony of Massachusetts, where any form of gambling was whacked with a gavel, those gavels flew out of the judges' hands when Massachusetts held lotteries to raise funds to offer bonuses to those who enlisted to fight the British.[55]

The British too used views of vice as moral muskets during the war. The Puritan colonies of New England and the Quaker colony of Pennsylvania had long banned plays, since members of the clergy feared the theatrical stage competed with their stage.[56] During the Revolution, however, when Boston and Philadelphia were occupied by British troops, England sought to woo less zealous colonists by quashing their bans on theater. In 1775 they permitted a production of *The Tragedy of Zara* in Boston.[57] Notably, this play by the acclaimed French intellectual Voltaire depicts love being crushed by religious intolerance. Take that, ye Puritan descendants. To round out the bill, the play was paired with *The Farce of the Citizen*. Not hard for most to get that message. For those who were hard of messaging, advertisements for the double bill ended with the phrase "Vivant Rex & Regina"—Long Live the King and Queen. The phrase appeared as well in ads for plays produced in British-occupied New York, Philadelphia, and Savannah, assuring that theatergoers knew who was buttering their theatrical bread.[58]

After the war, the British authorities were gone. But other authorities remained, one of which emerged with more power than ever before: white male property owners. On the other hand, in terms of views of vice, the Bill of Rights was written in 1789. And with it, moral tail chasing picked up its pace in the United States.

2

A "Virtue-ly" New Nation

"You ask me what news? Nothing indeed new, but all in the old ways." So began the "Extract of a letter from Connecticut," published in New York City's *Daily Advertiser* on September 9, 1790. "But we are become so liberal of late," this letter went on to say, "that a man may openly commit adultery and keep half a dozen mistresses. . . . The truth is, my friend, times are altered." Apparently the letter writer couldn't decide if things were the same or different. Closer to the truth would have been to say, "The *myth* is, my friend, times are altered."

Today it may appear that there was at least one significant change in views of vice, that being the Bill of Rights, if for no other reason than its prohibition of "cruel and unusual punishments." That view, however, had been voiced over a century earlier in Massachusetts's 1641 Body of Liberties. Cruelty, however, was in the eye of the beholder of the whips that continued to be used in the opening decades of the United States. Even Thomas Jefferson, the Founding Father who penned the phrase "the pursuit of happiness," did not view as cruel castration for a male homosexual act or cutting a hole no less than a half-inch in diameter in the nose of a convicted lesbian.[1] He proposed these punishments to replace Virginia's death penalty for these acts. The majority of the Old Dominion's legislators, however, preferred to continue its tradition of not enforcing the death penalty. It's pretty clear who was asserting power by maintaining the death penalty for homosexual acts, but what source of power resulted in the law's penalty not being imposed? To find out who these people of influence were, we would need to examine Early American Closets.

That the biggest winners in the American Revolution were wealthy white men soon surfaced in conflicts with less wealthy white men, and one of the most hotly contested conflicts had to do with booze.

Whiskey was the object of the first federal excise tax in the United States. It was the brainchild of the wealthy white man who was the nation's first secretary of the treasury, Alexander Hamilton. For him, the beauty of taxing whiskey was akin to the view of James I taxing tobacco. "As far as habits of less moderation in the use of distilled spirits," Hamilton declared, ". . . rendering the article dearer might tend to restrain a too free indulgence of such habits."[2]

But, as often with laws designed to bop vice, the effort turned into Whac-A-Mole—though, in this instance, the "moles" whacked back in what became known as the Whiskey Rebellion. Vehement resistance arose among the many considerably less than wealthy white men who eked out a living in the regions of the Appalachian Mountains—but not because they were a bunch of jug-guzzlers. For these Americans, the whiskey tax was an act of discrimination by the nation's more settled and wealthier easterners. Corn growers in the Appalachian regions faced the obstacle of transporting their harvest farther, not to mention through mountainous terrain, to reach the large markets in the more established cities of the East. To reduce both the bulk and perishability of their crop, they converted much of their corn into whiskey.

In an effort to placate their anger (indeed, their threat of violent rebellion), Congress enacted another excise tax—this one aimed at what some considered a vice of gluttony by wealthy Americans: carriages. Owning your own enclosed carriage was that era's sine qua non of elegance for well-qualified buyers.[3] "I should not be sorry to see the duty on carriages increased so far as to amount to a prohibition," declared one pissed-off pedestrian in a letter to the editor that shook its fist at the rich by declaring, "I have no idea [why] those citizens who cannot afford to ride are to be suffocated in dry weather with the dust raised by the carriage wheels of these pretended advocates of equality."[4]

Back in colonial days, no effort had ever been made to restrict the fun of riding in a fancy carriage. After the Revolution, the gradually increasing power of less wealthy Americans led, also gradually, to less restriction on their less costly forms of fun—up to a point. John Hancock, the Founding Father with the eye-popping signature, praised the Massachusetts legislature in 1793 for reenacting colonial laws, now "founded in the principles of the Constitution." As governor of the state, he went on to hold up as the most shining examples of such laws those that "guard the avenues of the heart against corruption and depravity. These prohibit lewdness, intemperance, gambling, idleness, levity, and dissipation of manners."[5]

Levity a prosecutable vice?

Idleness, so susceptible to crime it should be a crime?

Clearly not eye-poppingly large for Hancock was that "pursuit of happiness" in the Declaration of Independence, upon which he affixed his famous jumbo-size signature, whereas the Bill of Rights, to him, was evidently the fine print we tend to skip.

The relationship between power and views of vice was voiced loud and clear in one 1804 editorial when it declared, "The flood gates of vice and iniquity opened in the repeal of the naturalization law." The law, enacted under President John Adams and repealed under his successor, President Jefferson, had increased restrictions on immigration. The warning regarding vice, however, was employed to impose the power of the Federalist Party over Jefferson's Democratic Republican Party. Federalists feared (probably correctly) that immigrants would be more likely to identify with Jefferson's party, which focused on the interests of farmers and laborers to strengthen the country, as opposed to the Federalists, who believed the best way to strengthen the nation was to fortify its manufacturers and merchants. But who wants to be viewed as defending the rich? Consequently, the editorial draped the debate in views of vice. "When, therefore, the country shall have become corrupted and virtue lost her influence on the heart," it concluded, "then may we expect to reap the harvest of the labors of the President [referring to Jefferson]; a harvest of death and desolation through scenes of blood to slavery and despotism."[6]

Also thanks to Jefferson, a different slew of foreigners became citizens during his presidency—in this case, not because they came to this land but because their land became ours with the Louisiana Purchase. The jewel—or, in terms of vice, canker—in this vast 1803 acquisition from France was New Orleans. The Big Easy. Of which its residents said then, and still do, "Laissez les bons temps rouler!" Let the good times roll!

To most Americans back then (and for many years to follow) ooh-la-la and France went hand in hand. Virginia's *Alexandria Gazette* groused that New Orleans was "peopled principally by Frenchmen... exhibiting, particularly on the Sabbath day, scenes of the most licentious wickedness."[7] Diddling with slave girls, for instance—whether consensually or not—was one thing in the nation's original (British-descended) states, but these French guys practically married them! They even had a word for it: *plaçage*. Literally translated, *plaçage* means "veneer," but in this context it referred to a man setting up a separate household for his nonwhite mistress. Moreover, among Louisiana's wealthy planters there existed a low high society with a veritable social season of gatherings attended by these men and their mixed-race mistresses.[8]

In addition, the Louisiana Purchase brought a whole new vice into the nation's now enlarged borders: voodoo. Though rooted in African religion, voodoo was, and remains, viewed by most Americans as a superstition at best and as witchcraft at worst. Under the Constitution, however, witchcraft was no longer illegal. And Louisiana, with all its *plaçage,* had hordes of free nonwhites protected by that document. But as John Hancock and his cronies in the Massachusetts legislature had shown, what difference did that make?

Still, African American spiritual gatherings dating back to colonial times continued in an area of New Orleans called Congo Square and continued to include voodoo.[9] Despite the fact that nearly all whites viewed voodoo as a vice, no laws were passed to prohibit it. Did nonwhites in New Orleans, a great many of whom were enslaved, nevertheless possess sufficient power to circumvent the prohibition of voodoo? Or were they so lacking in power as to be of no concern?

The truth is that nonwhites had more power than was apparent. In the politically and militarily shaky decades that followed the Revolution, the power of all nonwhites in the United States was enhanced by the possibility that they could link their fortunes to

England, which had not entirely given up hope of regaining some hold on regions of this newfangled United States. Consequently, whites tended not to press too hard with nonwhite groups, that is, until the end of the War of 1812. After that, the British threat began to diminish, and bopping voodoo commenced. As far away as New England, an 1820 news item reported on a raid in New Orleans at a gathering for "the idolatrous worship of an African deity called Voodoo."[10]

The crackdown on voodoo not only increased white power but also sought to strengthen Christian power. The grip of religious authorities had slipped a bit when the Constitution forbade the establishment of an official religion. In addition, laws were expunged from colonial legal codes that allowed "benefit of clergy"—a procedure that enabled defendants to lessen their sentences by reading or reciting sections of the Bible.[11]

But the power of words relies on their interpretation, in which other powers participate.

John Hancock, in his previously cited speech in which he brandished the Constitution as the basis for his state's laws against depravity, also spoke of laws "calculated to inspire the citizens with a reverence for religion." Hancock so-proudly-we-hailed, "In this class are the laws against blasphemy and profanity, and also those which enjoin the observation of Holy Time."[12]

Indeed, religious authorities remained powerful, even with the political shifts embedded in the laws of the new United States. "You have been indicted by the Grand Jurors of the County for the crime of blasphemy . . . and the Jury has found you Guilty," a Vermont judge declared to defendant Eli Hamilton in 1806. The judge separated freedom of speech from blasphemy by reasoning, "We sit not here to avenge by human punishment the indignity offered to the Supreme Being . . . [but] to sentence you for an offence . . . which directly tends to disturb the peace of society[,] . . . to corrupt the rising generation, [and] to violate the feelings of the great body of a believing people." Still, evidence of the shift in the grip of religious leaders on the law is the *sentence* Eli Hamilton received. Under Vermont law, the judge could have imposed a sentence up to and including death. He opted for one hour in the stocks plus court costs.[13]

On the other hand, each of the first thirteen states enacted what had been their colonial prohibitions of fun on Sunday. So too did the new states of Vermont, Ohio, Kentucky, and Tennessee as they entered the Union. But then there were the French. What was now the state of Louisiana enacted no such laws. Devolving from whatever it was in their culture (and whatever it was, tourists flock to it even now), most Louisianans did not view Sunday recreation and amusements as vice. One who did was Samuel H. Hadden. A relative newcomer to New Orleans, he managed to get elected to the legislature, where he promptly proposed a number of Sunday prohibitions. Hadden, a Methodist Church leader, encountered opposition from fellow legislator Pierre Dornemon, whose name reveals his French lineage. In Dornemon's view, Sunday prohibitions were "unjust, impolitic, and immoral ... [since they sought] to prevent the exercise of those enjoyments to which the Creoles of this country, from their ancestry, have been accustomed." Hadden replied with a vice-fighting shot across the bow of racial power, calling the Creoles "people [who] have always exercised habits in direct contravention of acknowledged morality." Dornemon, for his part, used a moral glove to slap Hadden's face by referring to him as having been one of the "inhabitants of the northern states, who are a melancholy-thinking set of beings and whose character is naturally hypocritical."[14]

Let's leave them to their *mots de trash* and cut to the chase. Power in Louisiana was still mainly in the hands of its preponderant population of French descent. Pour cette raison, Hadden's proposal failed to pass. Over time, however, the demographics changed. But as they did, another group was emerging that challenged the power of both these groups: abolitionists. This threat led both groups to set aside their power struggle, with its weapons of Sunday dos and don'ts. Only after the Civil War and the military occupation that followed did Louisianans get back to this fracas for influence. This time around, however, Louisiana was no longer so français a state. In 1886 it enacted restrictions for businesses on Sundays.

After the Revolution, the question of whether or not theater should be a punishable vice became a brawl involving several groups seeking to secure their power now that the Brits were gone. Advocating on behalf of religious leaders seeking to regain the influence they once had (and, for himself, seeking the votes of their congregants), one Pennsylvania assemblyman urged the reinstatement of the state's ban on theater by declaring in 1785, "Theatrical performances give an alluring color to vice and wickedness."[15] In 1795 a Connecticut resident railed about morals in an attempt to assert the power of the upper class when he said that producers of plays were motivated by "the emoluments arising from them, and this emolument being in a considerable degree derived from the less refined and less informed part of mankind . . . there is the utmost danger that the exhibitions will be calculated for coarse and vulgar amusement."[16] Some employed this view of vice not to project power over other Americans but simply to project American power. "If, on the American stage, we are to be entertained with dramatic productions exhibiting the theatrical foppery of fretful, passionate kings, pouting queens, rakish princes, and flirting princesses . . . better that we are without them," a 1793 editorial asserted.[17]

Bans on theater were reestablished in New England and Pennsylvania, with efforts to do likewise throughout the new United States. Here again, the Bill of Rights was more the Bill of Little Difference. "It will be questioned by the friends of the theater whether the legislatures have a right to interfere with their amusements," one fun-unloving New Yorker wrote in a letter to the editor of the *New York Packet*, going on to justify the prohibition of theater by asking "whether an individual or individuals should be permitted madly to erect for their diversion a tower which, by its height, would be a terror to its neighborhood, and by its fall spread round extensive devastation."[18]

With these laws, theatrical Whac-A-Mole commenced. Philadelphia impresario Lewis Hallam Jr. tap-danced through the wording of the law by producing what his advertisements called *A Lecture on Heads*. The lecture consisted of "a poetical address . . . [on] the most eminent dramatic authors—serious, comic, and satire . . . diversified with music, scenery, and other decorations." Over time, his programs came to include several "lectures," some of which were nonverbal, such as a pantomime titled *Harlequin's Frolics*, while others entailed other realms of scholarship, such as the "musical entertainment of Darby and Patrick . . . with new scenery, machinery, music, etc." Hallam's technique for evading the law soon spread to that bastion of stage fright, New England. Even Boston's authorities could not find a way for their law to stomp out *Feats of Activities*, a 1792 "lecture" advertised as a (presumably academic) examination of "DANCING ON THE TIGHT ROPE . . . TUMBLING . . . SONG . . . the whole to conclude with a pantomime entertainment called *Harlequin Doctor*."[19]

Theatrical Whac-A-Mole spread westward as Americans migrated into these regions, founding communities created by their own influential groups. Theaters sprang up in Pittsburgh, Cincinnati, and Lexington, Kentucky.[20] "It appears to be a sad evidence of depravity, and ominous of much evil to society, if to the vain pleasures of balls . . . must be added the fascinating and corrupting entertainment of the stage," an 1815 editorial lamented in regard to a community theater being formed in Ohio's original state capital, Chillicothe.[21]

With all this elbowing for influence in the new nation, some groups sought to join forces. From Portland, Maine (technically still part of Massachusetts), through New England, New York, Pennsylvania, and westward into Ohio, Americans began for the first time to form organizations devoted solely to fighting vice.[22] Emblematic was the 1814 mission statement of the Connecticut Society for the Promotion of Good Morals: "The considerate and sober are always on the side of such efforts," it stated, the vice it most sought to stem being drunkenness, ". . . but the power of the Most High is employed in aid of those who, according to His will, use the means He gives them."[23] Thus the society, like its counterparts in this era, sought to assert religious power through its view of vice, but, by virtue of being a coalition, it did so without privileging one religion or sect over any other.

With advances in the printing press during these years, another vice became increasingly prevalent: pornography. The Massachusetts Society for the Prevention of Vice received accolades in 1818 for "its recent efforts . . . [to combat] the distribution of obscene books and pictures."[24] What, you may wonder, did the society consider obscene in 1818? Here's a sample:

> He seized me and, smothering me with kisses, without losing a moment he threw me on the settee, stripped up my shift, and in spite of the resistance I made, which only served to inflame his lust, got the head of his engine into my belly. . . . He soon became ungovernable, tearing me without mercy, his thrusts growing more and more furious, and after causing me a great deal of pain, thrust it at last up to the very hilt. . . . [S]o keen was the sensation I felt, when I received the emission of his seed, that I scarcely knew if I had any life in me, and soon expired in the arms of the murderer of my virginity in an agony of bliss.[25]

Yowser.

This spicy tidbit from a book called *Venus School Mistress* was not the only or the most widely read pornographic novel in early America. That genre's runaway best seller was *Memoirs of a Woman of Pleasure*, first published in 1749 but read even to this day, though now more popularly known as *Fanny Hill*.

But even with these groups combating vice by pointing to *where* and demanding that *there* judges' gavels should be whacked, the effort proved ineffective. "It appears that moral societies . . . have almost wholly failed," New York minister John Chester told his fellow members of the Albany Moral Society in 1821, going on to share considerable insight when he said, "The principles upon which these societies rose were mistaken, or misapplied. . . . The great object has been to enact penal laws for the suppression of immorality, and to enforce them with rigid exactness upon offenders."[26]

How They Ho'ed in the New Nation

"Prostitution prevails to a most shocking degree," a 1788 article exclaimed in Boston's *Massachusetts Gazette*.[27] This was considered news for the same reason that it periodically is considered news: as a weapon for power. Notable in this regard was the article going on to ask, "To what cause shall we attribute the great prevalence of prostitution? To female folly, or to the villainy of man?" As we shall see, in the years between then and now, views of prostitution will shift back and forth as to who is to be punished—the prostitute or those who use her for pleasure or profit?

One of the ways American religious authorities sought to regain power in this era was through a less punitive, though still biblically based, view of prostitutes as "fallen women." Though the phrase itself did not surface until 1820, in a poem by Lord Byron, the effectiveness of this view is reflected in the name of the first organized effort in this country to combat prostitution, the creation in 1800 of Philadelphia's Magdalen Society—named after the New Testament's Mary Magdalene, a follower of Jesus widely (though possibly incorrectly) believed to have been a prostitute.[28]

But a different and hidden hand was also pulling the strings in this view of this vice, that being, quite simply, the power of sexual attraction. See if you can spot it hidden in this 1789 tract on prostitution: "A slight view of the wretchedness of many once respectable and virtuous females, now cut down by the cruel shafts of the seducers, must swell our bosoms with the most poignant anxiety."[29] Had that sentence spoken of the wretchedness of, say, alcoholics or gamblers in terms of "cruel shafts" and "swelling bosoms," readers would react with confusion. But not in regard to prostitutes, because we're talking sex. In that context, *swelling bosoms* and *cruelly shafted* are words well crafted to purvey this view of vice.

Thus, back then, when one Daniel Harrington was convicted in 1816 for operating a brothel in Troy, New York, no charges were brought against the women. When in 1823 brothel operators John and Polly Evans were arrested in Portland, Maine, not only were the women in the brothel not charged, but one news account referred to the women as "enslaved."[30] Indeed, those aspects of prostitution viewed as nonconsensual were embodied in the nation's initial state laws. Typical in this regard was an 1821 Connecticut statute that penalized those who operated "houses of bawdry and ill fame" but not the women employed in them.[31] The same principle was more explicit in the laws of new states and territories created prior to the Civil War. Consent formed the basis of an 1838 Arkansas law, much as in other emerging states, when Arkansas directed its penalties at anyone "who shall take away any female under the age of fifteen years, from her father, mother, guardian or other person having the legal charge of her person, without their consent . . . for the purpose of prostitution."[32] The girl, however, based on her presumed lack of consent (or lack of informed consent), was considered a victim.

Myth also played an important role in using views of vice—or, more accurately, *occluding* such views—to maintain power. An 1839 newspaper report about the jailing of (notably, in terms of power) a newspaper editor charged with libel told readers, "Mrs. Adeline Miller was then proffered as bail for him, and she was examined on oath as to her competency, and having sworn that she was possessed of property to the amount of $20,000 and upwards, her bail was taken."[33] Unstated (and thus occluded from view) was the source of her wealth. Adeline Miller was one of New York City's preeminent madams.

Even when news accounts did identify brothels, enforcement of laws against prostitution remained spotty due to the combined power of sex and money influencing views of vice among police and politicians. In 1841 New York's *Hudson River Chronicle* reported, "A three story brick building in Leonard Street, owned and occupied by a notorious character named Julia Brown, was nearly destroyed by the falling of the back wall of the theater, and a young female named Margaret Yahger, who had but a few days previously left her parents in Philadelphia and 'taken board' with Julia Brown . . . was burned almost to a cinder."[34] Though Julia Brown was well known as the operator of a brothel, no action was taken to enforce New York's law prohibiting her from operating a whore house.[35] Likewise, the *Times-Picayune* in New Orleans made no mention of any action against the operators of what it identified as a "house of ill fame" in its report of an 1837 murder that took place there.[36]

When actions were taken in this era to eliminate brothels, often they revealed who was imposing power over whom through enforcement of this view of vice. An 1825 news report in Rhode Island's *Newport Mercury* told readers of a mob attacking a house "occupied by a colored man named Gray, who had been convicted of keeping a house of ill fame."[37] A Massachusetts newspaper reported in 1827 on the conviction of "John Mumford, a black," who used his "house in Salem for purposes of prostitution . . . [for] the corrupt and abandoned, of both sexes and colors."[38]

Whites were not the only group to use views of prostitution in the service of racial power. An 1856 article in an African American newspaper on a speech by a black leader revealed him seeking to acquire power for his race through his view of theater as a vice. "Our theatre-goers came in for a share of that rebuke which they so fully deserve," the article approvingly reported. "[They] boldly assert their God given rights throughout the day, while at night they are found garretted in the third tier of those sink holes of Satan [more often referred to today as balcony seats], surrounded by base and profligate women."[39]

While women in brothels got off the hook, not so their colleagues who worked on the street. The reason can be seen in one of the first American laws that used the word "prostitute." In the early 1800s New York added that word to its list of illegal no-goodniks that included beggars, fortune tellers, and jugglers (yes, still no) who could be arrested because they "live idle without employment."[40] In this justifying phrase, we can spot this view of vice being used for purposes of power, since employment is precisely what street prostitutes are engaged in. But street walkers, by virtue of being (or, if working for a pimp, appearing to be) "sole proprietors," were viewed as consensually engaging in prostitution, unlike their counterparts in brothels. Moreover, the privacy of brothels concealed patrons who could afford fees higher than those charged on the street.

This public/private distinction often forms our view of sexual vice. Strolling about in the nude, for example, is not a punishable vice in the curtained privacy of one's home, but doing so in public is a punishable vice. Usually. Here it gets more complicated but continues to reflect who holds power.

Back when there were more isolated regions in the world (which is to say, geographic privacy), a greater number of tribal groups did not view as vice their women going about with bared breasts. Influential members of the tribe felt little need to control who made babies with whom in seeking to ensure reproduction of their group. For the rest of us, however, cultural differences account for groups having considerable concern regarding reproduction—and empowering those concerns by viewing public nudity as a punishable vice. It behooves other powerful groups too to confine nudity (and the consent it can suggest) to controlled realms. Business owners, for instance. Even Hugh Hefner, who amassed millions marketing nudity as the publisher of *Playboy*, would undoubtedly have taken a dim view of his magazine's staff coming to work in the nude.

Shifts in power later altered the view of some people that public nudity was a vice—those people being nudists. As we shall later see, they organized into a movement that also sought to acquire power through views of vice—or, in their case, not-vice.

Views of Vice Lending a Hand in Acquiring Land

Prior to the Revolution, England sought to curtail the growth of American power by restricting the regions where its colonists could settle. Even after the Revolution, however, citizens of the new United States seeking to settle in those once-restricted regions faced a hurdle, that hurdle being the Americans already settled there. The Chickasaw, Choctaw, Creek, Sauk, Osage, Chippewa, Miami, and Winnebago—between 1820 and 1830, these tribes were among those that signed treaties ceding land to the United States. Needless to say, power (in the form of either military force or the threat of it) helped put pen to paper when Native American leaders signed these agreements. But to enlist more widespread support for such force, white people in positions of power used views of vice to persuade those who might otherwise have had misgivings.

Watch closely as John C. Calhoun, one of that era's most masterful politicians, demonstrates how to do a U-turn in views of vice. Rather than viewing Indians as vice-spreading savages, Calhoun depicted them as *vice-susceptible* savages when, as secretary of war in 1820, he asserted, "Many of the Indian tribes have acquired only the vices with which a savage people usually become tainted by their intercourse with those who are civilized." Calhoun went on to urge, ostensibly on behalf of Native Americans, "They must be brought gradually under our authority and laws, or they will insensibly waste away in vice and misery."[41] Yes, he was one of the nation's leading racists, but the elegance of that moral backflip is as impressive as it is abhorrent. In its way, it set the standard for future moral salchows and double axels that elegantly landed with justifications for enslaving fellow humans.

Just as vivid a use of views of vice in the service of power, albeit not nearly so elegant, was an 1847 law ostensibly enacted to combat the vice of drunkenness among Native Americans. By then, massive numbers of Indians had been relocated to reservations under treaties that provided annuities to each member of the tribe in compensation for surrendering ancestral land. Forking over all that cash was no fun for Congress. There were so many Americans who, unlike Indians, had voting rights to whom this money could be distributed in ways that would enhance the power of the politicians. To get their hands on these funds in a way that would win the approval of most voters, Congress stipulated in 1847 that none of the money "shall be paid or distributed to the Indians while they are under the influence of any description of intoxicating liquor, nor while there are good and sufficient reasons for . . . believing that there is any species of intoxicating liquor within convenient reach of the Indians."[42]

Ker-ching!

Within Native American tribes, views of vice also functioned as servants of those who held power. Among the Cherokee, who dwelt at the time primarily in regions of present-day Georgia and Alabama, the views of their leaders regarding drunkenness appeared to be identical to those of white political leaders. In truth, however, those views were rooted in their power struggle with whites. Out of deferral to, or admiration for, the power of whites, the Cherokee had created a tribal government modeled after that of the United States. In 1827 its legislature enacted laws against drunkenness and prohibited alcohol at tribal events. But in legal cases involving alcohol that entailed jurisdictional disputes between the Cherokee and Georgia, the federal government supported Georgia by refusing to recognize the legitimacy of Cherokee laws. Which is precisely what the Cherokee leaders meant to challenge by enacting their own laws to combat this vice.[43]

This use of views of vice for political leverage became evident in what Cherokee leaders did next. They responded both to the problem of drunkenness and to the challenge presented by state and federal power by teaming with missionary societies to establish temperance groups in their settlements. Missionary views of vice emanated from the power of religion. Religious leaders also often conflicted (then and now) with federal and state political leaders in regard to authority. Siding with the Cherokee, prominent missionary Jeremiah Evarts quoted a phrase in the tribe's 1791 treaty with the United States that stipulated that their agreed-upon land was not "within the jurisdiction of any state." He then asked, "Within what jurisdiction is it, then? Doubtless within Cherokee jurisdiction; for this territory is described as 'belonging to the Cherokees' [emphasis in original]."[44]

While the interests of Cherokee and missionary leaders led to their joining forces to oppose Georgia and the federal government taking command of efforts to combat drunkenness among Native Americans, those same interests led to differences in other views of vice. Christian missionary Sarah Tuttle described the Cherokee as a people who "know not that there is such a thing as sin."[45] One such sin, according to the Bible, is homosexuality. At that time, however, Native Americans did not view it as sin. Different tribes perceived such love in a variety of ways, but none in a way that was deemed punishable.[46] In 1830 John Tanner, an American who had been held captive by the Ojibwa in present-day Michigan, wrote of one member of the tribe: "This man was one of those who make themselves women, and are called women by the Indians. There are several of this sort among most, if not all, the Indian tribes. . . . This creature, called Osaw-wen-dib, was now near fifty years old and had lived with many husbands . . . [and] was very expert in the various employments of the women, to which all her time was given."[47]

The acceptance of various sexualities that John Tanner described was one of several Native American customs that whites viewed as vice. He also described what whites then would have viewed as licentiousness on the part of women—made even vicier by the notion of women smoking: "I was standing by our lodge one evening when I saw a good looking young woman walking about and smoking. She noticed me from time to time, and at last came up and asked me to smoke with her. I answered that I never smoked. 'You do not wish to touch my pipe; for that reason you will not smoke with me.' I took her pipe and smoked a little, though I had not been in the habit of smoking before. She remained some time and talked with me, and I began to be pleased with her." Tanner wrote of his captivity in order to convey how it changed so many of his views, most notably in his falling in love with and marrying this pipe-smoking woman.

While John Tanner, by writing in his memoirs of the Ojibwa acceptance of men who identify as women and of women who smoke pipes, sought to influence attitudes toward Native Americans via his recently adopted views of what he no longer viewed as vice, other instances in American history reveal efforts to hide very similar views held by a famous white man—but also in the service of power. An 1855 newspaper article seeking to promote Sam Houston as a potential presidential candidate told readers of his service in the War of 1812 and his subsequent election to Congress and the governorship of Tennessee, from which "he resigned his office and took up abode among the Cherokee in Arkansas. . . . [S]ubsequently, during a visit to Texas he was solicited to allow his name to be used . . . to form a constitution for Texas . . . which led to war and finally to the independence of Texas, and the election of General Houston as President of the Republic." The article closed by saying how this "venerable hero of the Indian and Mexican wars" was now a U.S. senator from Texas.[48]

But hold your horses there, hero. What was that thing about taking up abode with Indians?

In point of fact, Sam Houston did more than hang out with the Cherokee in the way one might today go to a dude ranch or backpack in the woods. As a teenager, Houston ran away from home and was adopted, under tribal traditions, by the chief of the Cherokee in his region of Tennessee. As did John Tanner, Houston became what we would call a naturalized member of a Native American tribe. Years later, a personal crisis believed to be related to his wife and his views of vice triggered his resignation as Tennessee's governor and flight back to his adopted father, who helped him desist from engaging in another vice: a drinking binge. None of which, needless to say, was mentioned in the newspaper. Nor did it mention what would be viewed as vice in clothing: Houston's earlier participation in a Cherokee delegation that met with Secretary of War John C. Calhoun in 1818, at which meeting Houston wore tribal garb. That fashion statement didn't fit with Calhoun's view that white vices infect Indians with decadence, since in this instance it appeared to be the other way around. Calhoun had the choice of being perplexed or pissed off. Being more powerful than Houston, he picked pissed off, and, indeed, Houston's career took a punishing stumble at this point.[49]

Uncle Sam's Advice to Teens

During the first half of the nineteenth century, the decline (albeit slight) in the influence of religion as a result of the rising influence of civic powers in a democracy can be seen in the always fun reading of advice books for teens. While minister George W. Burnap referenced the Bible when he wrote in 1840, "In order that low company should be sought and delighted in, there must have been committed the *original sin* of voluntary defilement of the thoughts and imagination," the statement that followed deferred to words emanating from industrialization: "There is a profane and immodest curiosity, a prying into the *animal economy* that seeks its gratifications in obscene books or impure descriptions, which is itself *polluting* and defiling to the soul [emphasis added]." Ultimately, religion totally yielded the lectern to secular forces in Burnap's admonitions. Rather than brandish the fear of damnation, he warned that vice "undermines the habits of industry and applications to business."[50]

Burnap's word choices in *Lectures to Young Men on the Cultivation of the Mind, the Formation of Character, and the Conduct of Life* revealed not only this shift in the pecking order between religious and secular authorities but also the extent to which, at that point in time, this shift resulted in views of vice being used to influence *men* as opposed to *women*. Note the italicized (by me) words in the following excerpt from Burnap's book: "By association with such [low company], the *natural* modesty of youth becomes gradually *soiled*," he said of males, then said of females, "The *sacred* charm of moral association, which invests woman to an unsophisticated mind with an inviolable *sacredness*, is slowly dispelled." Burnap used environmental terms ("natural," "soiled") when speaking of males, but for females his terminology ("sacred," "sacredness") was religious.[51]

Then again, Burnap was a guy. What about comparable books written by women for women? In 1830 Virginia Cary published *Letters on Female Character Addressed to a Young Lady*. In her book, religion and civics *shared* the lectern in her dispensing advice on female virtue and vice. In some instances, Cary emphasized the approval of others rather than the approval of God, as when she said in regard to vice in fashions, "A correctly brought up girl will be ashamed to wear anything that... will lead the world to cast aspersions upon her own prudence." In other instances, Cary, like Burnap, viewed vice through one lens, then switched to another. When advising young ladies on how not to accessorize, Cary first put forth a religious view: "Let us hope then... that the rising generation will learn to prefer the ornaments of a meek and quiet spirit. ... To effect even the smallest approximation to this general blessing will require a strict and cordial union among the disciples of the meek and lowly Jesus." Then, switching to a secular view, she concluded: "The woman who attracts attention by excess of expense, or eccentricity of fashion, invariably draws upon her the disapprobation, if not the contempt, of sensible, respectable people."[52] The key to whose power was being imposed in this latter view of vice resided in the word "respectable." Who bestowed respectability? Not God. (Were Mary Magdalene's counterparts in this era widely viewed as respectable?) Wealthy white men and their wives, that's who.

Like Burnap's views of female vice, so too Cary's dos and don'ts ultimately were in the service of religious power. Her views of vice in fashion and entertainment, for example, concluded with the hair-raising warning, "What young lady would not shrink with horror from the idea of falling dead in a cotillion or a waltz?" Of course, no guy would want to drop dead during a waltz, either. It would totally upend his future. But for females, according to Virginia Cary, the dread is the future. "What belle," she asked, "would be reconciled to the idea that she was suddenly to exchange the elaborate decorations of her ball night, and the affluent magnificence of her dancing apparel, for her last garment, the shroud?" Carey then took this religion-based view into far more profound realms than being caught dead in a prom dress. "Has anything, save Christianity, been yet discovered, of sufficient power to arrest vice in its mad career?" she asked.[53]

There is an additional dimension to the way in which Virginia Cary's and George Burnap's views of vice served the interests of the powers-that-be. Their respective religious/secular dualities rejoined God and Country. "The standard of the gospel," Cary aptly observed, "is about to be twined with our 'star spangled banner.'"[54]

A New Force Blows In

By 1850 new forces were amending conventional views of vice to acquire influence. Particularly notable was a fictional colonial era woman who expressed a far more modern view of vice in a book still sold today. That woman is Hester Prynne, the heroine in Nathaniel Hawthorne's now classic novel, *The Scarlet Letter*, set in colonial Massachusetts. Hester is convicted of adultery and sentenced to wear a capital A for the rest of her life. But she also endures an additional punishment: *her inner feelings of shame and guilt.* In Hawthorne's view, it is this second punishment that reforms Hester, so much so that ultimately, rather than being ostracized, she comes to be sought out by other women seeking guidance regarding their passions. The letter A that Hester continues to wear, Hawthorne tell us, comes to represent the word "Able." Hawthorne's novel was widely (though not unanimously) praised.[55]

This shift in views reflected a newly organizing force entering American society at that time, albeit with some sputters and backfires: behavioral science. "A new and complete system of intellectual and moral philosophy" was the subject of an 1836 book titled *Phrenology: Proved, Illustrated, and Applied,* by Orson and Lorenzo Fowler. Based on what proved to be a faulty premise that measurements of the skull revealed one's cognitive and emotional faculties, phrenology nevertheless marked the entrance of a behavioral science into the larger, and itself increasingly influential, realm of science. Within that realm, as will be seen, behavioral science would go on to become a highly influential force in the United States, acquiring much of its power through its views of vice.

Indeed, through its views of vice, phrenology, for all its flaws, did more than wedge its foot in the door to sell ceramic heads illustrating the sections of the brain. It too put forth views of vice such as, in the Fowler brothers' 1836 book, its viewpoint on sex. They criticized the "false modesty, that sickly delicacy, that double-refined fastidiousness which pervade every civilized community in regard to it, and which are far more detrimental to virtue and purity than anything and everything else could be."[56] Phrenology's ceramic heads were cracked, but they paved the way for Sigmund Freud and legions of psychologists who would project new views of vice and not-vice into America's culture.

For all of phrenology's significance as a sign of major changes to come, it had little influence in its day. Hawthorne, for example, made no references to the size or shape of Hester Prynne's skull. Indeed, the prevailing view toward this more psychological view of sexual vice—particularly how that prevailing view served the interests of those in power—can be seen in another American novel dealing with the inner torment of adultery. Five years after *The Scarlet Letter,* Mary Gove Nichols published *Mary Lyndon* in 1855. Reviewers were revolted. (More on that word shortly.) "Fatal to all social purity," the *Sandusky Register* opined. "A book which no decent person would keep in his, or her, house," according to the *Milwaukee Sentinel.* "Strenuous efforts should be made to prevent anything of the kind falling into the hands of children," the *Newport Mercury* warned.[57]

By comparison, the few bad reviews of *The Scarlet Letter* looked like a nitpick here and a tut-tut there. Since both books depicted the inner turmoil of a woman coping with extramarital passion, why did critics praise *The Scarlet Letter* but pan *Mary Lyndon*? Particularly since, in *Mary Lyndon*, the struggle is depicted up to a point shortly before the point where *The Scarlet Letter* begins: that being the moment of adultery. *Which Mary decides not to commit.* What gives with these reviewers? Or, more to the point, what were these reviews giving their readers?

None of these reviews maintained the book was actually pornographic, since nothing in the book could support that claim. Nor can we assume the criticism was because its author was a woman, since numerous highly regarded authors in the nineteenth century were women, many of whom wrote of struggles with romantic passions.

Which brings us to the word "revolted." Specifically, its core meaning: revolt. Hawthorne, in *The Scarlet Letter*, minimized an aspect of his story that, in *Mary Lyndon*, occupied center stage: both women, through their journeys, ceased to be dependent on men. Because this quest for independence was central to *Mary Lyndon*—and since sex was central to her quest—it was viewed as vice. But to view female independence as vice, reviewers hid from view the fact that Mary's quest included opting not to commit adultery, since their readers would have viewed that as virtue.

In fairness to the critics—even though they weren't fair—there was another reason this book raised their hackles. Though the novel did not advocate free love, its novelist did. Mary Gove Nichols and her husband, Thomas Low Nichols, were among this era's leading advocates of what was known as the free love movement.[58] Those in the forefront of this movement were not, as its name seems to suggest, advocating promiscuity. They opposed marriage laws, since such laws impose government power over intimacy and, at the time, imposed male power over women in regard to property and child custody.

As far back as 1792, British women's rights advocate Mary Wollstonecraft, condemned by many for her views on free love, pointed out how views of marital virtue and vice served the interests of those who held the most power. Rejecting an advice book for young women by a prominent minister, Wollstonecraft quoted its claim that "men of sensibility desire in every woman soft features and a flowing voice, a form not robust, and demeanor delicate and gentle," to which she rejoined, "Is [this] not the . . . portrait of a house slave?"[59] By 1855 free love advocates in the United States were likewise but more forcefully asserting, "Marriage is the slavery of woman. . . . The slave's earnings belong to the master, the earnings of the wife belong to the husband. . . . [T]he clothes they wear and the food they eat is the property of the master."[60]

During these years, a free love colony was founded in Berlin Heights, Ohio. In the variety of views expressed by its neighbors, we can see how those who pulled the strings of American morals in colonial days, when the Mount Wollaston settlement caused so much rage, had since been joined by other sources of power. One 1857 letter to the editor of the nearby *Sandusky Register* intertwined God and Uncle Sam (though the writer did so very differently from Virginia Cary or George Burnap) when it defended "their 'God-given right' to locate and remain in Berlin [Heights] or anywhere else, in the enjoyments of all their peculiar notions." Still, that old-time religion was not gone. Another letter in the same day's paper expressed the "wish that the whipping-post and ducking stool of old might be revived, for the better instruction of 'Free Lovers.'" Yet another in the batch published that day used language that reflected the influence of a newcomer to the scene from after the Revolution—industrialization—when its letter writer supported the effort to oust this free love community "which is *polluting* the moral atmosphere [emphasis added]."[61]

Industrialization: Immigrants, Cities, and Vice

"The late United States census . . . calls attention to the extraordinary tendency of Americans to agglomerate in cities," an 1852 editorial in Brattleboro, Vermont's *Weekly Eagle* noted as a springboard to a moral cannonball dive on newcomers to the United States. "With luxury and refinement come many of the most interesting features of an advanced civilization," it said on its lofty rise, then tucked its virtuous butt to splash, "but, hitherto at least, a laxity of morals . . . is no doubt one of the results of the enormous immigration to this country." Taking another plunge at newcomers, this time it added a twist: "The Irish, who form the greater portion of this immigration, are eminently gregarious and social in their habits and have little taste for the life which Daniel Boone led in the forest, or which the New England pioneers lead in Oregon and the far West."[62] To this day, Americans feel revivified by a clean fresh breath of Daniel Boone— one of this nation's most morally pure myths, filtered as it has been of facts such as Boone having married a Shawnee woman, despite the fact that he was already married.[63]

But why be satisfied with one newspaper in Brattleboro, Vermont, when up at the northern end of that state whom should we find but Nathaniel Hawthorne, moseying around the industrializing town of Burlington? "Nothing struck me more in Burlington than the great number of Irish emigrants," he wrote of his visit. "It is difficult to conceive how a third part of them should earn even a daily glass of whiskey, which is doubtless their first necessary of life."[64] When touring a dam being constructed to power industry along Maine's Kennebec River, Hawthorne described "an old Irishwoman [who] sat in the door of another hut, under the influence of an extra dose of rum," as being "a true virago" (a woman of masculine strength) by virtue of the way she spoke to his host, one of the project's owners, about her resolve not to vacate her company-owned "hut." As for her husband, Hawthorne viewed him as doubly viceful in being both unmanly and brutish: "Meanwhile her husband stood by very quiet, occasionally trying to still her, but it is to be presumed that, after our departure, they came to blows, it being a custom with the Irish husbands and wives to settle their disputes with blows."[65] Note his assuming the presumed violence to come was consensual.

Hawthorne doesn't look good here—to us today, that is. But wait, it gets worse. It becomes even more evident how Hawthorne's views of vice served to maintain the social status quo when these remarks about Irish immigrants are compared to statements he made about French Canadians who came to Maine to work on the dam. Hawthorne viewed alcohol as engrained in their culture, too. But in their case he didn't view it as vice. He described, for example, a "Monsieur S—— shaving himself yesterday morning" as being "in excellent sprits . . . breaking out into scraps of verses of drinking songs, '*À boire! À boire!*' [To drink! To drink!]," going on to admire how this fine fellow "turned foolery to philosopher by observing that mirth contributed to goodness of the heart, and to make us love our fellow-creatures."[66] What was the difference between Irish drinking and Canadian drinking? Unlike the Irish, these French Canadians presented no challenge to the social order of the United States, since their intention was to return to Canada.

Au revoir. À boire!

Hawthorne, however, as seen in *The Scarlet Letter*, was no simpleton. His views of adultery in that novel were and remain profoundly insightful. Likewise here, other remarks reveal that his views of vice were more complex. And their complexity reveals competing sources of power. Regarding that ramble through the company-owned shanty town, Hawthorne also wrote of two "very pretty and modest-looking young women," of whom he said, "Amid all the trials of their situation, [they] appear to have kept up the distinction between virtue and vice." Maybe they did, maybe they didn't, but there is little question as to what formed Hawthorne's view of Irish virtue: sexual attraction. So much so, it circled back to those seeking to maintain power through views of Irish vice. "It seems strange," Hawthorne wrote when commending these comely lasses, "that man should have the right, unarmed by any legal instrument, of tearing down the dwelling-houses of a score of families, and driving the inmates forth without a shelter."[67] While one might be inclined to attribute this view to Christian influence, neither mercy nor salvation played a part in Hawthorne's view of the older and less attractive Irish woman or his view of her unmanly/brutish husband.

Those seeking to maintain white Protestant dominance included a once preeminent group: rural Americans. Amid the growing power of industrialists and the flood of foreigners arriving to work in factories and the infrastructures needed to support them, agricultural Americans began increasingly cultivating views of vice to maintain their influence. "In our great cities," the *Salem Gazette* warned its still agricultural community in 1831, "vices the most disgusting, brutal intemperance, crime in its most hideous and appalling forms are congregated and form a mass of corruption rendered more deleterious from the mixture of imported depravity."[68] Such views of vice were fertilized with moral myths, as when the *Farmer's Cabinet* said of young men who had already moved from the farm to the city: "When he contrasts the profaneness and depravity of his present companions with the sacredness of all he ever heard or saw in his father's dwelling, many will be the dreary and dissatisfied intervals when he shall be forced to acknowledge that in bartering his soul for the pleasures of sin, he has bartered the peace and enjoyment of the world along with it."[69] It is doubtful that "all he ever heard or saw" on the farm was virtuous. Still, then and now, moral myths of rural life pack a powerful punch, and not just in the United States.

Comparable efforts were made to dissuade daughters from the lure of urbanizing America. "Fashion, that juggernaut of great cities," was Virginia Cary's warning to rural girls in her previously cited book. Like Hawthorne, her advice on urban vice served to promulgate the social status quo, as when she advised young women who did live in cities, "You should be careful how you give to the poor girls around you such things as may nourish a taste for finery. This mischief making passion has destroyed as many women as the vice of drunkenness has destroyed men."[70]

Urban industrialists were not the only group acquiring power in this era. Coalescing in their wake were their workers. In 1840 early labor advocate Orestes Brownson vindicated their vices when he wrote, "The great mass wear out their health, spirits, and morals, without becoming one whit better off than when they commenced labor." At the same time, Brownson pointed at what he viewed as a vice of their employers—gluttony—when he said, "And yet there is a man who employs them to make shirts, trousers, etc., and grows rich on their labors. . . . He passes among us as a pattern of morality and is honored as a worthy Christian."[71]

As seen in Hawthorne's observations, Irish immigrants were particularly prominent among those joining the migration to factories in this era. Fleeing poverty that turned to famine in the 1840s, when a potato disease caused Ireland's staple crop to fail, multitudes of Irish flooded into the United States. Adding to Ireland's woes was the widespread alcoholism that we saw forming the focus of Hawthorne's attention. So many Irish arrived in so short a time that antivice societies sprang up anew, this time more singularly devoted to abstinence from alcohol. Ossining, New York's *Hudson River Chronicle* devoted an editorial to this nationwide response, applauding these efforts to enlighten drunkards about "the misery, ruin, and distress which follow in the train of intemperance to the poverty and want entailed upon such family."[72] Though these groups had genuinely magnanimous motives, their view of this vice served the interests of industrialists by distracting attention from the low wages that kept so many workers mired in poverty and despair.

Still, among Irish immigrants, this incarnation of the temperance movement did have considerable success. In Philadelphia, for example, every Catholic parish established a temperance society. More than five thousand of that city's Catholics, a vast number of whom were Irish immigrants, pledged to abstain from alcohol.[73] Why, if the approach was so wrong-headed (or industrialist-headed), was it working so well? Because one aspect of this view of vice at this point in time projected Irish power. Most Americans, however, got only a glimpse of it, as in a brief news item from 1840 that read, "In consequence of the late difficulty among the Irish laborers on the [Western Railroad], near Pittsfield, the contractor discharged a large number of them and went to New York . . . to engage a supply of fresh emigrants from Ireland, every one of whom had Father Mathew's Temperance Medal hung to his neck."[74]

Theobald Mathew was a priest in Ireland who in 1838 commenced a temperance movement in that land. Ireland had been under the direct rule of England since 1801, when the British government abolished Ireland's parliament. As in this country with Native Americans, snuffing out self-rule was part of a larger conflict: Who gets what land? England had coveted Ireland since before the twelfth century, when it first invaded. Long story short, by the nineteenth century, those native Irish—still religiously and patriotically Catholic—had been reduced to dire poverty and, as with Native Americans, were shackled by laws limiting their political power. Also as with Native Americans, alcoholism ran rampant.

Temperance, under Father Mathew's crusade, became a patriotic act, since it dovetailed with a struggle taking place in Parliament for Irish independence led by Bishop Daniel O'Connell. Here, then, is where this view of vice asserted Irish power, as it had for Native Americans during the cultural revival that dovetailed with Pontiac's Rebellion.[75] When, however, O'Connell's struggle failed to achieve self-rule for Ireland, Father Mathew's temperance crusade rapidly lost its fuel, much as alcoholism surged anew among Native Americans following the failure of Pontiac's Rebellion.

Views of Vice as Weapons in the Civil War

More starkly than any other aspect of American history, the conflict over slavery entailed views of vice being employed by those who adhered to one side or the other in that clash between the North and South. Here again, long story short: two tales from the era reveal this use of vice as a servant of power.

In Harriet Beecher Stowe's 1852 classic antislavery novel, *Uncle Tom's Cabin*, a slave owner's wife invokes a religious view of vice when she declares to her husband, "It is a sin to hold a slave under laws like ours—I always felt it was—I always thought so when I was a girl—I thought so still more after I joined the church." Employing such views on behalf of industrialists, Stowe included a subplot involving a factory owner to whom a slave named George is leased. Not surprisingly, she depicted the factory owner as a kindly man under whom George "had free liberty to come and go."[76]

The Planter's Northern Bride, by Caroline Lee Hentz, served as the flip side to *Uncle Tom's Cabin* and sold well when it was published in 1854. In this instance, a plantation-owning husband says of industrialists to his antislavery bride, "It has often been said that there need be no such thing as poverty in this free and happy land; that here it is only the offspring of vice and intemperance. . . . Whether this be true or not, let the thousand toiling operatives of the Northern manufactories tell; let the poor, starving seamstresses, whose pallid faces mingle their chill, wintry gleams with the summer glow and splendor of the Northern cities, tell."[77]

Today, *Uncle Tom's Cabin* remains widely remembered, whereas very few Americans have even heard of *The Planter's Northern Bride*. The powers in the North, after all, won the war. Still, even though the North won, racism did not lose. Over time, however, its power has ever so gradually declined. Today, many readers (especially among African Americans) view the character of Uncle Tom as having a vice: servility. Which is to say, the acceptance of unempowerment.

3

"Free at Last" with Liberty and
Must-Nots for All Kinds of Stuff

Emancipation not only paved the way for African Americans to become increasingly influential (albeit in the face of massive and violent resistance) but also sparked efforts to achieve equal treatment by other groups, most notably, women, Chinese Americans, and Native Americans. Many of the leaders of these groups—and of groups resisting these quests—expressed views of vice that enhanced their group's power. Another group, too, was making its way by joining in these frays. Scientists, until now bit players on the American stage, began getting bigger speaking roles by expressing views of vice that, in some instances, enhanced the power of one of the groups and, in other instances, enhanced the power of its opponent—but in all instances enhanced the power of scientists.

Not surprisingly, most scientific views of vice served the interests of those who held the biggest whip. "In the city of Charleston," statistician Frederick L. Hoffman reported, "the number of deaths from syphilis for the period 1889–94 was 66 among the colored population, as against 10 among the white population." Hoffman also collected data on drunkenness, drug addiction, and crime. From this data, he concluded, "The root of the evil lies in the fact of an immense amount of immorality, which is a race trait. . . . It is not in the conditions of life, but in the race traits and tendencies that we find the causes."[1] In other words, relax, white folks, the vices of blacks have nothing to do with you. The correlations in Hoffman's data are startling. Left out, however, was an even more startling statistic: over 99 percent of all murderers drank milk as children. This example is an axiom of data analysis—*correlation does not prove causation*—an axiom that Frederick Hoffman, a professional statistician, opted to ignore.

Bad science, but not bad for scientists, based on the hypothesis of the biggest whip. "It is the best book yet issued on the subject, the fruit of close study of the subject and absolutely free of bias," proclaimed the *New Orleans Times-Democrat*. South Carolina senator Benjamin R. Tillman expressed hope that it would become required reading for "every student of our political sociological and ethnological conditions."[2] Ohio State University professor Matthew Hammond cited Hoffman's data to support his own research coming to the conclusion that "it is not to be regretted that the majority of negroes . . . have not acquired ownership of land."[3]

Not all scholars were fooled. One professor at Atlanta University identified the faults in Hoffman's data analysis (and the data itself), then spoke, in effect, of the use of views of vice when he declared that this kind of science was an example of how "Anglo-Saxon prejudice had shut nearly every avenue of advancement in [African American] faces."[4] The byline of this book review bore one of those four-word names no college kid wants to argue grades with—William Edward Burghardt Du Bois—more widely known today as W. E. B. Du Bois. He was the first African American to earn a doctorate from Harvard University, and he went on to become one of the preeminent voices of his generation for equal rights.

In his 1903 book, *The Souls of Black Folk*, Du Bois pointed out how racism was often intertwined with views of vice to maintain the power of the well-to-do. "In the higher walks of life," he wrote, ". . . the color-line comes to separate natural friends . . . [but] at the bottom of the social group, in the saloon, the gambling-hell, and the brothel, the same line wavers and disappears." Du Bois's own background, racially and economically, straddled those lines. For this reason, perhaps, even he spoke of the vice of "shiftlessness" in *The Souls of Black Folk*. Commenting on an instance in which he witnessed laziness and irresponsibility by two African American workers, he wrote, "Shiftless? Yes, the personification of shiftlessness." But Du Bois vindicated this vice by writing, "They are careless because they have not found that it pays to be careful; they are improvident because the improvident ones of their acquaintance get on about as well as the provident."[5] In this remark, Du Bois became one of the first to maintain that when views of vice are used to maintain inequality, the inequality they maintain contributes to vice. As time will tell, he was correct. And not only in the case of African Americans.

During this same era, many scientists also put forth views of vice that served to advance their influence by enhancing that of those seeking to suppress the growing power of mankind's oldest nemesis: womankind. "The weight of the average female brain," A. Hughes Bennett, MD, told readers in the February 1880 issue of *Popular Science*, "has been estimated at from five to six ounces less than that of the average male brain.... As the organ of intellect in the female is smaller and lighter than that in the male, we may fairly assume ... her weaknesses and vices are greater."[6]

May we? How, then, can we explain, beginning in 1848, the extraordinary political organization taking shape at annual woman's rights conventions? Not to mention (though we will later) the leadership of women in the temperance movement? Both of these movements amassed enough power to get the Constitution amended.

One way to explain these indications of women's intelligence, if one opted not to believe it, was through views of vice. In 1848, that landmark year for woman's rights, Columbus, Ohio, enacted an ordinance prohibiting women, or men, from appearing in public wearing the clothing of the opposite sex. Coincidence? If so, it's a curious coincidence, since going around in drag was already punishable in Ohio—and every other state. As early as 1805, for example, a Connecticut law stated, "If any man shall wear women's apparel, or if any woman shall wear men's apparel ... such offenders shall be corporally punished or fined."[7] Why, then, was Columbus, Ohio, enacting this ordinance in 1848? Indeed, why did more than thirty other cities and states enact similar laws between 1848 and 1920, the year in which the Nineteenth Amendment, giving women the right to vote, was ratified?[8] The answer can be seen in an 1851 editorial on the woman's rights movement. "Termagants [shrewish females or, in the parlance of contemporary insults, bitches] and men-women may hold conventions and pass resolutions about the rights of the sex—the inconvenience of their dress, the tyranny of men, etc.," the *Cincinnati Times* scoffed, then, for adornment, it wove another vice (public farting) into the same sentence when it concluded, "But they are the gaseous exhalations of the corruptions of the times, as fleeting as the air."[9]

Phew! That was one crowd-fleeing use of views of vice.

As if women joining together to challenge the status quo wasn't enough, Chinese people began arriving in the United States about this time, having been attracted by the 1848 discovery of gold in California. Industrialists discovered gold of a kind, too: Chinese workers. Coming from what was then a deeply impoverished nation, workers from China were willing to accept lower wages than their American counterparts. One way white workers combatted this challenge to their wages, which already hovered around the level of bare subsistence, was by using views of vice. The recently formed Workingmen's Party of California (WPC, though the party could have doubled the Ws, the added one standing for White) declared of the Chinese neighborhood in San Francisco: "There we behold dens of iniquity and filth, houses of prostitution of the vilest sort, opium dens, [and] gambling houses." Much as scientists sought to enhance their power by promulgating views of vice that served the interest of groups with more power than they, so too the WPC sought to enhance its power by viewing vice in ways that added to the influence of a more powerfully established group: scientists. The WPC statement said of San Francisco's Chinatown: "There it is from whence leprosy, this inherent factor, this inbred disease of Chinese, is infused into our healthy race by the sucking of opium-pipes, which have been handled by those already afflicted."[10]

But did scientists return the favor? Some in California did, since the gold rush there was where their bread was buttered. Two San Francisco physicians, for example, were among those who signed the WPC statement. But numerous physicians in the United States and elsewhere had already noted that leprosy's infectiousness was not so simple, and American doctors knew the disease was more prevalent in areas of Louisiana and the Midwest than in Chinese-infested San Francisco.[11] By opting for empirical facts that, over time, proved more valid than moral myths, these physicians ultimately increased the influence of their group.

As for industrialists, they tended to view Chinese vice—and virtues—differently. "The aptitude of Chinese for commerce surpasses even that of the Anglo-Saxon, and to that aptitude there is joined a scrupulous probity"—probity being legalese for morality, and these words being those of an attorney whose client supplied Chinese labor to industries. "I do not think the Chinamen are all angels," he conceded, but in his view, "not one out of twenty uses opium." Agreeing with the WPC about the crisis of vice in California, this mouthpiece for business interests U-turned that concession into a moral whack at white labor when he said, "California was originally settled by gamblers and this early passion has continued to the present day. . . . It is no cause for surprise that our boys and girls—our boys and girls, not those of the Chinaman—do not grow up the models of virtue and propriety. We furnish billiard rooms, whiskey saloons, dance cellars, melodeons, and brothels all over town."[12]

The Chinese Exclusion Act closed the gates to their entry in 1882, but what about the ones who were already here? To whack that, Congress passed another law in 1909—the first of its kind on the federal level: the Opium Exclusion Act. With its enactment, America's national war on drugs commenced.

And was declared on a group whom most whites did not want.

Drug Power

Opium was big business, as is the drug trade today. Back then, however, the muscle that most effectively enforced the will of the drug lords was the British military, often along with that of France and later the United States. To varying degrees, these nations engaged in two Opium Wars with China (1839–42, 1856–60) and intervened to suppress its Boxer Rebellion (1899–1901), which threatened Western opium dealers. Officially, these wars were for trading privileges; unofficially, those privileges included paying for Chinese products not with silver, as Chinese law required, but with opium, which China's emperor forbade. In nineteenth-century China, opium was a popular pain reliever for poverty and hopelessness, despite its side effect: addiction. When, midcentury, Chinese workers began pouring into California, opium smokers were among them.

Before the federal government enacted the Opium Exclusion Act, California had already passed antiopium legislation, and before that San Francisco had given it a go.[13] As had been the case with colonial laws prohibiting whites from providing alcohol to Indians, these opium laws turned out to be largely ineffective. More to the point, and also as with their colonial counterparts, these laws were not enacted to protect substance abusers; they were enacted to protect those in power and their loved ones. That cat was let out of the bag when, soon after San Francisco passed its 1875 antiopium law, a news item from the *Los Angeles Herald* reported, "The first raid under the new ordinance against white persons who frequent opium dens was made at two o'clock this morning by a force of police."[14] In point of fact, the ordinance did not specify white persons. In point of reality, however, the statement was accurate. As one New Hampshire newspaper told readers, "It is a familiar fact that the Chinese inhabitants of the United States are almost entirely addicted to the use of opium, but it is not so generally known that there are fully 200,000 victims of the pernicious drug in this country, more than two-thirds of whom are from the best classes of the white race."[15] Again, factually not even close, but absolutely accurate in regard to whom these laws sought to protect: white people. The WPC cited opium in its list of Chinese vices that "destroy . . . the manhood and the health of our people." But laws emanating from this view of vice weren't aimed only at protecting manhood. "Young white girls are frequently enticed into [Chinese] laundries and opium joints, degraded and ruined," one book from the era asserted.[16] Unexplained but intriguing is how one entices a girl into a laundry.

Not all Americans viewed opium use through the lens of race. Viewing it through the lens of (and thus seeking to acquire influence for) behavioral science, John V. Shoemaker wrote in 1904, "There is a certain class of young people who are weak enough to look on such experiences as an evidence of their knowledge of the world."[17] Wanting to be like adults—a more empowered group than youth—many teens, then and now, will vindicate a vice (despite its risks) in an effort to assert their individual power. Adding to that allure back then were a number of influential figures in the Opium Users Hall of Fame. They included the widely read poets Samuel Taylor Coleridge and Alfred, Lord Tennyson, and Thomas De Quincey, author of one of that century's longest-running best sellers, *Confessions of an English Opium-Eater*.[18]

Also widely admired at the time was Ezra Jennings, an opium-smoking detective in what was for several decades a highly popular novel from 1868, *The Moonstone* by Wilkie Collins (who was also known to use opium). Though Ezra Jennings is all but forgotten today, take a look at this sequence in which his client expresses uneasiness about drug use and see if this opium-imbibing detective reminds you of anyone:

"I thought the influence of opium was first to stupefy you, and then to send you to sleep."

"The common error about opium, Mr. Blake! I am, at this moment, exerting my intelligence—such as it is—in your service, under the influence of a dose of laudanum."[19]

More on laudanum (a mixture of opium and alcohol) shortly, but what about the voice of Ezra Jennings? Sound like that still-popular drug-using sleuth Sherlock Holmes?

Making his debut two decades later, Sherlock Holmes continues to astound readers with his amazing mental powers. Unlike for Ezra Jennings, however, the drug of choice for Sherlock Holmes was cocaine, the significance of the difference being that opium "had connotations of association with low-class Chinese," in the words of Martin Booth in his biography of Holmes's creator, Arthur Conan Doyle. "Such a drug as opium would never do for such a high-class man as Sherlock Holmes."[20]

In the United States, the view of opium use as a Chinese vice emanated less from the groups in power than from a group seeking power: white industrial workers. As for cocaine, neither America's powers-that-be nor powers-that-wannabe viewed the use of cocaine as a vice of high-class men. In 1902 the *Atlanta Constitution* reported on "the alarming growth of the use of cocaine among the negroes." A state law already existing in Georgia required a doctor's prescription for cocaine. But here we find one of those gaps in which so much history is stashed. "No effort has been made by the authorities to enforce it," the article reported. Why wasn't it enforced? Check out the sentence that followed: "Physicians state that if the habit among the negroes is not suppressed . . . it will mean the utter ruin and final extermination of the race in the South."[21] It wasn't enforced because, in the words of the previously mentioned veteran of television vice, Homer Simpson, "Just because I don't care doesn't mean I don't understand."

Many, if not most, whites feared blacks. And if physicians and other scientists said that cocaine was, in effect, causing self-genocide, those whites preferred that outcome to law enforcement helping to sustain that race. But the science guys were wrong. Genocide wasn't the result. Crime was. By 1914 it was abundantly evident that to obtain this illegal substance, addicts did illegal things. To provide added power to law enforcement, moral myths were deployed. Black cocaine users were now characterized as "a constant menace" by (why am I not surprised?) a medical doctor, Edward Huntington Williams, who informed white America, "His whole nature is changed for the worse by the habit. Sexual desires are increased and perverted, peaceful negroes develop a degree of 'Dutch courage' that is sometimes almost incredible." But the doc was just warming up his myth pitches. He went on to get a second opinion from a police officer whom he quoted as saying, "The cocaine nigger is sure hard to kill," before adding,

"Many of these officers in the South have increased the caliber of their guns for the express purpose of 'stopping' the cocaine fiend when he runs amok."[22] Even that "fact" was just this physician's opening moral myth pitch. Check out his depravity spitball, on which he'd affixed police chief D. K. Lyerly of Asheville, North Carolina:

> In attempting to arrest a hitherto peaceful negro who had become crazed by cocaine, Lyerly was forced to grapple with the man, who slashed him viciously with a long knife. In self-defense the officer drew his revolver, placed the muzzle over the negro's heart, and fired—"for I knew I had to kill him quick," the chief explained. The revolver he used, be it understood, was not the short-cartridge, pocket weapon carried by most Northern policemen, but a heavy army model . . . [that] will kill any game in America. And yet this bullet did not even stagger the crazed negro, and neither did a second bullet which pierced the biceps muscle and entered the thorax. So that the officer had finally to "finish the man with his club."[23]

For the record, Edward Huntington Williams, MD, wasn't some isolated quack. He was a widely respected professor of medicine at Iowa State University, and these statements of his were reported at length in newspapers and cited in scholarly journals.[24]

The moral of this story is that moral myths, used to promulgate views of vice that are in turn being used to impose power, are more than intellectually interesting. They can be deadly.

Still, why were white Americans now using such heavy artillery, both literally and with extraordinary myths about blacks and cocaine? Crime alone can't account for it; Frederick Hoffman, as we saw, was cooking up statistics on black vice and crime twenty years earlier.

In the interim, however, an organization was created that, if its growth went unchecked, could challenge white dominance. The National Association for the Advancement of Colored People (NAACP) was formed in 1909. To make matters worse (in the view of white supremacists), its founders included a handful of influential whites. In the past there had also been whites who viewed blacks as equal, but, being few and far between, they never formed an organized movement. In response to efforts such as the creation of the NAACP, an amped-up view of "Negro vice" became one of the weapons of white supremacists.

A Treatment for Unhappy Housewives: Vice

Housewives were another group that appeared as a result of industrialization. In agricultural regions, wives in middle-income and even in many upper-income rural families engaged in tasks required to maintain the farm or ranch. Not so among their urban counterparts. Urban families that had sufficient wealth promoted the view that industriousness was virtuous by viewing as indolent or incompetent men whose incomes required their wives to work. As for the wives in those more fortunate families, they only had to clean the house, cope with the kids, and cook the meals—or, if they were more "fortunate," not even that. Many found these tasks mind-numbing and depressing. But a new form of relief appeared in the nineteenth century: laudanum. Having the added benefit of not being viewed as either a Chinese or a Negro vice, it became the drug of choice among housewives.

Laudanum addiction was by no means limited to women, but when data began to be collected in the early twentieth century, the statistics indicated addiction to it among housewives far exceeded that of their husbands.[25] Obtaining the drug was no problem, as laws did not yet restrict its use. It was frequently sold as a pain reliever or cough suppressant or, for some, simply as a perker-upper. And it wasn't some bogus elixir: for each of these maladies its mix of opium and alcohol did the trick. Few at first were aware of its addictiveness, including pharmacists and physicians. By the mid-nineteenth century, however, this risk was well known. As was the reason so many housewives, even knowingly, took it. "Its effects upon her spirits were most exhilarating," one physician wrote of a laudanum-addicted patient in 1867. "She felt lively and cheerful, and could accomplish almost any amount of household work."[26]

By the turn of the century, some number of housewives acquired an addiction to another opium derivative: morphine. "Many authorities have pointed out the danger of morphinism in women," physician Thomas Crothers wrote in 1902. We might assume that Dr. Crothers's views on morphinism in women, as opposed to men, were based on facts rather than myths, since he was a scientist. But no. "Capriciousness of mind, irritability, selfishness, restlessness, and excitability are the natural characteristics of many women, who quickly become morphinists," he pseudoscientifically asserted.[27] In other words, relax, guys, none of her problems have anything to do with you.

Still, something had to be done about drug-addicted women, if for no other reason than the housework wasn't getting done—though there were other reasons. Love, for one. One husband repeatedly told his local pharmacist not to sell laudanum to his wife, but the husband didn't have the power to dictate to whom the pharmacist sold what. The husband could, however, sue the pharmacist on the basis of—and here's where power resided in this view of this vice—*damaging the husband's property*. And he won. As did other husbands, because, in the words of one such ruling in 1897, "The husband, as a matter of law, is entitled to [his wife's] time, her wages, her earnings, and the product of her labor, skill, and industry. And it seems to be a most reasonable proposition of law that whoever willfully joins with a married woman in doing an act which deprives her husband of her services . . . is liable to the husband in damages for his conduct."[28]

But the lawsuit route was cumbersome and costly. Lawyers may have liked it, but another group suggested a different approach. "Laws should be enacted forbidding the sale of preparations containing the [addictive] drugs, except on prescription only," physician J. J. McCarthy told readers in the August 1910 issue of *Pearson's Magazine*.[29] Which is to say, give this power to doctors.

Which is not to say it was a bad idea.

Four years later, Congress did just that. In 1914 President Woodrow Wilson signed into law the Harrison Narcotics Act, which required a doctor's prescription for "opium or coca leaves or any compound, manufacture, salt, derivative, or preparation thereof."[30]

Add Vice on How the West Was Won

During the same years that various groups were engaged in combatting urban vice, out on the western frontier, Uncle Sam's favorite nieces and nephews, white people, were beleaguered by a different problem, that being the Apaches, Lakotas (aka Sioux), Navajos, Hopis, and others whose tribes were native to those lands. Among the weapons used to overpower these people were views of vice.

In the realm of drugs, peyote, a hallucinogen derived from a type of cactus, was the first upon which the crosshairs of vice were trained. Members of several tribes in the Southwest used peyote to transport themselves into spiritual realms during religious rituals. In 1889 the Bureau of Indian Affairs made it a criminal offense for them to do so.[31] One might be inclined to think the intention of this regulation was good, though its proponents provided no evidence that peyote use in these tribes was harmful.

Ironically, this dictum was undermined by a separate effort to weaken tribal power. Two years earlier, passage of the General Allotment Act commenced a program in which the federal government altered the ownership of tribal land. Rather than being owned by the tribe, the land was distributed in a way that the head of each family in the tribe owned (and could sell) his allotted parcel. Along with this shift toward, shall we say, the American way of life, those Indians now acquired citizenship. And thus Uncle Sam's right hand whacked its left, since, as citizens, Native Americans could claim that their religions were now protected by the Bill of Rights. In 1918 the dictum on peyote was downsized to permit its use in religious rituals. By then, however, it and other weaponry had sufficiently succeeded in scattering the western embers of Native American power.

Peyote was not the only Indian tradition targeted with views of vice. In 1899 Oklahoma's territorial legislature outlawed the practices of Indian medicine men. The reasoning was based on the view that, as the *Chicago Tribune* reported, "the magician and prophet of the American Native is a power for evil."[32] Or, in other words, witchcraft.

Witchcraft wasn't the only colonial era vice summoned from the past. Views of dancing as punishable vice were also brought back to the moral armory of the powers-that-be. What, we may wonder today, was the big deal about Indians getting together to dance? The big deal for many whites was that Native American dance ceremonies were viewed (correctly) as gateways to tribal cohesiveness—and tribal cohesiveness was strength.

In this respect, whites most feared the Ghost Dance. Commencing in the late nineteenth century among the Lakotas/Sioux in present-day South Dakota, this dance ritualized their growing belief that the arrival of a Native American messiah was imminent. This messiah would reunite the Indians with their dead ancestors and replenish their hunting grounds with new earth that, in some versions, would cover all white people. The Ghost Dance thus aroused fears that it presaged an uprising.[33] "Reds Must Stop Dancing," headlined a front-page story in the November 25, 1890, *Chicago Tribune*, reporting that U.S. troops were positioned outside the Pine Ridge Reservation to make clear to the Sioux, in the words of Gen. Nelson Miles, that "there will be no nonsense about quelling an outbreak."

And indeed no outbreak occurred, though violence did. On December 29 the troops entered the reservation in the vicinity of Wounded Knee Creek. By day's end, over 150 of the tribe's men, women, and children lay dead, with some 100 more mortally wounded. Because of a dance.[34]

At the risk of repetition, using views of vice to impose power can be—and not infrequently is—deadly.

Other Native American dances were also viewed as punishable vice during this era. The federal government prohibited the Sun Dance, an integral part of the ceremony in which boys were inducted into manhood in several of the tribes that inhabited the Great Plains. Its self-inflicted violence was horrific to white culture. The ritual, however, was entirely consensual—a fact that was known and reported at the time. "No Sioux is obliged to undergo it," the *Washington Post* told readers in a December 28, 1890, feature. "The youth has his choice, when arrived at manly age, of being a woman-man or of proving by the tortures of the Sun Dance that he is fitted to be a warrior."[35] Expansionist whites particularly needed to weaken the cohesiveness of Indian tribes with men fit for war. Among the ways to overpower them was emasculation via the imposition of white views of vice.

Which brings us to another cohesive view of Native Americans: male sexuality. "If he prefers to be a woman-man," the *Post* article continued, "he will not be ill-treated or even scoffed at. . . . He must dress like the women, and like them he is left at home when the braves go hunting or to battle. In fact, this treatment is such a matter of course that a stranger might visit a camp and encounter any number of these persons and have no reason to suppose that they were other than women."[36]

Which, in turn, brings us to how views of sexual vice helped win the West. The federal government also cracked down on sexualized dances that were rituals among some of the tribes. Tippy-toeing between reporting the news without getting whacked for obscenity, one 1923 newspaper article referred to an "unprintable report" describing such dances among the Hopis in New Mexico and Arizona and agreed with the federal government's Bureau of Indian Affairs that "the time has come when the Indians should be discouraged, at least in his abandonment to filthy and immoral practices."[37] And, by federal fiat, they were.

Since it's no longer unprintable, let's take a peek at that government report (which, to keep these various reports clear, was written in 1915). It described dancers "imitating animals in the act of sexual intercourse," then went on to say of a group of male dancers costumed as what whites would call clowns, "Each pulled his penis from under his breech cloth and . . . women marched by either kissing or taking a bite of the clown's penis." Yikes. Though they may have been wagging clown cocks, since elsewhere this same report told of various fruits and vegetables carved to resemble male and female sexual organs.[38]

The newspaper article that refrained from printing these details approvingly cited the government's justification for prohibiting such

Indian dances, noting that "girls and boys, after careful instruction in morals in the boarding schools, go back to the Hopi villages to be engulfed in filthy practices and immoralities that too often accompany the dances." Explicitly employing this view of vice on behalf of white power, a teacher from one such school was quoted as saying, "Unless we attend to the uncivilizing influences among the Indians, we might as well stop our attempts toward civilizing."[39]

Witchcraft, drugs, and dancing weren't the only realms in which views of vice were used to stomp out Native American power. So too was what in the white world was called free love, along with its handmaiden, alternate views of marriage. "The marriage relation is one requiring the immediate attention of the agent," Secretary of the Interior Henry Taylor declared in an 1883 report that called for the suppression of several Indian dances. In addition, Taylor expressed alarm at those tribes that accepted "plural marriages" and at tribes in which "the marriage relationship, if it may be said to exist at all . . . is exceedingly lax in its character."[40]

In contrast to the declining power of Native Americans, a new group whose power was rapidly rising was the Mormons. Though the early history of the Mormons is obscured by the dust and blood of claims and counterclaims, clearly there were reasons to fear that the Mormons who followed Brigham Young to present-day Utah may have considered the possibility of forming their own nation. After all, whites in the South were doing the same thing. Although there were some military skirmishes between the Mormon militia and the United States Army, the most effective weapon used to overpower the Mormons was a view of vice.

That vice was polygamy, which was and remains widely viewed as a punishable vice in the United States and many other parts of the world.[41] Mormon leaders, for their part, used their view that polygamy was not vice as a means of acquiring power—and not just, if at all, power over women. Though polygamous, the Mormons in Utah granted women the right to vote in 1870, preceded only by (curious as it may seem today) Wyoming. Congress, however, had the power to revoke that right, since Utah and Wyoming were still territories and therefore did not have the power that states then had to regulate marriage. And revoke it Congress did. In Utah. In Wyoming, Congress let women vote. Wyoming had few Mormons and a law against polygamy. Here, then, is one of this country's clearest examples of views of vice being employed for purposes of power. It was the weapon of choice in the duel for power between the Mormon Church and the federal government.

En garde: In 1862 Congress passed the (inadvertently but aptly punned) Morrill Act, which banned polygamy in the Utah Territory. But for any law to work, the government has to be able to convict those who violate it. "Would you call on twelve petit jurors with twelve wives each to convict?" Senator Stephen A. Douglas asked when this approach was proposed.[42] Douglas's doubts were correct. Lunge deflected.

While some may call it bad form, Congress did achieve a *touché* in 1882 when the Edmunds Act authorized the federal government to confiscate the assets of the Mormon Church, based on the church conducting federally forbidden polygamous marriage ceremonies. The law also required monogamy oaths in the Utah Territory in order to vote or serve on a jury. Such oaths enabled the federal government to bring perjury charges against anyone who lied in order to vote or serve on a jury. Of course, as with the 1862 law prohibiting polygamy, its effectiveness depended on there being jurors willing to enforce the perjury charges.

While the 1882 oath requirement may appear to have been little more than a legislative *coupé flick*, the scratch that resulted ultimately proved fatal for polygamy. During the 1880s, the growing population of Utah came to include an increasing percentage of non-Mormons, so much so that the *Chicago Tribune* reported on February 12, 1890, "The gentile [non-Mormon] victory in the municipal election at Salt Lake City strikes another deadly blow at the Mormon iniquity. . . . The test oath, which disenfranchises all who cannot satisfy its provisions, succeeded in purifying the lists and the battle was won." As for the confiscation enabled by the 1882 law, the article went on to credit that provision with "the complete paralysis of the power of the

Mormon Church as a political agency." Nine months later, the Mormon Church announced it would no longer sanction plural marriage. Eight years after that, Congress was convinced that the Mormons no longer threatened the nation's established powers and elevated Utah to statehood.

Which brings us to what might be called the State of Vice: Utah's neighbor, Nevada. Gambling galore. Legal whores. But that's now. Back then . . . Actually, gambling was legal then, too. As for prostitution, on that Nevada law was clear: "It shall be unlawful for any owner, or agent of any owner, or any other person to keep any house of ill-fame, or to let or rent to any person whomsoever [etc., etc.] . . . for the purpose of prostitution [etc., etc. again] . . . situated within four hundred yards of any school house or school room used by any public or common school."[43]

What? Whorehouses were okay so long as they weren't within shouting distance of a schoolmarm?

Why would Nevadans have such a different view of vice? Were there no religious leaders? There certainly were in Utah. Or were there no others whose interests were threatened by commerce in sex? Indeed, in Nevada there were not a lot of either. Nevada is comprised almost entirely of land its neighboring states did not want. Called by geographers: the Great Basin. Called by the rest of us: desert. Aside from some precious metals to be mined, Nevada had little arable land other than one small region with abundant vegetation, known to colonial era Spaniards as *las vegas*. To make money in Nevada took some doing.

Still, even though Nevadans vindicated gambling and prostitution because of their need for the revenue, why would Congress allow these activities while, at the same time, getting its feathers all flustered over polygamy in Utah? Not only did Congress turn a blind eye to legalized gambling and prostitution in the Nevada Territory, it relinquished its power to prohibit them when it granted statehood to Nevada in 1864. Was Nevada too sparsely populated to matter? Only 6,857 white people lived there, according to the 1860 census. According to Abraham Lincoln's Republican Party, however, its white population was between 30,000 and 45,000. Why such wildly different numbers? For the same reason that Congress turned a blind eye to legalized gambling and prostitution in Nevada.

Power.

The fact is, there weren't 30,000 (let alone 45,000) white folks in Nevada in the early 1860s. Consequently, those who did gamble and frequent whorehouses from among Nevada's 7,000 or so whites constituted very little threat to the nation's power structure. On the other hand, the fiction that 30,000 to 45,000 whites lived there was necessary for Nevada to qualify for statehood during those Civil War years. The Republican Party, with its narrow plurality in the Thirty-Eighth Congress, hoped to endear itself to Nevadans and thereby better enable Union troops to secure the route to gold-rich California. Plus, President Lincoln had reason to fear his bid for reelection in 1864 might be very close, and even Nevada's votes might make the difference.[44]

What we have, then, is the vindication of gambling and prostitution to gain power in wartime conditions. Which you could call a gamble, or you could call prostituting one's morals. Or you could call it what Congress did: Nevada.

4

Careers in Vice for Crusaders and Purveyors

There is money to be made in vice. And not just in fields such as drug dealing, prostitution, and producing the orgies of violence Hollywood calls "action movies." (What would be an *in*action movie?) There's also money to be made as a professional moral reformer. It is a prestigious career—prestigious implying influential, which in turn implies power, which leads to this career tip: unless connected to the powers-that-be, few people will fill your vice-fighting coffers. How successful do you think a Muslim immigrant would be spearheading an effort in the United States for tighter regulations on Internet porn?

Blazing the trail in this country for this profession was Anthony Comstock. When this Civil War soldier returned and joined the workforce in New York, his idea of fun was attending lectures at the YMCA. Many of those talks sought to dissuade young men such as himself from all the immorality running rampant in the streets. Spotting an opportunity, Comstock approached the organization's leaders, volunteering to organize a drive to get New York City to enforce the laws against vice. Since he sought nothing from them in return, the leadership gave him the nod.

Comstock's overture to the YMCA leaders resulted from another opportunity knocking from Washington. Congress enacted legislation in 1865 tidying up this and that in the postal system—including inserting a provision that specified that any "obscene book, pamphlet, picture, print, or other publication of a vulgar and indecent character" could not be sent through the U.S. mail. Comstock now proceeded to comb through newspaper ads and order copies of books with titles such as *New York Naked*, *The Adventures of a French Bedstead*, and *Lord K's Rapes and Seductions*, to name but a few from this era of porn. When one of the books arrived, rather than open the package, he presented it to the New York police as evidence of the publisher sending obscene material through the mail and demanded that that publisher be charged.[1]

Still, none of this was making Comstock any money. Nor even much in the way of prestige, since his name remained little known—except among lowlifes in New York. But once again he spotted an opportunity. In November 1872 an exposé appeared in a radical feminist newspaper called *Woodhull & Claflin's Weekly* regarding an adulterous relationship between two members of New York's elite: Reverend Henry Ward Beecher and Mrs. Theodore Tilton. It caused quite a fluttering of fans and fidgeting with cigars among New York's upper crust, as winks and snickers from those less empowered buffeted their class a bit, I dare say, uncomfortably. Beecher had been prominent in the abolitionist movement and was also the son of the famed minister Lyman Beecher and brother of the previously mentioned author Harriet Beecher Stowe. Theodore Tilton was a renowned newspaper editor and poet. But more prominent at the time than both—and the brass ring for which Comstock was reaching—was Victoria Woodhull.

Victoria Woodhull and her sister were the first women to obtain seats on the New York Stock Exchange.[2] When economic conditions caused their investment company to go belly-up, they made a career change, leaving Wall Street to publish a feminist newspaper. Its circulation rose as Woodhull climbed platforms to give speeches connecting the newspaper's views to issues in the women's movement, including the legal inequities and frequent moral hypocrisies of marriage. Though women did not yet have the right to vote, nothing prevented them from running for president, which Woodhull did in the November 1872 election—the same month in which her newspaper's sexual exposé appeared. Put it all together and you have, in Anthony Comstock's eyes, the ideal woman to screw—in the mean-spirited sense of the word that, in its way, resulted in the birth of the first professional moral reformer in the United States.

Woodhull's newspaper stated that it was publishing the tawdry details of this adultery to expose Reverend Beecher's hypocrisy about the sanctity of marriage. It quoted Theodore Tilton having said of

Beecher: "That that damned lecherous scoundrel should have defiled my bed for ten years, and at the same time have professed to be my best friend! . . . [T]o have him creep like a snake into my house, leaving his pollution behind him, and I so blind as not to see, and esteeming him all the while as a saint—oh! It is too much."[3]

Pretty good stuff. And it gets better.

"It was not the fact of intimacy alone," Woodhull wrote, "but, in addition to that, the terrible orgies—so [Tilton] said—of which his house had been made the scene, and the boldness with which matters had been carried on in the presence of his children."[4]

Woodhull was not just talking dirty; from Anthony Comstock's point of view, she just went postal.

Comstock (posing as his wife) promptly ordered a mail subscription to *Woodhull & Claflin's Weekly* and, when it arrived, did his thing with the cops about sending obscenity through the mail. Because of Victoria Woodhull's prominence, her arrest made national news. More importantly for Comstock, mention was made of the citizen who complained. "Mr. Comstock is a young New York merchant who is destined to have his name somewhat widely known," the *Chicago Tribune* wrote.[5]

Interesting prediction. Evidently this journalist's insight followed from knowing, and reporting, "[Comstock] has been engaged for a year in seizing vile literature and bringing men engaged in the trade to trial and often to the penitentiary." And poignantly adding, "He has been doing this work at his own cost."[6] Who do you think told the reporter that? I'd say Comstock. And I'd say what Comstock was really saying was: *Hint, hint, you financial backers of the YMCA*. Those backers being banker J. P. Morgan, toothpaste magnate Samuel Colgate, and the like—rich men who wanted to be liked by religious leaders, since they sure weren't liked by the vast masses of labor. And indeed, as we'll see, they got the hint and soon ponied up a paying position for Comstock.

Woodhull, for all the brouhaha, was acquitted. The judge ruled that newspapers were not among the kinds of publications specified in the law barring obscene material being sent through the mail. This oversight, Comstock realized, was not the only aspect of the law that hindered its enforcement. Having proven his abilities to the money men who backed the YMCA, he now convinced them to send him to Washington in an effort to strengthen a law.

So skilled was Comstock in spotting opportunities that he got Congress to redo the law. In addition to enlarging the scope of what was considered obscene, the law now authorized federal judges to issue warrants forcing postal inspectors to search specific packages based on a citizen's suspicions. Citizens such as Anthony Comstock. And he got more. While in DC, he got himself appointed as a postal inspector, albeit on an unpaid basis.

Which brings up another career tip: in this instance, the unpaid part was a shrewd move. Not being a paid federal employee, Comstock remained free to pursue other aspects of his crusade and earn money from them. One such source of income was another item Comstock got Congress to add to the law. Henceforth, the government would pay a bounty to the person responsible for the arrest and conviction of anyone sending smut through the mail. In 1874 Comstock collected $675 in bounties, which he could add to other income he was now beginning to garner. The following year he raked in $1,250 in bounties. The average American at that time earned $776 a year. All in all, he was so instrumental in the enactment of what Congress called "An Act for the Suppression of Trade in, and Circulation of, Obscene Literature and Articles of Immoral Use" that the rest of the country came to call it the Comstock Act.[7]

After the enactment of the act in 1873, Comstock convinced the financial backers of the YMCA to create a separate organization for his crusade. Thus began the New York Society for the Suppression of Vice, with Anthony Comstock as its director. He had now achieved what no American had before: a salaried position as a full-time moral reformer.

But wait, there can be even more in store for this line of work. Comstock's salary grew considerably after he convinced the state legislature, when it approved his organization's charter of incorporation, to grant the New York Society for the Suppression of Vice "one-half of the fines collected through the instrumentality of this Society or its agents." Two years later, he got the state legislature to empower his organization to make arrests.[8]

"Anthony Comstock's Raid" (1879), "The Hunter's Point Dens Raided by Anthony Comstock" (1882), "Raid by Anthony Comstock—Improper Songs Given in Phonographs" (1897) were among the headlines that appeared in the years that followed. In addition, he branched out beyond New York. Headlines such as "Mr. Comstock's Western Raid" (1876) and "Anthony Comstock on Art—He Establishes a Branch Association in Baltimore" (1887) followed his crusade as it went nationwide.[9] In addition, he wrote books, adding to his fame and finances.

Though remembered today for his raids on those dispersing material involving sex, a number of his arrests were for publications such as circulars sent through the mail to young women in the hinterland luring them to cities with the promise of employment with impressive potential for income. The employment, not surprisingly, turned out to be prostitution. For arrests such as these, Comstock was applauded even by those who opposed his role as self-appointed censor in chief. Which was not hypocritical on their part, since these acts very clearly lacked informed consent.

Whose power was being projected by Comstock's crusade can be seen by comparing who got framed and who didn't. After a widely reported raid by Comstock on the Art Students League in New York, a reporter asked the director of the Metropolitan Museum of Art if he was concerned about his institution being raided, what with all its paintings and sculptures of nudes. He wasn't worried. Nor was his joint raided. Nor did Comstock ever raid an art dealer who purveyed such works to wealthy collectors. Because Anthony Comstock knew, even if only instinctively, that he should never touch a rich man's peccadillo.

Likewise, it was rich men—several being the same ones who funded his career—who funded the creation of the New York Public Library. Which Comstock never raided, despite the fact that its shelves held classics by Boccaccio, Rabelais, and Balzac that this latter-day Robin

Good deemed so indecent he often led his band of unmerry men in raids on bookshops offering them.

As do all of us, occasionally Comstock erred. In 1905 he sought to prevent George Bernard Shaw's play *Mrs. Warren's Profession* from opening on Broadway—her profession being proprietorship of a whorehouse for London's elite. George Bernard Shaw was himself one of London's elite, being both a highly acclaimed playwright and a cofounder of the London School of Economics. Thus in this match-up Anthony Comstock found himself taking on the backers of Broadway shows (who are rich), influential intellectuals, and, having read in the news of this Big Time Bout, "between 2,000 and 3,000 people seeking to buy tickets [who] had to be turned away," according to the *New York Times* report.[10]

For all that *Mrs. Warren's Profession* got Comstock hot and bothered, he refrained from raiding such real-life establishments in New York—despite this being the era in which the city's Tenderloin District was in its heyday. Brothels proliferated and raked in big bucks in this area of midtown Manhattan that ranged from 23rd Street to 42nd Street between Fifth and Seventh Avenues. Why did Comstock not blast such blatant vice? He never said, but we can take a pretty good guess. For one thing, he couldn't be sure whom he might uncover, quite literally, in raiding a top-tier bordello. The odds, however, were pretty good that he'd find some influential rich guy or powerful politician. Their power caused him to ignore what, in low-cost books, he viewed as vice, just as their power caused him to overlook looking for vice in museums and the city's prestigious library.

As to the women in those brothels, Anthony Comstock likely shared the view that prostitutes were usually more sinned against than sinning. Indeed, this perspective came to be embedded in another federal law, also inadvertently but aptly punned, the Mann Act. Enacted in 1910, it applied to prostitution the approach to obscenity used in the Comstock Act by making it a federal offense to transport a woman across a state line for purposes of prostitution. Note that it is the transporter of the woman, not the woman being transported, at whom this law is aimed.

Note also that, in a blatant revelation of power forming views of vice, the Mann Act was more familiarly known as the White Slave Act— "white slavery" being a term then used to mean forced prostitution.

Why white?

Why even ask?

Literary Art or Literally Obscene?

Though edited for length, thus ends the 1920 novel *Ulysses* by James Joyce:

> Ill put on my best shift and drawers let him have a good eyeful out of that to make his micky stand for him Ill let him know if thats what he wanted that his wife is fucked yes and damn well fucked too up to my neck nearly . . . he can stick his tongue 7 miles up my hole . . . yes O wait now sonny my turn is coming . . . O that awful deepdown torrent O . . . and then he asked me would I yes to say yes my mountain flower and first I put my arms around him yes and drew him down to me so he could feel my breasts all perfume yes and his heart was going like mad and yes I said yes I will Yes.[11]

And, yes, a full-scale war over censorship commenced.

"Improper Novel Costs Women $100," the *New York Times* announced on February 22, 1921, in what turned out to be the opening salvo. The women, Jane Heap and Margaret C. Anderson, were editor and publisher, respectively, of the *Little Review*, a literary magazine that had serialized *Ulysses*. Each was fined $50. Not a lot of money, but, as the *Times* announced not long after, "War on Censorship Opens on Big Scale."[12]

Why, at this particular point, was this "war on censorship" declared? Anthony Comstock had been digging up books he wanted buried for the past forty years—why hadn't an assault against censorship been launched then? The reason is revealed in a number of in-depth articles from that era that included discussions of *Ulysses*. Fortunately for us, we can just read their titles in order to glean what we need to know: "Our Post-War Novel." "The Post-War Novel." "The Post-War

Novel in England." "A Bird's-Eye View of What the War Has Done to Contemporary European Literature." Each appeared in an American publication during these years because—much as with emancipation in the aftermath of the Civil War—the grip of those whose hands held the levers of power had slipped amid the upheavals of World War I. In this first instance of the United States participating in a European war, more than fifty-three thousand Americans fell dead, with some two hundred thousand returning home wounded, and countless others with injuries unseen but deep.[13] All for causes that, to Americans, were murky.

Ulysses was one of the first fruits in the harvest of uncertainties that followed. A group calling itself the Joint Committee for the Promotion and Protection of Art and Literature was the subject of the headline announcing that the "war on censorship" was about to get big. The coalition consisted of Actors' Equity, the Motion Picture Directors Association, the Screen Writers' Guild, and other performing arts organizations, all of whose members had been targets of moral crusaders. In this period of postwar uncertainty as to who held the nation's reins, these groups joined forces to issue a manifesto declaring their "right to speak or to write as we please." More to the point, the manifesto sought to increase awareness regarding views of vice when it went on to state, "Not only does every age have its own interpretation of vice and virtue, but every race, every creed, and, it might almost be said, every community."[14]

Intellectuals also took this opportunity to speak out against the ban on *Ulysses*, since the ban imposed on it via the Comstock Act (and thus by those powers behind enactment of that law) impinged upon the power of highbrows and scholars. "*Ulysses* is not immoral—not so, at least, in the sense of tendency or capacity for leading any reader, young or old, into vicious courses," an unnamed *New York Times* reviewer opined.[15] In explaining why phrases such as (though not cited in the article) *fucked yes and damn well fucked too up to my neck nearly* and similar literary tropes lacked the capacity for leading readers toward immoral "vicious courses," this erudite reader stepped on the necks of others in order to climb higher in the tower of power when going on to say, "Its offending lies in its occasional violations of what, by common consent, is decency in the use of words . . . frequently to be heard in the places, chiefly barrooms, frequented by the personages described and quoted in *Ulysses*. That most people would find the story incomprehensible and therefore dull is, perhaps, its complete vindication from the charge of immorality." And who are such personages who'd find it dull? The less educated, whose level of comprehension is lower than this intellectual, who views their capacity for immoral "vicious courses" as greater.

Which, in turn, explains why this "war on censorship" was declared on *Ulysses* as opposed to, say, *Married Love or Love in Marriage*, also published at this time and described in the *Brooklyn Eagle* as having "numerous passages so disgustingly obscene and filthy that they cannot be reproduced in any decent newspaper." Far more "personages" were far more likely to comprehend *Married Love or Love in Marriage*. But as the *New York Tribune* noted (more accurately than not), "Nobody, not even the most radical of the literary Futurists has been able to make out what James Joyce has been writing about in *Ulysses*."[16]

Still, not all working-class readers opted out of this fight against the censorship of *Ulysses*. With influence in America so up for grabs, some leaders of blue-collar workers weighed in. In an article on the banning of this book, one leftist labor leader declared in an article reprinted in several publications: "The reasons why . . . morality is so much on the rampage at this particular moment, are quite clear. . . . What really corrupts and depraves people is the economic system under which we live. . . . The system has lately had a tremendous shaking, and we have seen how frantically and insistently the politicians of our race have had to invoke a specious morality to bolster their efforts to uphold it."[17] None of which is to say that if Marxists such as this writer were the prevailing power, they would not also employ views of vice to maintain their authority, as indeed this writer's fellow Marxist leaders were doing in the Soviet Union.

Last but far from least in this moral free-for-all were physicians and scientists. Most notable among their entrants was neurologist Joseph

Collins, who wrote at length about *Ulysses* in his 1923 book, *The Doctor Looks at Literature*. Along with scholars and intellectuals, Collins recognized that what at first seemed incomprehensible in *Ulysses* was, in fact, the characters' unedited thoughts. With his insights from neurology, Collins navigated this stream of consciousness and emerged from the ride giving *Ulysses* a thumbs up. As for its sexual passages, Dr. Collins raised an empirical question: *Is there evidence that immorality in art causes immorality in life?* And just to get the discussion going, since there was no evidence one way or the other, he tossed in his two cents. "To make the state share the parent's responsibility may lessen the burdens of parenthood," he wrote, "but it is unlikely that it will improve the child's chances."[18]

If the public's reception of Joseph Collins's book is emblematic, physicians and scientists may well have been the group that gained the most ground in the uproar over *Ulysses*. Madison, Wisconsin's *Capital Times* told readers that Collins's book "should be read ... [as] a new standard of criticism." Even the *New York Times* bowed to his perspective "as a neurologist and psychiatrist" rather than that of a "guardian of the public morals."[19]

As for the novel at the center of this storm, *Ulysses* was released in book form in the United States in 1927. Its publisher was Samuel Roth, until then a little-known owner of a bookstore and small publishing operation in New York. With *Ulysses*, he made a name for himself— though that name was mud. Not only did many revile him for publishing a banned book, others reviled him for publishing *Ulysses* without its author's permission or any indication that Roth intended to pay royalties to Joyce.[20] All kinds of court cases followed. Still, anyone considering a career purveying vice would do well to keep an eye on Samuel Roth. He'll be back. Big time.

Observing this entire fray from his office at the high and mighty publishing company Random House, its celebrated editor Bennett Cerf sensed that the time had come for publication of *Ulysses* to go mainstream. Unlike Samuel Roth, Random House opted to play by the rules, but its lawyers also knew the rules of views of vice. Shrewdly, they aimed their effort at the spot where the ban on *Ulysses* would most expose the use of views of vice by those who have power. In this particular case, that spot was the U.S. Customs Service.

Among the legislative successes of Anthony Comstock was a law barring entry into the United States of material the Customs Service deemed obscene. But it also enabled Customs officials to make exceptions, which they periodically did when wealthy collectors, *including J. P. Morgan, one of the founding donors of the New York Society for the Suppression of Vice,* sought to bring in sexual artifacts from other cultures for their personal collections.[21]

This provision was the arena in which Random House wanted the fight to take place, since in that arena it could turn the power of men such as J. P. Morgan against themselves. And it's where it did take place when Random House's effort to import a copy of the book for purposes of publishing it in the United States got blocked at the gate by a Customs agent. And where, on December 6, 1933, federal judge John M. Woolsey ruled that *Ulysses* was not obscene.

America's First Professional (De)Vice Crusader

Typically we think of moral reform as an effort to get others to toe the line, but it can also entail efforts to make others get their toes off our lines. Such was the quest of Margaret Sanger, who sought to get those who were not invited to do so to keep their contraception-picking fingers out of women's wombs. In many ways, Sanger built on that which came before—including, ironically, following a path set out by her foremost opponent, Anthony Comstock, in demonstrating how one could earn a living as a professional moral reformer.

When a nurse at New York's Henry Street Settlement early in the twentieth century, Margaret Sanger saw firsthand the medical and social maladies that abounded in that city's impoverished and overpopulated Lower East Side. Most heartbreaking to Sanger were abortions, which she opposed on moral grounds and which, being illegal, were often botched by the amateurs in whose hands these desperate women placed their lives. To raise awareness of ways to prevent pregnancy, Sanger wrote a monthly newsletter on birth control called the *Woman Rebel*. As its title suggests, its views were not in the service of industrialists or powerful religious leaders. Since many of the families on New York's Lower East Side were Jewish, and virtually all were connected to the then-organizing working class, the newsletter sought to acquire more influence for the least empowered of the working class—that being women—by asserting that every woman ought to be the "absolute mistress of her own body."[22]

When Sanger commenced publishing the *Woman Rebel* in 1914, she very likely knew she was taunting the aging but still kicking Anthony Comstock. Repeatedly, he had her arrested. Which enabled Sanger, repeatedly, to get her newsletter mentioned in newspapers, much as Comstock's early efforts got his name mentioned in the press. In 1916 Sanger formed an organization not unlike the New York Society for the Suppression of Vice, except for the fact that it was one many viewed as spreading vice, since her organization was a network of birth control clinics. Also like Comstock, she published books, and, again like Comstock, she focused on Congress—though in her case, seeking to get the Comstock Act amended so that birth control devices and information would not be deemed obscene.[23] In addition, she gave speeches, which Comstock had also done, although Comstock's speeches urged police to arrest those who sold stuff that shouldn't be seen or heard, while Sanger's dared police to arrest *her* for being seen and heard.

And they did. And in so doing, they generated more news stories about Sanger and her birth control clinics. Following one such arrest in 1921, the cops had to contend with the audience of several thousand massing around them and following them to the station, creating an incident that was reported nationwide.[24] It was also an incident that revealed the jostling for power taking place in the United States in the wake of World War I. Women, who were very much among the groups in that national fray, finally achieved a constitutionally protected right to vote at this time. As for Sanger, in 1921 she refashioned her network of clinics into the American Birth Control League, an organization that remains in existence to this day, though its name was later changed to Planned Parenthood.

In these initial years of her now full-time paid career as a campaigner for birth control, Margaret Sanger faced her greatest opposition from religious leaders. But not all religious leaders. Theological reasons for opposing birth control were offset, in the views of numerous ministers whose congregants were well-off whites, by concern that the birthrate among Catholics (who constituted a disproportionate percentage of the working class and immigrants) was so much greater than the birthrate in their fleecier flocks. One *Washington Post* headline from 1935 pretty much summed it up: "Churchmen Hit Cardinal's View of Birth Control—Protestants and Jews Join in Reply, Citing New Concept of God."[25]

To say, however, that Catholic clergy were theologically obstinate or that they wanted a rapidly growing Catholic population, no matter how impoverished and plagued, vastly oversimplifies their view. Catholic leaders feared a means of suppressing power that, in those years, was becoming frighteningly influential. Among scientists, whose influence had been steadily increasing, some got another rung up the tower of power by advocating a selective form of birth control called eugenics. So named in 1883, this branch of science theorized that birth control was "the surest and supremely important means of improving the human race" by using it to limit reproduction among those who were not the cream of the crop. "As long as the procreative instinct is allowed to run reckless riot throughout social structure," one proponent wrote, "... grandiose schemes for security may eventually turn into subsidies for the perpetuation of the irresponsible classes of society." That proponent who said those words was Margaret Sanger.[26]

Catholic priests at the time well recalled all the ways those of their faith had faced discrimination in the United States. Five of the first thirteen states prohibited them from holding public office.[27] In the 1850s Americans opposed to Catholics and immigrants created the Know Nothing Party. And in 1928 voters expressed intense opposition to the Democratic Party's presidential candidate, New York governor Al Smith, because he was Catholic.

By toting up the victories and defeats of Margaret Sanger and other birth control proponents in the 1920s and 1930s, we can get a rough measure of who held power and how much. Sanger repeatedly failed to persuade Congress, many of whose members represented a considerable number of Catholics, to take birth control devices and publications off the list of obscene materials in the Comstock Act. Judges, however, generally did not have to answer so directly to those who vote. Consequently, court rulings trimming the Comstock Act commenced. Mary Ware Dennett, whose 1929 conviction for sending a sex education booklet through the mail will be discussed in more detail below, appealed her case to a higher court, which reversed the decision. In ruling that her booklet was not obscene, this decision became the new legal standard when the government opted not to pursue the case to the Supreme Court. In 1937 the courts further chipped away at the Comstock Act in a suit brought by Margaret Sanger. In this case the court ruled that the confiscation of contraceptive devices sent to her by a physician was a violation of the Constitution.[28]

Equally revealing were all the court cases that never took place. Adherence to and enforcement of the Comstock Act were now so lax in this realm—due to a decline in power of those groups whose influence had led to its enactment, relative to the increasing power of women and physicians—that by 1930 Arno Press, a major publisher, released a guide titled *Seventy Birth Control Clinics*. It was but one of many sexual guides now on the open market. The March 9, 1930, *Chicago Tribune*, for example, carried advertisements for *Physiology of Sex Life*, *Love Rights of Women*, *Aspects of Birth Control*, and *Essays on Sex*—all offered for sale by mail.

The Nation Begins to Get Carried Away

While Margaret Sanger was the first woman in the United States to carve out a career as a professional moral reformer, she was by no means the first American woman to become a celebrity crusader. That honor goes to Carrie Nation, the hatchet-wielding grandmother who in 1900 commenced a campaign raiding bars, where she smashed bottles of booze and barrels of beer.

Beginning in her home state of Kansas, where booze was banned, Nation's first foray made headlines because her hatchet job brazenly dared the authorities to charge her with destruction of property that was illegal. But arrest her they did.[29] Which, as she'd hoped, generated sufficient publicity to fuel her forays into other states (in these cases, places where alcohol was legal), assuring more arrests—and more publicity. She too wrote a book and, as did Comstock and Sanger, added lecture tours, though hers included souvenir sales of miniature hatchets—a nice touch to help defray costs, since (career tip) the vandalism biz has high overhead.

Carrie Nation's crusade revealed a good deal about power and vice in that, discomfitingly, perhaps, she smashed the commonly held belief that power resides in government—particularly in the United States, with its (presumably freely, as opposed to expensively) elected officials. Power is far more fluid than that.

And booze is the fluid that proved it.

In 1880 Kansas had prohibited the manufacture or sale of alcohol, preceded only by colonial Georgia in 1732 (where the effort flopped and the law was rescinded) and the state of Maine in 1851 (where in 1911 a referendum was held to rescind it). Clearly, prohibition wasn't faring too well in Carrie Nation's home state either. After enacting its law, Kansas had to strengthen it by banning not only the manufacture or sale of alcohol but also the possession of it. Slight oversight. But this effort too went down the drain, often literally, as quaff-loving Kansans didn't obey it. So Kansas upped the stakes with another law, this one allowing the authorities to confiscate "saloon fixtures" from public establishments—akin to later antidrug laws that, similarly unsuccessfully, sought to whack cannabis by prohibiting the sale of bongs, hash pipes, and related paraphernalia. Kansas also permitted prosecutors to summon citizens and bring charges against them if they refused to answer questions regarding whether or not they had bought liquor and, if they had, from whom.[30] Even then, the Fifth Amendment protection against self-incrimination wasn't the only thing going down the hatch in Kansas, as evidenced by the fact that Carrie Nation still felt the need to take up her hatchet. As seen in other vice laws, lack of adherence or enforcement reveals in that gap the presence of hidden or rising sources of power.

One such group in Kansas were the purveyors of alcoholic beverages (though they likely viewed drunkenness as vice). Money—the quintessential example of the fluidity of power in being, by definition, a fluid means of exchanging power—formed most of this group's views of booze. But booze producers and purveyors also employed the flip side of views of vice—that being views of virtue—to hawk their product. The sales pitch for a 1913 book entitled *Straub's Manual of Mixed Drinks* said of its author, "As a celebrated connoisseur, his name is known and his recipes are used in the best places of this country." It thus sought to project a virtuous view of ɒ the well-to-do who hobnob "in the best places of this country," such as Chicago's tony Blackstone Hotel, where Jacques Straub was the wine steward—and thus one of those best places where America's most refined (or you could say rich, or powerful) could appreciate "a beverage the excellence of which is a real source of enjoyment to the most exacting palate."[31]

Clink-clink.

But more than America's well-heeled were needed when, due in part to hatchet wielders such as Carrie Nation, the notion of national Prohibition began to loom over Congress. Seeking to combat this threat to their business, purveyors of alcohol sought to acquire added influence by associating their products with powerful groups viewed as virtuous. "For Your Medicine Chest," headed a local ad in 1917 for a bar with the rather non-health-conscious name of the Falstaff Saloon. "You always need and should have on hand, ready for an emergency, a little pure WHISKEY, BRANDY OR WINE." The proprietor of the Falstaff Saloon informed the community, "I keep in stock especially for this purpose some of the best and purest goods possible to be distilled." And he urged all who wished to learn more of their wonder-drug effects to "call and sample them."[32]

An additional hurdle confronted the brewers of beer. Unlike liquor, whose history in America began five or ten minutes after white men set foot on its soil, beer production didn't become an industry until the influx of Germans in the mid-nineteenth century. This beverage, so prized by these foreigners—often at beer gardens on *Sundays*—was not only alcoholic but, in the minds of many in the shadows of World War I, un-American. In hopes of refuting these views of vice, the big brewers (many now headed by second- and third-generation descendants of their German immigrant founders) deployed the tried-and-true de-vice: views of virtue through a lens of truth or myth, it mattered not which, so long as it was very American virtue. As in this ad from 1915:

> ### BENJAMIN FRANKLIN—"FATHER OF AMERICAN DIPLOMACY"
>
> America has never produced a greater statesman than Franklin, who was revered by the people second only to Washington. ... He was possessed of robust health ... of a wise but merry nature ... a conspicuous figure in any assemblage of great men. He was a moderate user all his lifetime of Old Madeira and barley-malt brews. It is safe to say he toasted the New Republic with every great man of Europe and America. ... Today, wherever Americans go for health, or business, or pleasure, their famed brand BUDWEISER is there.[33]

Topping this off with the attractive froth from another source of power, the ad added that Bud was so popular with the American public that "7,500 people are constantly employed to keep pace with the ever-increasing demand."

Prohibition: A Patchwork Quilt of Power

Though not the first to do so, the temperance movement, the suffrage movement, and the birth control movement each sought to acquire more power by threading together patches of each other's views of vice. The fact that the woman's suffrage movement included, for example, Catholics who viewed birth control as vice did not stop birth control advocate Margaret Sanger from praising the suffrage movement and connecting its aims to hers. Nor did Sanger, who was by no means a teetotaler, shy away from saying of hatchet-wielding Carrie Nation and her fellow female saloon bashers, "Woman is smashing and hating and loving and sweeping the world into a new age."[34]

And she was right. The ascent of women as a political force in the United States had as great an impact on views of vice—and altering views of what constituted vice—as any other group in the nation's history. Prohibition being Exhibit A. As we have seen, efforts to outlaw alcohol date back to the colonial era and continued, via temperance groups and various vice-fighting societies, throughout the nineteenth century. But not until women had acquired sufficient power did Congress pop its nonalcoholic cork, amending the Constitution in 1919 to ban the manufacture, sale, and transportation of alcohol in the United States.

That said, it should also be pointed out that moral myths about Prohibition abound. More importantly, the reasons they abound have to do with various groups seeking to maintain or acquire power. *Myth 1: Women winning the right to vote resulted in Prohibition.* Bad counting. The *Eighteenth* Amendment inaugurated Prohibition; the *Nineteenth* Amendment (enacted the following year) guaranteed women the right to vote. Any question as to what group promulgated this myth? (Hint: three-letter word beginning with *m*.)

But members of the *m*-word group were not the only ones grinding their axes on moral myths. Which brings us to *Myth 2: Women did not have the right to vote until the Nineteenth Amendment.* By the time the Nineteenth Amendment was passed, fifteen states had already accorded women full voting rights. The significance of the amendment is that it extended this right nationwide by declaring that states cannot disqualify a citizen from voting based on sex.

Myth 3: Prohibition did not exist until the Eighteenth Amendment. When it was passed by Congress, thirty-three states had already enacted laws prohibiting the consumption of alcohol.

Trivia questions, or do they matter? They matter. Moral myths, whether employed to impose power or acquire it, often seek to contain power by hiding the fact that it is actually *very fluid*. Within the temperance movement, for instance, its supporters came from a variety of groups that sought to maintain or acquire power for those various groups through this view of vice. On the other hand, while temperance advocates often joined together, sometimes they did not. Women were barred from participation at the 1854 World's Temperance Convention in New York. Similarly, in 1873 Annie Wittenmyer did not create a World Temperance Union; she created the Woman's Christian Temperance Union (WCTU). Among the 168,000 who joined the WCTU by the turn of the century, some had done so to advance the influence of its C through this view of vice; others joined to use this view of vice to acquire more power for its W.[35] It isn't the devil that's in the details; it's power.

Physicians and scientists had also acquired considerably more influence by 1870s compared with the 1850s. As did women, they employed views of alcohol as a vice to garner added power. And many joined forces with those American-born women who used this view to oppose a potential source of power pouring into the nation's mix: immigrants. Scientists plugged in by publishing in professional journals articles with titles such as "Alcoholic Drink and the Immigrant," "Alcohol the Barrier to Patriotism," and "The Drink Curve and the Immigration Curve."[36]

"Foreigners drink," *The Cyclopedia of Temperance, Prohibition, and Public Morals* stated in a two-word opening sentence in its entry titled "Drink as a Hindrance." It went on to inform readers: "Saloon keepers are frequently the most effective leaders of the new industrial immigrants. There is hardly a drinking place in a large foreign colony which does not have its political club. The brewers do everything possible to create a feeling of antagonism among the units of the new immigration against the 'Puritanism' of the Anglo-Saxons." Making no secret of the fact that, in this instance at least, Prohibition had as much or more to do with imposing power as with opposing drunkenness, it concluded, "Immigration will prove a blessing only if the immigrants take on the main characteristics of native Americans. [Presumably not meaning Native Americans.] The greatest hindrance to this absorption of the new immigration is the saloon and the liquor traffic."[37] This from the book's scientific editors? Actually, no. Though this book's title implied academic objectivity, its publisher was the Methodist Church. Misleading? Not misleading?

Take a whack at that question if you wish; this much is known: sew it all together and you get Prohibition.

A related event demonstrates the fluidity of power *even more* than the uses of this view of vice by many women, physicians, religious leaders, foes of Catholics, and foes of immigrants. That event is the failure of Prohibition.

The Eighteenth Amendment went into effect on January 17, 1920. On December 3, 1933, the Twenty-First Amendment rescinded it. What went wrong was a failure to recognize the fluidity of power and, because of its fluidity, all the nooks and crannies in which power can reside. The millions of Americans who slipped into the millions of liquor-nipping nooks that added up to the inability of moral reformers to stomp out alcohol use all had one thing in common: consent.

It is precisely that power that was overlooked in the metaphors employed by the leader of Maine's temperance crusade, Neal Dow, when he wrote in his half of a dual-authored article, "Like war, [alcohol] wastes the products of industry and kills the worker, or so mutilates and maims him that he is unfitted for work. . . . It is like pestilence, ravaging any community where it is tolerated, cutting down the brightest, bravest, and best."[38] Disease, mutilation, and maiming are not consensual. Nor for many is war, and for those who are gung-ho to go into battle, the products of industry are not wasted—provided their side wins. Faulty analogies are not just grist for English teachers' mills; they often lead to faulty laws.

How did Dow, a former Civil War general and later successful and popular mayor of Portland, Maine—in short, obviously a very intelligent and insightful individual—fail to see that his metaphors were faulty? Possibly he knew they were faulty, but even if he didn't, either consciously or instinctively what he did know was that those metaphors were powerful moral myths. As for the many other Americans back then, were they less insightful than Americans today? Or were they struggling so hard to maintain the status quo or acquire higher station in it that they believed moral myths? Just as we do today, for the same reasons, across the political spectrum.

Another temperance advocate from back in the day lays to rest any question of Americans from earlier eras being less insightful. "A vice is a harm I do myself in the pursuit of pleasure," Dio Lewis wrote in his half of the 1884 article that presented his and Dow's opposing views. "A crime is a harm I do to another with malice. . . . Legislation that ignores this distinction between vice and crime must prove a muddle and a failure."[39] Which very aptly points to the fact that consent is power—and enough of it, even among unorganized individuals, can make a muddle of legislation.

The failure back then to recognize Dio Lewis's distinction between vice and crime is particularly evident in an April 13, 1888, *Washington Post* item regarding a dinner party that went awry. The police, after becoming curious about "a number of strange looking women" entering an apartment house from which the police heard "revelry" coming from a unit on the third floor, decided to look in on things.

> The officers quietly mounted the stairs and, directed by the noise, burst open the door of the room in which the social was being held. . . . The room was handsomely furnished, and in the center of it was a table spread with a luxurious supper. About the board were seated about fifteen men dressed as women. Some of the dresses were of rich material and were made according to the latest fashions, while their wearers, in order to heighten the effect, wore wigs of long wavy hair and were decked out with ribbons in a style that was simply dazzling.[40]

Simply dazzling! But bedazzling be damned, they were arrested for being illegally dressed for dinner.

Two years earlier, a physician in Germany named Richard von Krafft-Ebing published his view of sexual attractions deemed to be vice in which he coined a new term: homosexual. After his book, *Psychopathia Sexualis*, was translated into English in 1892, this new word arrived in the United States, where it competed with—and soon bested—"sodomy." This bit of linguistic trivia is telling, since the root of the word "sodomy" is religious (from the biblical account of Sodom and Gomorrah), and the root of the word "homosexual" is Latin, the language adopted and adapted by science. While both groups, at the time, viewed this behavior as vice, the way in which they viewed it became a weapon in the competition for influence between science and religion.

So important a weapon was this view of vice that both religious leaders and scientists employed the heavy artillery of certitude that is packed into moral myths. "We know that the sexual desire originates in the cerebral cortex," neurologist Smith Ely Jelliffe declared in 1912, confidently asserting, "Homosexuality is therefore parallel to insanity, and it becomes the duty of the state to guard the population against this evil by enforcing certain measures, as it does in insanity." Refuting this view on behalf of those religious leaders who thought such behavior punishable sin, an editorial in Michigan's *Ironwood Times* fired off moral myths when it said, "Science could probably make out a convincing case for the mental condition of the savages who attacked the pioneer stockade of early days, but the business of the pioneers was to protect their home, their church, and their school. So they shot down the savages and preserved their civilization."[41] The pioneers, however, did not consent to those attacks, just as Native Americans did not consent to attacks on their settlements. Thus they had nothing in common with consensual physical intimacy between people of the same sex. Indeed, the power of consent in this realm has been demonstrated by the fact that, throughout history, moral reformers engaged in various versions of Whac-A-Gay (or, more accurately, its vernacular term today, "gay bashing"), making countless hits—inflicting immeasurable cost and pain on so many— and have still lost.

Still, in the shifting ways these crusades have whacked, shifts in power can be witnessed. In 1915 North Dakotan William McDonald could have cited Krafft-Ebing till he was blue in the face, but it likely would have had little impact on the judge who "lectured the defendant severely" before sentencing him to ten years at hard labor for his homosexuality. North Dakota was not unique. In New York at that time, homosexual acts were punishable by up to twenty years in prison.[42] Over the next several decades, however, sentences for homosexual acts not only lessened in severity, but in some instances judges imposed confinement in mental hospitals rather than prisons. In 1938 Illinois became the first state to inscribe such sentences into its law.

Also commencing at this time and, thirty years later, forming itself literally into a fist to assist its views of virtue and vice in acquiring power was the gay rights movement.

The Vice Biz

While careers as professional vice crusaders date back only to the late nineteenth century, careers purveying vice date back to the snake in the Garden of Eden. Thus since colonial times there have been Americans who earned some or all of their income peddling sex, selling drugs (beginning with alcohol and tobacco), or purveying violence in entertainment. As with laws against hooch and cooch, lack of adherence and enforcement also undermined laws prohibiting violent entertainments. Cock fights, for example, were illegal in all the colonies, but those laws were so poorly enforced that authorities took no action when Giles Jacob's *The Compleat Sportsman* was published in 1718, a book that devoted a chapter to cock fighting and enjoyed brisk sales for fifty years. Even in colonial communities, where those in positions of influence were far more powerful by virtue of there being far fewer groups, power was far more fluid than the moral myths embedded in schoolbooks would have us believe.

Consent, that itchy niche those in power can't whack or scratch, also figures prominently in violent vices. Still, bear in mind: while those who sponsor or attend cock fights do so by consent, the animals do not. As in its more modern-day counterpart, dog fighting, the violence is imposed upon the animals by their being trained and goaded into attacking each other by those with the power to do so.

Among humans who fight to provide entertainment for which others pay, the violence is far more likely to be consensual. The history of laws and regulations regarding boxing, the longtime preeminent form of prizefighting in America, also reveals who held what power. Within the boxing community, rules were originally a matter of consent between the contestants or their managers until the twentieth century. A 1743 guide, however, carried considerable clout, both out of mutual self-interest between the contestants and by virtue of its having been written by one of England's most widely admired bare-knuckle boxers, Jack Broughton. Along the same power lines, the requirement that boxing gloves be worn appeared in 1867, when Scotland's Marquess of Queensberry published an amended set of rules. Royalty packed more punch in what is now the United Kingdom than in the United States, but the American boxing community, seeking greater acceptance outside its arena and fewer deaths inside it, got in step with this upper-class fan of fist fights for fun and fortune.

Nevertheless, there was a sustained crusade against prizefighting, one that continues to this day—and one that, because of the power of consent, continues to fail to deliver a KO punch to such events. Just as in colonial days, prizefighting was illegal in the early states and most of the later states in this country. But prizefighters and their followers eluded these laws. Often they simply paid off the authorities. Sometimes they back-stepped beyond the authorities' reach, as when the *Baltimore Sun* reported on September 2, 1867, "The prize fight between Aaron Jones and Mike McCool took place today in a grove adjacent to the railway, some 26 miles from Cincinnati." The article made no mention of the fact that prizefights were illegal in Ohio but did note, "There were nearly three thousand people present."[43]

Eventually, boxing delivered a KO punch to those crusading against it—and it did so in a way that, as we shall later see, other vice-purveying industries would eventually replicate. It took responsibility for its power by using it to regulate itself instead of using it to fight its powerful opponents. Or gave the appearance of regulating itself. Or (most accurately) did both, to varying degrees in various situations. This vice device commenced in New York when its boxing enthusiasts proposed the creation of a state-sanctioned commission that would establish and enforce rules for the sport. The legislature gave its consent, and in 1911 the New York Boxing Commission was formed. Numerous states soon followed suit.

Those considering careers in vice should also take note that the market is largest for a vice when strictures against it are too. Take, for instance, the arrest of Mary Ware Dennett for sending her sex education book, *The Sex Side of Life*, through the mail. With the censorship of her 1929 book making headlines, one New York theater producer made hay with a play loosely based on the book—loose enough to enable the producer not to have to obtain the rights and to stage whatever he could get away with behind the mask of Mrs. Dennett's news-making book. Strictures against obscenity also created a market for books purporting to educate readers about immorality in, shall we say, greater detail. For works such as these there was a far larger market, one that existed long before and after the appearance of Mary Ware Dennett's primly written primer on reproduction. Best sellers in this sexucational genre have included *Female Convents: Secrets of Nunneries Disclosed* (1834), *Paris in America* (1863), *Bed Chamber Secrets: The Revelations of a Doctor* (1910), and *Hollywood Babylon* (1965), one of the last books authorities in the United States attempted to ban.

Rather than purvey vice under the cover of education, money could also be made by purveying it as news. In this realm, the *National Police Gazette* set the American standard, earning big bucks by exposing vice with "news reports" such as, just in its June 5, 1880, issue: "Illicit Love Terminates in a Public Scandal at Erie, Pennsylvania," "A Frisky Old Sinner," "Satan in Petticoats," "San Francisco Belle Gets into a Funny Fix," "A Cleveland Boarding House Landlady, a Male Boarder, and a Colored Lecturer."

That same issue of the *Police Gazette* made mention of a relatively new vice soon to capture widespread attention. In an article headlined "The Ladies' Lunch—Which Includes Champagne, Tobacco, Some Toilet Secrets, and a Cachuca [a Spanish dance!]," the *Gazette* reporter told of witnessing a woman smoking and overhearing:

"Bell, where in heaven's name! Where did you get these cigarettes?"
"They are a special brand, my dear."

"I should fancy so, especially adapted to be smoked by ladies."

Which, for starters, puts the lie to the 1968 advertising slogan for a new brand of cigarettes, Virginia Slims: *You've Come a Long Way, Baby; You've Got Your Own Cigarette Now*—since Bell's brand was "adapted to be smoked by ladies" some eighty years earlier. Most significantly, however, is that both manufacturers sought to hide the damage known to result from smoking by tacitly projecting women's rights—the suffrage movement in one case; the feminist movement in the other.

In the vice-purveying biz, selling tobacco wrapped in thin cylinders of paper dates back to the late 1600s. Not until 1842 did the French add their diminutive suffix *ette* to the word *cigar*—and when they did, it was specifically in reference to *women* smoking these things.[44] Not unrelated, at the time, women in France and England were (just a few years ahead of their American counterparts) joining organizations that advocated for equal rights. Similarly, while opposition to tobacco dated back to James I, crusades to combat the habit increased markedly in the wake of women acquiring increasing political influence, with some of these crusades aimed solely at *women* smoking— revealing, yet again, muscle masquerading as morals. "What is at best a doubtful habit when followed by men, becomes more than doubtful when a woman takes it up," a feature on "Women and the Cigarette" declared in the March 26, 1887, issue of *Harper's Bazaar*. "A woman who deliberately breaks the barrier of that conventionality, even with so slight a thing as a cigarette, puts herself under suspicion of a reckless readiness to break down other barriers," the article warned.[45]

Seeking to maintain their elevated status, some number of well-to-do Americans also employed the view that smoking was a worse vice in women than in men. The same *Harper's Bazaar* article stated, "We know that Indian squaws have always smoked. . . . After all, they are squaws. We know, too, that certain old backcountry crones have their clay pipes or their cobs; well, they are backcountry crones, making no pretension to be better than their old pipes." Turning to foreigners, it informed readers, "We hear also stories, of strange sound to our ears, of the women of southern Europe with their dainty cigarettes. . . . But that women among ourselves of this Western world, given for the purification of the people [in other words, given by God, superior], . . . women of intellect, of cultivation, of any fine breeding, of any decent manners, of any gentle society or family [in other words, wealthy], should be guilty of smoking—that is something which strikes us involuntarily with the same qualm as their cigarette gave them."[46]

Nor was *Harper's Bazaar* alone in this view. An 1885 article in the *Youth's Companion* reported of school girls on a train: "Several of them were smoking cigarettes and, leaning back on their seats, puffed the smoke out of the windows of the car." And these weren't just any old youngsters. These girls were "well dressed and appeared to belong to a respectable class of society."[47] That class being, needless to say, well-to-do, native-born, and white.

But power was shifting, though not without a struggle in which views of vice were used as weapons. In 1908 the city council of New York commenced such a battle with an ordinance that prohibited women from smoking in cafés. But the mayor vetoed it.

Indeed, power had already shifted enough to get the attention of the makers of Lucky Strike cigarettes. In the 1920s, the company commenced an advertising blitz featuring an attractive woman with a cigarette and the slogan, "Reach for a Lucky instead of a sweet."

The crusade against cigarette smoking was not solely aimed at the ascending power of women, for there is another major element in the history of cigarettes. In the 1880s new machines came into use that could produce cigarettes one hundred times faster than before. Consequently, their cost dropped enormously. Consequently, a lot of kids could afford them, too.

Articles soon appeared, such as "The Use of Tobacco by Boys"—which, nevertheless, made a point of noting, "Women and girls also make every year a larger contribution to the revenue derived from cigarettes." In 1899 an Anti-Cigarette League was founded "to combat by all legitimate means the use of tobacco by boys." Tennessee, Iowa, Kansas, Arkansas, and Utah enacted laws totally prohibiting the sale of cigarettes. Even the tobacco-growing states of Virginia and North Carolina enacted laws prohibiting the sale of cigarettes to youth (usually defined as under sixteen years of age). With these laws, smoking became a punishable vice for the first time since the colonial era. Now, however, those primarily responsible for this view were not religious leaders but physicians and scientists. Nevertheless, as in the days of James I, each of the states that totally prohibited cigarettes repealed those statutes in the 1920s due to lack of adherence to the law and to get needed revenue by taxing tobacco. Nevertheless, virtually all Americans shared the view that young people did not yet possess sufficiently mature judgment to give informed consent regarding temptations such as cigarettes—a view recently buttressed by empirical data.[48]

And yet—whack, whack—there's this: Why, back then and still today, do Americans so admire that famous adolescent smoker, Huckleberry Finn? In Mark Twain's 1884 novel, Huck not only smokes but expounds on its joys while rafting down the Mississippi with the runaway slave Jim. Or why, during both world wars, did virtually all Americans support the inclusion of cigarettes in soldiers' rations?

In both instances, what caused Americans to vindicate the vice was power. In the case of the fictional character of Huck, it was the powerful moral myth embodied in his and Jim's efforts to free themselves of society's confinements. The soldiers, on the other hand, were not fictional characters. They were actually laying their lives on the line for our power to be free.[49]

5

Vices That Roared between World Wars

In the proverbially vice-ridden Roaring Twenties, who or what was roaring? Typically, machine guns in the hands of gangsters come to mind. Or the roar of jazz, a musical form created by African Americans. Or the sass of flappers, young women in that era who were more provocative than those who came before because of the way they (or simply because of the fact that they) spoke out. And smoked. And wore shorter hair and less clothly clothes. Taken together, however, this roar resulted from those in power having lost their bite, or at least several teeth, in the social upheavals that accompanied World War I. Notably, as an example, it was in 1921 that the last known conviction for blasphemy occurred in the United States.[1]

Another example of this loose-tooth roar in the 1920s can be heard in one of its natural habitats, the *North American Review*. "The silk stocking has for many a year been a provocative simile for social exclusiveness," Henriette Weber, pianist, lecturer, and declawed wealthy woman declared in its pages, "a label for class distinctions, and finally a bit of political slang, sarcastically applied by those who can see in social contrasts nothing but an unjust distribution of wealth." Meaning, as she went on to clarify, the Irish. "Just because the Colonel's Lady and Judy O'Grady are sisters under the skin, they naturally— from Judy's viewpoint—want to be as nearly as possible of the same class on the outside of their epidermises. So Judy goes to work to obliterate all class distinction as well as she possibly can, and in no other country in the world do the Judys accomplish their ends with such success." As, for example, "two gum-chewing flappers" whom Weber described: "There they were in tight fitting, black satin coats; of a dubious quality to be sure, but satin for all that, and with a bit of dead white cat about the neck. Smart little felt hats topped off their perfectly correct bobs—the hats imitations of Paris's latest cry, but costing, at the most, about one-tenth of what an original French model would bring. And there was the long expanse of leg encased in silken stocking, nothing less."[2] Shocking. To well-to-do whites, that is, worried that their power was being challenged by the belles of the beaus who had just come home from fighting, in President Wilson's words, "to make the world safe for democracy."

And not just the Irish. "Saunter along Hester Street," Weber wrote of the bustling thoroughfare bisecting the Jewish immigrant enclave on New York's Lower East Side. Noting all the "cheap and standardized ready-to-wears," she asked, "[The] picturesque old immigrant women . . . what do they think, one wonders, at the manners of their flapper granddaughters and the cheap and perishable finery with which they bedeck themselves?" In her effort to reassert her group's power by likening expensive fashions to imperishability, she concluded, "Sedition? Pouf! Our women know how to dress well by instinct."[3]

Instinct? As in genetics? Here there is a quick-as-a-flash dagger use of views of vice in an effort to maintain power.

And not just Henriette Weber. And not just Irish and Jews. When it comes to using views of vice to maintain power, never underestimate America's ability to pack blacks into their vice-fighting weapons. Reverend William C. Allen loaded up at that arsenal before setting off to attack flappers in order to reassert the turf of religious leaders. "And there is the paint," he wrote in regard to the use of cosmetics by flappers. Going on to recall his days as a missionary, Miller said of African women, "In proportion to the quantity of paint dabbed on the smooth cheeks of scantily-clad native ladies, I have seen their pride soar and flutter." Which he then brought home by concluding, "Now numbers of our own fair women follow their dusky sisters."[4]

Nor did Mrs. Max Oberndorfer miss the opportunity to use African music. As head of the music division for the General Federation of Women's Clubs, she sought to reassert the influence of its well-off white membership by writing, "Jazz music, in its original form, was used as the accompaniment to the voodoo ceremonies by which the uneducated, almost barbaric Negro aroused his most sensuous nature." While one could not propose prohibiting or regulating jazz in the United States (something Nazi Germany did do) Mrs. Oberndorfer announced that the federation was sending a model music curriculum to public schools throughout the country—the hope being that its use would convey an appreciation of the kind of music where everyone plays their prescribed part.[5]

Then, of course, there was that frequently seen bugaboo of moral reformers: dance. In the 1920s younger Americans began dancing to jazz with the Charleston and the Black Bottom. The first was named for the city in South Carolina that had long had, and at the time still had, a black majority population that generated a vibrant African American culture; the second was named after an African American ghetto in Detroit—though the dance also celebrated the pun. The previously mentioned Reverend Allen, again drawing on his missionary days among African tribes, stated, "The Charleston is basically a Kaftur dance." All in all, he lamented of flappers and the men from well-behaved families they entranced, "Already with barbaric joy had we borrowed the wild dance from the sable sons of Africa. Already had we become debtors to half-naked blacks who live in round huts into which you crawl on hands and knees." Nor was he alone in viewing black dance steps as vice in order to reassert power. A magazine article devoted to the Charleston described it as a dance in which "smart young women and loose-jointed, slightly imbecile young men do astonishing Negroid things with their knees and ankles." The article's moral gunpowder included scientific terminology (and moral myth, since the statement wasn't scientific) to add to its power: "The wretched thing has spread like some dreadful epidemic over this fair land."[6] A point worth repeating, since it occurs so often with moral metaphors and vice: incidents such as disease epidemics are not consensual.

As for viewing these aspects of African American culture as vice, those Americans of African ancestry tended to see them differently. "This race has the greatest of the gifts of God, laughter. It dances and it sings," W. E. B. Du Bois wrote in 1923. "If you will hear men laugh, go to Guinea, 'Black Bottom,' 'Niggertown,' Harlem."[7] From his perspective, jazz and the dances developed to accompany it were not vices but virtues.

Humpty Dumpty Had a Great Fall from the Wall (Street) and the Wagon

When the stock market crashed in 1929, setting off the Great Depression, which extended through the decade that followed, not only did those directly or indirectly connected to Wall Street take a tumble as well but, as in the nursery rhyme, America's equivalent of king's horsemen and men couldn't put the egg that reproduced their world together again. The first of their power-imposing views of vice to get scrambled was Prohibition. Like Wall Street, it too had failed to do what the powers behind it had promised. Which is not to say the old guard was now powerless. The Twenty-First Amendment repealed *federal* prohibition of alcohol, not state or local laws. For a time, Kansas, North Carolina, Mississippi, Oklahoma, and Texas resumed efforts to enforce their laws against alcohol. Not until 1966 were all these state laws repealed. To this day, however, numerous local ordinances remain in place, reflecting who has power where.

Moreover, just because it was open season for power didn't mean the season was open to all. Federal Prohibition, for instance, continued to be imposed on Indian reservations, as Native Americans were among the least empowered people in the United States and because it behooved most of those groping for more of a grip on the levers of power to keep it that way. And, as with the rest of America, Prohibition continued to fail in the case of Native Americans, despite being buttressed by the (now discredited but still widely believed) moral myth that Indians are genetically predisposed to alcohol addiction. Here too, the key element in laws failing to have the power to whack vice is the fact that drinking alcohol is a consensual act and that consent contains power. And many Native Americans used that precious cranny of power as an act of resistance, even while they knew it was self-destructive. But if they felt they were at the bottom of the nation's totem pole, then how far could they fall?

Indeed, the issue of consent is precisely what drew the attention of the federal overlords of Native Americans during this free-for-all for power. "For the past several years it has been the policy to have these [alcoholic] Indians voluntarily attend sanatoriums for periods of from three to six months," Interior Secretary Harold Ickes told the chairman of the House Committee on Indians Affairs in 1935. "In practically every instance the Indian on his return from the sanatorium, continued the use of liquor or narcotics."[8] Ickes urged legislation that enabled involuntary commitment to rehab, thereby seeking to whack that piece of consent. But that legislation also addressed a far larger question regarding consent. *When one becomes addicted, is the addiction no longer consensual?*

Harold Ickes was by no means the first to raise this issue. In the late 1840s Swedish physician Magnus Huss advanced the view that alcohol addiction resulted more from physiological failures than moral failures. Huss called this particular addiction "dipsomania" (in contrast to the term used by religious and industrial leaders, "drunkenness"), and his view soon spread to the United States. In the competition for power, these two terms became ammo when the weapon used was views of this vice. Reporting from this battlefield, *Littell's Living Age* told readers in 1858, "In the progress of events, new scientific terms are continually making their appearance; the last is perhaps Dipsomania—a craving for intoxicating liquors. . . . The law, which always drags heavily at the heels of general intelligence, has not yet been able to make any distinction in the drinking species."[9]

But the law did make distinctions in the punishment of vice. Data collected in 1910 revealed that African Americans, who constituted 10 percent of the population at the time, constituted nearly 41 percent of those sentenced for a term of one year or longer for any crime. (The data did not distinguish between felonies and misdemeanors nor between convictions for vice versus convictions for acts that harmed others. Later researchers arrived at more detailed correlations of racial disparity in sentences for comparable offenses.)[10] Interpreting this initial data, the human bean counters at the Bureau of the Census delicately observed, "While these figures will probably be generally accepted as indicating that there is more criminality and law breaking among Negroes than among whites, and while that conclusion is probably justified by the facts, it should be borne in mind that the difference between the two races in this respect may very well be . . . to some extent the result of discrimination in the treatment of white and Negro offenders."[11] More effectively cloaking racism (and class distinctions among whites) while imposing power via views of vice, judges frequently levied fines to reduce or replace time in jail. "It is probable that the Negro is more often unable to pay the fine than the white man," the Census Bureau noted in interpreting its data, "and is therefore more likely to be sent to jail." As already seen, this vice device for power dates back in this country to its colonial era and was, even then, an inheritance from Europe.

Curious as it may at first seem, among those who got a grip on a bit of power during this era were alcoholics. In 1935 a group of Americans addicted to drink joined together to form Alcoholics Anonymous, thereby claiming for themselves the power to combat their addiction. As with everyone else, their views of vice were formed by the influences in their individual lives. Thus this new group, like any group, did not exist independently of powerful groups. Its cofounders were physician (and alcoholic) Robert Holbrook Smith and businessman (and alcoholic) William Griffith Wilson, both of whom acknowledged that their approach had its roots in a Christian-based mutual-support organization in England known as the Oxford Group.[12] Thus Alcoholics Anonymous viewed confession, faith, and fellowship—plus recognition of consent—as virtues, using that view to amass the power to combat this addiction.

Keeping One's Power Fashionable

In the same way that leaks plagued the effort to seal the power of many white, native-born Protestants by imposing Prohibition, so too were there leaks in the effort to seal the nation's portals to immigrants through laws that increasingly closed those gates.[13] By far the largest leak involved Mexicans—largely because agricultural powers found ways to wedge openings so that Mexicans could pick produce for a pittance of what U.S. citizens would need to be paid for a living wage. To make matters worse for those who sought to seal in white Protestant power, these not-quite-white Spanish-speaking Catholics weren't particularly vice-ridden.

So vices were invented.

"Drug peddlers in Gary [Indiana] have recently made a systematic effort to enslave high school students to marijuana, or 'loco weed,'" the *Chicago Tribune* warned readers in 1927.[14] Here again words served as ammo in using views of vice to impose power. This news report deployed Spanish—*marijuana* in lieu of a previously used term such as *cannabis* or *hemp*, and *loco* rather than *crazy* or *inebriating*. Even within English the choice of words in that one sentence revealed their use as ammo. The longtime designation of cannabis/hemp as a *plant* was supplanted by calling it a *weed*—aptly paralleling the way many native-born Americans viewed these newcomers. The horticultural distinction between a weed and a plant is that a weed is an unwanted plant. And the article deployed myth when it noted that marijuana "grows wild in Mexico and the American southwest." Which it does, since it thrives pretty much everywhere between latitude 60° north and 60° south—or, to save you a trip to a globe, from Norway to Australia.

This report was not the first of its kind. In 1919, when many Americans were clamoring for Congress to close the gates to immigration, numerous publications began to refer to marijuana as a weed of the Mexican desert.[15] As any knowledgeable pot-head knows, one of the few places where the plant does not do well is in deserts. Nor did Mexicans introduce it to this country. It was propagated here during the colonial era—primarily to make rope, but even in ye olden days colonists were aware of its effect when ingested.

And they liked it.

Suspecting perhaps that anything people liked might be viewed as vice, purveyors of pot in the eighteenth and nineteenth centuries pedaled it as having medicinal benefits. Nevertheless, the writer of one 1857 ad couldn't resist a dash of vice in pitching it with the spin:

$1000 REWARD!

The above reward will be paid to any person who will show that one half as many have been cured of disease by any other medicines as have been cured by Dr. James' Extract *Cannabis Indica* .... We have certificates showing that Consumption, Bronchitis, Asthma, Liver Complaint, Coughs, Colds, Sore Throat and General Debility have been cured.[16]

Views of marijuana as a Mexican vice were first employed to whack at leaks along that border when a series of skirmishes occurred during the uproar over immigrants, which rose to a crescendo in the years leading up to major gate-closing legislation in 1921. "Cocaine, opium, and morphine are nursery tonics compared to marijuana," the *New York Sun* informed its readers on August 26, 1915, in a story headlined "Worst Vice in the World." The article went on to elaborate on this myth, telling readers, "One who takes it becomes instantly mad and proceeds to do whatever is in the mind with an insane courage." Then, firing this view of vice across the border, it noted that the leader of Mexico's revolution, Emiliano Zapata, was believed to smoke marijuana—which, if you bought into the myth, lent credence to the claim that he was behind the spate of incursions by Mexicans along the border—rather than the alternate view that most who crossed with weapons were random rustlers and thieves. And if anyone doubted the *New York Sun*, one month later an entire page in the September 25, 1915, edition of Utah's *Ogden Standard* was devoted to a feature with photos headlined "Is the Mexican Nation 'Locoed' by a Peculiar Weed?"

When views of marijuana as a Mexican vice failed to keep them out, white Americans seeking to maintain their preeminent power invented a new vice they ascribed to Mexicans: the zoot suit, a men's fashion that, in fact, Mexicans did not introduce to this country any more than they did marijuana. Black jazz musicians are believed to have been the first to wear this clothing style, which sported extra broad shoulders on a loose-hanging jacket with loose and flared slacks.[17] But facts are anathema to moral myths. Revealing this transition from marijuana, a 1943 news report headlined "Zoot Suit Riots Held Anarchy" about violence between members of the military and Mexican American teenagers told readers, "The suggestion that the majority of the young rioters might be under the influence of marijuana was made by R. A. Sanford, state narcotics officer."[18]

That same year, efforts commenced to deem the zoot suit a punishable vice. "Ban on Freak Suits Studied by Councilmen" headlined a *Los Angeles Times* report on a proposal before the city council that "it be made a jail offense" to wear a zoot suit. The council opted not to enact the ban, but some judges did anyway. Two teenage Mexican Americans arrested that year in Los Angeles for disturbing the peace (they were described in one report as "being boisterous" in the presence of a police officer) were given a choice by the judge of three months in jail or disposing of their zoot suits. The boys surrendered their suits. A similar penalty was imposed that year on nineteen-year-old Adame Sanchez, convicted of being inebriated. Sanchez, however, sat in jail twenty days before finally agreeing to trade in his zoot suit rather than remain imprisoned for the full amount of time Judge Daniel A. Parsons could impose. In Tucson, Arizona, one judge announced that "anyone brought before him wearing a zoot suit would be found guilty."[19] In the view of these magistrates—and no doubt many other Americans seeking to maintain white power—the vice of Mexicans wearing zoot suits was worse than that of overindulging in alcohol, publicly engaging in boisterous behavior, or (at least in one Tucson courtroom) anything else on earth.

On the flip side, many Americans who sought to *acquire* power similarly used views of vice in fashions. "A fractious husband could not be more inhumanly punished than to be sentenced to wear for one week his waistcoat as closely fitted to his body as his wife habitually wears the waists of her dresses." This nineteenth-century female complaint was voiced by a man, physician Edward B. Foote, in his 1870 book, *Plain Home Talk: Medical Common Sense.*[20] Being a physician, he buttressed his views by citing medical harms from so tightly cinching the waist and, in warm weather, covering so much skin. In addition, he raised issues of empowerment by citing some of the remarks a woman wrote in an 1866 letter to the *Herald of Health*. In that letter she observed:

> From the sense of freedom I experience while wearing about the house a dress I originated merely for home use, I can obtain a slight realization of what it would be, were some such costume generally adopted and worn on all occasions. In the customary senseless dress of skirts and hoops, I am at once transferred to a state of the most thorough incapacity for all practical or sensible purposes.... [I] am unable to resist the cold weather even, and feel like curling myself down by the parlor register in a state of the most approved and fashionable vapidity. But in the other dress, ambition, health and spirits are in the ascendant; impossibilities become possibilities; feel capable of meeting and conquering any difficulty that presents itself.[21]

Dr. Foote had a prescription—though he knew his prescription would be viewed as vice. "Thousands of sensible women would adopt what is called the ... bloomer costume," he wrote, "were it not for the bigotry of fashion." Bloomers, named for Amelia Bloomer, a leading activist in the temperance movement, were loose-fitting pants that extended to the ankles, initially worn by American women under a shortened skirt. What stopped them, according to the doc, was that "they do not feel strong enough to face the ridicule."[22]

Ridicule is indeed a form of punishment, but more than that scared the pants off women. It was pretty big news in 1866 when New York City police arrested a woman named Mary Walker after she dared to wear bloomers in public. Mary Walker, however, turned out to be a distinguished physician who had served in the medical corps for the Union Army, during which time the fact that we were at war (that most powerful of forces) vindicated the vice of a woman wearing pants, as pants better enabled Dr. Walker to move in ways necessary for a surgeon. Nor was she wearing pants now simply because she wore them in wartime. Rather, because Dr. Walker wore them in wartime, and because she was an activist for women's rights, she now wore them to challenge male-dominating views of vice in female fashion. And she won. Upon learning who she was, the judge dismissed the charge, saying that Walker was "smart enough to take care of herself."[23]

Other women weren't so fortunate. Numerous bloomer-wearing women ended up paying fines or spending time in the pokey in the second half of the nineteenth century.[24] Combating such views of vice in women's clothing now became part of women's quest for equal power. The National Council of Women initiated an effort in 1891 "to secure the adoption of a much-needed, more comfortable and sensible form of dress for women engaged in business vocations." Corsets and high heels, the council declared, "handicap the female sex from competing with men," and it proclaimed that "the slavery of skirts must be abolished."[25]

Those who sought to keep this boundary of power in full no-bloomer bloom were far from defeated. Rather, they strategically retreated, directing their efforts at women who were less empowered. "Bloomer Girl Arrested" headlined an October 31, 1896, news item in the *Norfolk Virginian* that reported, "Rebecca Diggs, a colored girl who was progressive enough to introduce the 'new woman' at Newport News, was arrested by Officer Moss last night on the charge of obscenity." As for white women in bloomers, the battle was now waged in *places* where they were more vulnerable—as in a 1908 news flash that appeared in the *Los Angeles Times*: "Six Baltimore society ladies were arrested here today, charged with 'indecent exposure,' because they insisted upon putting on the nattiest little bathing suits on the beach."[26] The nattiest little bathing suits in 1908 sported short bloomers. While the bathing suit was not made of material one could see through when it was wet, the wet cloth did cling to the body. The news report informed readers that women's swimwear that allows "any lines of the figure to be clearly displayed" constituted indecent exposure.

In this instance, those most offended by the new bathing suits were, as it happened, other women. "The W.C.T.U.," the same news report stated, referring to the Woman's Christian Temperance Union, "started a war on the summer colonists ... and two days ago posted notices that they would cause the arrest of any persons seen out of the water in bathing suits" that delineated the figures inside them. Powerful middle-aged and elderly women fearing the power of younger women? Quite likely a factor. Powerful female teetotalers fearing that a day in the sun among shapely ladies could drive a man to drink? Very likely a factor. Cops empowered to enforce a law to impose the power of men through that law's view of female bathing suit vice? Maybe—but maybe not, as the article also noted that getting cops to enforce that law required finger-pointing demands by the foot-stomping-in-the-sand members of the WCTU.

Still, elsewhere men did initiate enforcement of such laws. "Have you a skin tight bathing suit?" the *Chicago Tribune* asked readers on June 12, 1912. "Better not wear it when you take your initial plunge into Lake Michigan this summer.... Chief of Police McWeeny [yes, that was his name] has sat in judgment on bathing costumes," the article stated, albeit with evident sarcasm, going on to say that the police had been ordered to arrest those whose bathing suits "do not come up to the chief's standards." It is unlikely, however, that Chief McWeeny was using this view of vice on behalf of the power projected between his legs. More likely in this and many other such instances, men with this view of female bathing suit vice used it—consciously or not—to maintain the power of any number of groups seeking (since time immemorial) to control sexuality—and thus fend off risks from whichever unwanted types that could result from unregulated reproduction.

For those in the women's rights movement who were aligned with Margaret Sanger, reproduction was something they too sought the power to regulate for reasons of female empowerment. Similarly, those aligned with that era's free love movement, with its opposition to marital laws, sought the power to regulate sex themselves. And indeed, as women representing these and the many other groups that comprised that era's feminist movement began to acquire greater influence, their views of bathing suit vice contributed to that achievement. Chief McWeeny, for example, saw the regulation he wanted enforced overruled in court one year later.[27] That 1913 ruling mirrored its 1866 predecessor involving bloomers on the sidewalks of

New York in that both resulted from the actions of women who had acquired considerable power challenging the law. In this instance, Rosalie Ladova, a physician active in numerous medical and political causes, donned one of the new bathing suits, got wet in Lake Michigan, and got arrested by police, who had been alerted by the press—who in turn had been alerted by Dr. Ladova.

Though Chief McWeeny and his colleagues in the war on bloomers were defeated, others followed in the effort to use a view of bathing suit vice to impose power over women's sexual decisions. Or, more specifically, *white* women's sexual decisions. Again in Chicago, as an example, the supervisor of parks and recreation announced in 1931 that any woman wearing a two-piece bathing suit would be ejected from the beaches in Lincoln Park along Lake Michigan on the city's North Side. Beaches on the South Side, where the city's African Americans lived by virtue of segregation, went unmentioned. That this view of bathing suit vice was used in an effort to control pregnancy in white women further surfaced when the park's supervisor stated, "The question is as to whether the suits would be detrimental to public morals. I don't believe that they would be among a certain class of civilized people. Among the more elemental types . . . I'm afraid they might arouse emotions that would be followed by immoral and unlawful acts." And who were these more elemental types? Blacks, of course, but they were pretty effectively confined to the city's South Side beaches. Who, then, were they at Lincoln Park's beaches? "Some of the people who go to [Lincoln Park's] Oak Street beach have not been in this country long," the park pooh-bah explained, "and misconstrue the statement that this is a land of freedom to mean that there is no restriction on the individual."[28]

This era also witnessed a battle over *topless* bathing suits, difficult as that may be to believe. Spoiler alert: the controversial suits were being worn by men. But the risk of misleading readers by making a sensational statement failed to stop not only me but also the *Los Angeles Times*. It ran a page 1 headline on April 18, 1931, that bellowed: "Bathing Suits' Limit—Upperless Vogue Intruding from Other Countries." Who could resist buying a copy of that paper?

As for those who viewed such bathing suits as vice, the reasoning reflected the same power: control of reproduction. Men, after all, are not the only ones attracted by the bodies of the opposite sex. And it played out the same way. "Undoubtedly, the newer generation, of a commendably athletic type, is going to demand broader latitude than has been allowed," Santa Monica's mayor was quoted as saying, essentially conceding that defeat was on the horizon. Hell, if they couldn't beat a bunch of girls in bloomers, no way could they take on muscular white men and win.

Final Frontier of Vice in (or, Rather, Not in) Fashions

"There will be no nudist sunbathing on Chicago beaches," the city's mayor, Anton Cermak, declared in 1932. The mayor was responding to a request from a nudist group to erect a stockade on one of the city's North Side beaches behind which those who wished could go *au naturel* at Lake Michigan. Explaining why this behavior was vice, the mayor said, "The whole thing makes me sick."[29]

If that were truly so, he should have seen a physician. At the time, however, men and women inclined to group nudity were supported by physicians—not a lot of physicians, but a few who were influential members of this powerful group that, at the time, was gaining even more power. In addition, nudists were aided by the fact that many people viewed as vice much of the behavior of a group whose hold on power had slipped in these years of the Great Depression: industrialists. Both elements were present in the views of one early advocate of nudism, Theodor Hahn, a physician in Germany who, in the 1870s, was associated with a movement called Lebensreform, meaning Life Reform. It sought to combat anxieties resulting from industrialization by a back-to-basics approach to diet and lifestyle. Dr. Hahn also prescribed periods of group nudity as an antidote to society's complexity by regarding the naked body as natural, not naughty. Though in terms of the sources of power being served by viewing nudism as not-vice, let's not dismiss *vah-vah-vah-voom*.

On this side of the Atlantic, needless to say, Americans took notice. And some took their clothes off. In 1911 police raided the sanitarium of physician H. E. Lane, who followed the precepts of Dr. Hahn in treating anxieties with a "simple life" regimen of raw food combined with nude sunbathing on the rooftop of his office. Misguided medicine perhaps, but lascivious it was not. The rooftop was partitioned to separate men from women. Aside from a few such instances, however, the view that group nudity was not vice failed to gain much traction in the United States until the Great Depression, suggesting that many of its new recruits, jolted by the failure of the nation's industrial powers, sought to rebuild their lives in ways less connected to material wealth—including, at times, material for clothing. In 1931 Maurice Parmelee published *Nudism in Modern Life*. Police in Washington DC confiscated it as obscene. Ironically, both sides sought much the same end: to combat what they respectively viewed as sexual vice. Strange as it may sound to some, nudism was a moral reform movement. Moral crusades are not limited to prudes. "Nudists Call on America to Take Off Its Clothes," trumpeted a 1936 headline in the *Chicago Tribune* on a nationwide nudist convention that was held in (don't ask me why) Valparaiso, Indiana.[30]

Efforts to whack this vice with police raids were countered in 1933 by an effort to whack the raids. Fred Ring, who with his wife, Ophelia, operated a nudist camp in Michigan, opted to challenge the law after the authorities descended upon them and their naked clientele. The trial of these nudist proprietors attracted the national spotlight. "A capacity throng of spectators," the *Chicago Tribune* reported, packed the courtroom in Allegan, Michigan, some thirty miles northwest of Kalamazoo. The Rings' nudist camp was seven miles from Allegan, the last two traversable only by a dirt road. But no place was too far to go "to catch every word of a new revelation about what went on in that nudist camp," in the words of the *Tribune* report. Among those offering testimony spiced with vice was Mrs. Mary Angier, an elderly Chicagoan who owned a summer house across a stream from the nudist colony. Though a hill had to be climbed to get a view through the foliage, that didn't stop Mrs. Angier, who stated she saw people "going around stark naked." If Fred Ring's defense attorney thought Mrs. Angier some dumb old biddy, he was quickly disabused. When he asked if she'd ever visited the Art Institute of Chicago and seen nudes there she replied, "Yes I have—but they weren't hobnobbing with each other."[31]

Found guilty of indecent exposure, Ring was sentenced to sixty days in jail and a fine of $300; his wife was given probation. He appealed, and the case ultimately came before the Michigan Supreme Court. It upheld the verdict. In the wake of the Michigan case, the powers-that-be quickly saddled their moral horses. In 1935 a person in New York "who in any place willfully exposes his private parts in the presence of two or more persons of the opposite sex whose private parts are similarly exposed" was now guilty of a crime.[32] But proving indecent exposure was up for legal grabs, since, within the confines of a nudist colony, none viewed it as indecent. Consequently, posses deployed against nudists also pursued other paths. Kentucky required a twenty-foot-high wall to enclose any area in which nudists congregated. Other states and municipalities did their best to block nudist colonies through permit processes. Yet another route was unsuccessfully sought by an Oklahoma legislator who proposed that those convicted of nudism be subject to life imprisonment.[33]

Whack, whack, whack, yet still these efforts failed to stop these folks from hanging out with each other in the buff. Moreover, views of such nudity were shifting even among Americans who opted not to join in. A *Washington Post* editorial put forth an offbeat way of measuring such shifts in public opinion. Noting that celebrities Walter Winchell, Eddie Cantor, and Jimmy Durante "have scarcely let a radio act go by without somehow working in a joke about nudists," the editorial presented its finger-in-the-wind gauge: "The surest way to judge a story for timeliness, is to ask, 'Has it been wise-cracked on the air?' If the answer is affirmative, it is no longer news."[34] Today, TV sitcoms likewise function as this version of the proverbial canary in the coal mine, detecting the presence of shifts in power through views of vice that trigger their laugh track.

Indeed, nudists were no longer news. Because nudists were so secluded, whether by choice or by law, Americans began losing interest. The national spotlight on vice now found more flesh in efforts to prohibit striptease. And, for the media, it was a hotter battle to follow, since crusaders against striptease dancing had to take on two very powerful forces: sex and money. Indeed, punishment for nudism now fell off the paddy wagon when, shortly before New York enacted its law against nudists, a judge in that state ruled that striptease was an art, not a crime. Which left law enforcement wondering whom they could arrest for what.[35]

Still, but by the same line of reasoning, nudist colonies all but cleared out with the nation's entry into World War II. To support the fight against Germany and Japan, most of those who had advocated a back-to-nature simple life now became proponents of America's industrial might. Such back-to-naturists would return after the war, naked anew, but in a land very different from before.

THAT FERTILE IMAGINATION.

1. Vice is in the eye of the beholder, as this 1888 cartoon reveals in mocking morals crusader Anthony Comstock. Library of Congress (*Life* 11, no. 293 [1888]: 18).

2. Race and vice. Had the couple in this 1896 *National Geographic* photo been white, the magazine could not have been sent through the U.S. Mail. Library of Congress (*National Geographic*, November 1, 1896).

3. (*Opposite top*) This 1901 *Puck* cartoon shows that as women gained power, views of vice came under review. Note at far right, Carrie Nation wielding an axe against alcohol; far left, physician Mary Walker cross-dressing. Library of Congress, Prints and Photographs Division (LC-DIG-ppmsca-25513).

4. (*Opposite bottom*) A picture worth a thousand words is illustrated by this 1904 article from the *St. Paul Globe* showing views of alcohol abuse changing as physicians gained greater influence. Library of Congress, Chronicling America (*St. Paul Globe*, April 10, 1904, 15).

A SUGGESTION TO THE BUFFALO EXPOSITION: LET US HAVE A CHAMBER OF FEMALE HORRORS.

The Newest Hope for Inebriates

MAYOR TOM JOHNSON, OF CLEVELAND, TURNS TO UNTRODDEN PATHS TO FIND A CURE FOR THE VAST GROWING EVIL OF MODERN LIFE

Sanitariums to Take the Place of Prisons and Medical Treatment to Succeed the Policeman's Vigorous Methods

TO GRAPPLE with the twin evils of *civilization, drink and drugs, the city of Cleveland, casting aside traditions, has stepped into a new field of municipal endeavor.*

STOP

SMOKING

Law should compel the poison symbol (skull and cross bones) on every package of cigarettes. Nicotine is not so violent a poison as Prussic acid, but it is just as deadly. Tobacco-Specific is a harmless vegetable remedy that can be given secretly in food or drink. It cures the craving, the appetite, for tobacco, brings back the bloom of health, the strength of youth and the energy and courage that is the birthright of every American. A postal card will bring you a free sample package. In hundreds of cases a sample has cured.

5. Power and vice. This 1905 patent medicine ad begins, "Law should compel the poison symbol, skull and cross bones, on every package of cigarettes." It ran in newspapers more than half a century before physicians gained more power than the tobacco industry, resulting in the surgeon general first opposing smoking in 1964. Library of Congress, Chronicling America (*St. Louis Republic*, November 12, 1905, pt. 5, p. 7).

6. (*Opposite*) Power's influence on vice can be seen in this 1915 ad enlisting a Founding Father during the clamor to enact Prohibition. Library of Congress, Chronicling America (*Goodwin's Weekly*, June 12, 1915, 14).

"FRAMERS OF THE CONSTITUTION OF THE U.S.A." NO. 5

Benjamin Franklin—"Father of American Diplomacy"

AMERICA has never produced a greater statesman than Franklin, who was revered by the people second only to Washington. He was a signer of both the Declaration of Independence and the Constitution of the United States, and his wisdom made the latter a possibility. The great Lord Chatham pronounced him not only an honor to the Anglo-Saxon people, but to human nature. In every capitol of Europe he was a welcome guest, and he it was who induced France to lend us ships, men and money during the darkest days of the Revolution. Upon his death Congress ordered a general mourning of a month. In France it was decreed that all members of the national assembly should wear mourning for three days. So long as Americans treasure the Republic and Personal Liberty as the noblest of all human blessings, the fame of Franklin can never perish. Personally he was possessed of robust health; he was a well-shaped man, of a wise but merry nature; he had the head of a Greek philosopher, while his grace, his noble bearing and winning personality made him a conspicuous figure in any assemblage of great men. He was a moderate user all his lifetime of Old Madeira and barley-malt brews. It is safe to say that he toasted the New Republic with every great man of Europe and America. Franklin considered his work in building the Constitution his greatest service to posterity. Upon the self-evident declaration of the Constitution of the United States Anheuser-Busch 58 years ago launched their gigantic institution. To-day, wherever Americans go for health, or business, or pleasure, their famed brand BUDWEISER is there. Its popularity, due to its quality, purity, mildness and exquisite flavor, has daily grown in public favor until 7500 people are constantly employed to keep p. e with the ever-increasing demand.

ANHEUSER-BUSCH
ST. LOUIS, U.S.A.

Visitors to St. Louis are courteously invited to inspect our plant—covers 142 acres.

George Olson & Sons

Distributors   Salt Lake City, Utah

Budweiser
Means Moderation

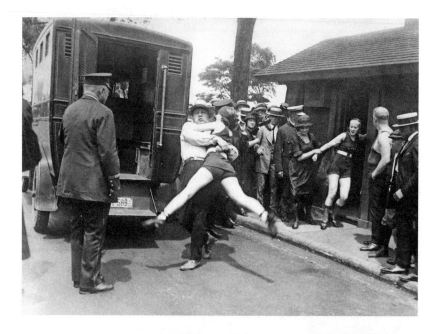

7. (*Opposite top*) When this news photo appeared in 1922, men wore very similar bathing suits . . . but the cops did not handle that like this. Getty Images.

8. (*Opposite bottom*) Sally Rand was famous—and frequently arrested—for her fan dance in the 1930s. Today her act would seem tame. Getty Images.

9. (*Above*) Book burning in America in 1935. New York Society for the Suppression of Vice leader John Sumner (right) joins New York City Police officials observing the burning of books deemed obscene. Getty Images.

10. Two views of vice in one. This 1936 film sought to purvey (and profit from) the view that marijuana is dangerous. If this poster seems over the top, it's because it was created in 1972 for a rerelease of the film when many viewed the earlier view as ridiculous. Getty Images.

He's one of the busiest men in town. While his door may say *Office Hours 2 to 4*, he's actually on call 24 hours a day.

The doctor is a scientist, a diplomat, and a friendly sympathetic human being all in one, no matter how long and hard his schedule.

According to a recent Nationwide survey:

MORE DOCTORS SMOKE CAMELS THAN ANY OTHER CIGARETTE

DOCTORS in every branch of medicine—113,597 in all—were queried in this nationwide study of cigarette preference. Three leading research organizations made the survey. The gist of the query was—What cigarette do you smoke, Doctor?

The brand named most was Camel!

The rich, full flavor and cool mildness of Camel's superb blend of costlier tobaccos seem to have the same appeal to the smoking tastes of doctors as to millions of other smokers. If you are a Camel smoker, this preference among doctors will hardly surprise you. If you're not—well, try Camels now.

Your "T-Zone" Will Tell You...

T for Taste . . .
T for Throat . . .

that's your proving ground for any cigarette. See if Camels don't suit your "T-Zone" to a "T."

CAMELS *Costlier Tobaccos*

11. As in the 1915 beer ad, this 1946 ad sought to influence views of vice by enlisting a member of a powerful group. From the collection of Stanford University (tobacco.stanford.edu).

12. This pre-zip code era ad (ca. 1950s to early 1960s) shows that not all changes in views of vice are more permissive. Co-Le Sales Company.

13. (*Opposite*) As in the 1946 cigarette ad, this 2013 ad to combat cigarettes used the same powerful group—physicians—to influence views of vice. In this instance, however, their power was enhanced by facts. Courtesy of the Centers for Disease Control and Prevention (CDC), 2013 *Tips from Former Smokers*™ campaign.

A TIP FROM A
FORMER SMOKER

RECORD YOUR VOICE FOR LOVED ONES WHILE YOU STILL CAN.

Terrie, Age 52
North Carolina

Smoking causes immediate damage to your body.
For Terrie, it gave her throat cancer. You can quit.
For free help, call **1-800-QUIT-NOW**.

#CDCTips

CDC

U.S. Department of
Health and Human Services
Centers for Disease
Control and Prevention
www.cdc.gov/tips

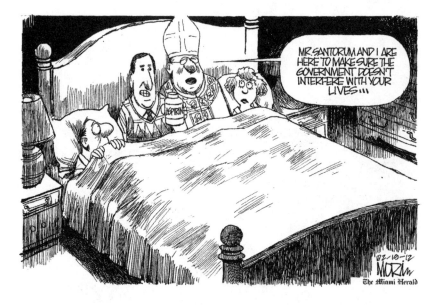

14. Since this nation's early days when heresy was still a crime, religious leaders have had to make room for many others who have joined America's powers-that-be. Nevertheless, they remain a powerful force and thus greatly influence views of vice. Jim Morin / *Miami Herald* / Morintoons Syndicate.

6

Moola and Ooh-la-la in Burlesque and Film

Movies were developed in the 1890s. Americans could see (but not hear, since sound track technology was yet to be developed) these first moving pictures as part of vaudeville shows or in shops whose owners added to their income by showing movies at night. By 1905 businesses dedicated solely to showing motion pictures began taking over, initially calling themselves "nickelodeons." That name bit the dust when the price went up.

As for those making the films, just as today, they often purveyed sex and violence. Back then these films had such vice-enticing titles as *In the Sultan's Power, Ingomar the Barbarian*, and *Airy Fairy Lillian Tries on Her New Corsets*. Needless to say, the nation's knights donned their moral armor and went to war. "Social Workers Will Censor Shows," headlined a May 3, 1907, article in the *Chicago Tribune*, reporting that members of this ascending behavioral science—comprised predominantly of members of another politically ascending group: women—would be assisting the Chicago police in "censorship over five-cent theaters." Censorship of more expensive amusements went unmentioned. Yet that same year, the *Chicago Tribune* carried theater ads for plays with similarly vice-enticing titles: *The Moonshiner's Daughter, Salomy Jane, The Time the Place and the Girl*, and *Miss Pocahontas* (the last boasting "Get Ready to Whistle and Whoop"). Middle-class and wealthy Americans, however, who comprised these audiences, were not the group at whom this view of vice was aimed. The working class was. More specifically, and far more significantly, views of movie vice in this era were employed to impose power on a rapidly growing segment of the working class: immigrants. Not only could they manage the nickel it cost for a ticket, but, by virtue of motion pictures back then being silent, non-English speakers could follow the movies' plots.

Joining with social workers were women's clubs, also comprised of well-off white Americans and—as with social workers, though in their own way—an adjunct of the women's movement. We can see these groups forming their nationwide crusade against film vice by splicing together, much as a film editor might, news items from across the nation: "The fight [against obscene films] made by the woman's church federation [is joining with other such groups]" (*Chicago Tribune*). "Among the societies and organization which have taken part in this campaign are the Women's Society for the Prevention of Cruelty to Children" (*New York Times*). "[When] the Civic Association held its monthly meeting . . . Mrs. P. G. Hubert reported concerning the ordinance which has been presented to the Council for action, providing for a Censorship Committee to pass upon moving picture films in this city" (*Los Angeles Times*). "The following committee was designated from the Federated Women's Clubs to censor and pass judgment upon the character of the moving pictures presented in the Atlanta moving picture theaters" (*Atlanta Constitution*).[1]

Joining this chorus were far more established voices of authority: religious leaders. "These men who run these shows have no moral scruples whatever. They are simply in the business for the money there is in it," Episcopal canon William Chase declared, aiming his view of movie vice, one might suspect, at those immigrant Jews who quickly grasped at this new industry not yet secured and sealed off by native-born Americans. Gustav Briegleb, a prominent Presbyterian minister in this era, ascribed the tendency of the studios to produce vice-filled films to his assertion that "eighty-five per cent of the industry is controlled chiefly by Jews." Using his view of vice to target the two major immigrant groups—Catholics and Jews—Briegleb said Hollywood movies depicted Protestant ministers as "weak-kneed, lady-like men," then asked, "Why don't those fellows take a Catholic priest or a Jewish rabbi and hold him up to ridicule?" Probably not being much of a moviegoer, Reverend Briegleb appears not to have seen the 1911 film *Story of the Nun*, roundly denounced by Catholics for its portrayal of a sadistic priest. That same year, Catholics also protested depictions of priests in *The Secret of the Confessional* and *The Price of Ambition* (in which a priest romances the wife of a congregant). Nor, evidently, did this minister catch, that same year, *The Yiddisher Cowboy*, a comedy that got laughs by ridiculing a Jew who'd ventured into one of America's most potent moral myths.[2]

Indeed, many if not most of that era's immigrant Catholics and Jews did not view films as vice—though their priests and rabbis often did. The Catholic Film Society was formed in 1914 for the dual purpose of urging boycotts of offensive films and the production of films by and for Catholics.[3] In 1909 Rabbi Stephen S. Wise, one of that era's most prominent Jewish leaders, became a founding member of the National Board of Censorship of Motion Pictures—a grand name for an unofficial organization. Nevertheless, it was comprised of enough National Grandly Regarded Americans that filmmakers coveted permission to include the organization's seal of approval on their films. Provided it didn't reduce the studio's bottom line.

Official or not, state and local censorship groups were not toothless. The Comstock Act and a concomitant federal law banning interstate transport of obscene material, along with state and local obscenity laws, fully equipped offended citizens to pressure officials to close or ban films on that basis. In addition, numerous jurisdictions enacted ordinances prohibiting films deemed as glorifying vice or crime.[4]

Even at the time, however, there were some who understood the underlying reason why such laws were ineffective. In response to one such proposed ordinance in Toledo, Ohio, its longtime mayor, Brand Whitlock, challenged all of America's moral crusaders. "All acts of which he does not himself approve are evil; a stop must be put to them at once, and the way to do this is to have a law," he wrote. Then, setting insults aside, Whitlock explained why the police are "incapable of carrying out such regulation" by cutting to the bottom line—the element of consent—when he said, "The difficulty is due to the fact that the old medieval confusion of crime and vice persists."[5]

Likewise there were those who knew this use of vice was rooted not in morals but in power. "The movies seem at once to be the object of a rare devotion from one part of the public and of a half-crazy, insensate, unreasoning hatred from the other," a November 27, 1916, editorial in the *Los Angeles Times* stated. "This pursuit of the movies . . . goes disguised under the name of 'reform.'" Likewise as well, this editorial employed views of vice (or, in this case, not-vice) on behalf of the film industry, which by then had acquired a considerable economic clout in that city. In doing so, however, the editorial also highlighted an example of power forming views of vice when it claimed that, among books popular with the nation's literati, "it was hardly possible to pick up a best seller without finding a story that would have placed a movie film in the hands of the police."

The *Times* was not wrong. Not long before, the *Chicago Tribune* told readers (with previously discussed canary-in-the-coal-mine humor) that a film based on a hoity-toity play ended up in the hands of the law because of its depiction of violence:

A fight which was arranged to come off yesterday in a five-cent theater was promptly called off by Police Lieut. Joel Smith. It was understood that the bout was arranged by one William Shakespeare, the contestants being Macbeth, the Cawdor heavyweight, and MacDuff, the Dunsinane Kid. In order to escape the police rule prohibiting prize fights, Shakespeare had arranged to have the fight given by means of moving pictures. But he couldn't fool . . . Lieut. Smith, who promptly declared the fight scene was a clear violation of the city ordinance as well as state law, and he was playing no favorites.[6]

But such laws were playing favorites. No stage production of Shakespeare had ever been prohibited in the United States because of its depictions of violence.

Censorship was not the only way those in power played favorites via views of vice in film. Often they did so in the opposite way. The number of films banned due to depictions of vice among or violence against African Americans, Native Americans, and Chinese can be counted on the fingers of one hand, revealing that those then in power sought to augment their influence by *displaying* rather than suppressing what they viewed as vice. One of very few films banned because of its ethnic depictions was *Free and Equal*. Released in 1918, it portrayed a light-skinned African American hired by a white philanthropist to raise living standards among less fortunate members of his race. The African American character availed himself of this opportunity by indulging in vices depicted as being inherent in blacks. *Free and Equal* was banned in some cities not because it was deemed offensive but because it was feared the film might anger African Americans to the point of violence against whites.

Not banned for that reason, however, was a film just as apt to enrage blacks but whose production was backed by far more power: *The Birth of a Nation*. Released in 1915, it glorified the Ku Klux Klan and climaxed with a heroically depicted lynching of an African American. Unlike *Free and Equal*, however, *The Birth of a Nation* arrived in theaters with far more influential credentials. In addition to having a highly esteemed director, D. W. Griffith, it was adapted from a highly successful Broadway play, *The Clansman*, by Thomas F. Dixon Jr., which in turn was adapted from his best-selling novel of the same name. While theatrical prestige hadn't been sufficient to vindicate (at least in Chicago) a film version of Shakespeare's *Macbeth*, an additional power was at work in the release of *The Birth of a Nation*. The author of its source versions, Thomas Dixon, had a friend from college days named Thomas Wilson who later went by his middle name, Woodrow. And, at the time, was president of the United States—the first, in fact, to view a movie at the White House. That movie was *The Birth of a Nation*.

African Americans in a number of cities initiated efforts to ban the film. None succeeded. Some efforts by whites, however, did succeed after incidents in which enraged blacks reacted violently to the film. Ohio and Kansas banned *The Birth of a Nation*, as did Chicago, Denver, Oakland and a handful of other municipalities—here too not because it was deemed offensive to blacks but because it was deemed dangerous to whites.[7]

In addition to being appalled by racial stereotypes, many nonwhites were as appalled as their white counterparts by films they viewed as purveying vice. Their views regarding vice functioned to maintain power for the same elements in their communities as in white communities. But they also served in the efforts to acquire greater acceptance and influence in white society. Still, to speak publicly of white depravity in films was risky business. Thus influential nonwhites opted to crusade within their communities for more moral performances by their actors.

"No actor who is not an accomplished star can afford to dictate," Sylvester Russell wrote in his 1911 "Annual Review of American Colored Actors." A former performer turned journalist, Russell advised black actors, "Too much cannot be said of . . . moral culture, good manners and . . . showing refinement at all times." To the extent that black actors could afford to accept only such roles, he urged, "All smut and suggestive dances would have to be omitted."[8]

Silent film actor and Lakota/Sioux chief Red Fox said of his screen appearances, "There were times when I wanted to go down to a clean stream and wash away my duplicity." In addition to accepting roles in which he attacked wagon trains and set the homes of white settlers ablaze—scenes with a basis in truth, but only one part of a far larger story—he also lamented, "I was pictured in war dances that a script writer must have dreamed up while in a nightmare."[9] Native American actors tried in vain to counter these and other abuses by forming the Indian Actors' Association in 1930.

Anna May Wong, among the most widely known Chinese American actors, found herself often salaciously cast in roles such as a Mongolian slave in *Thief of Bagdad* (1924) and, in the words of one film critic, "a lovely slut" in *Across to Singapore* (1928). As with African American and Native American actors, Wong struggled for nonstereotyped roles, even leaving Hollywood in 1928 to make films in Europe. Ultimately, however, the *im*moral myths about Asians proved too fixed in the film firmament of white people. Addicted to fame, as it were, Wong returned to the United States soon after box-office revenue skyrocketed when films acquired sound. And the sound of this born-and-bred American was one that many would view as the vice of faux-Chinese inflections. "We can't go back," Wong later wrote. "We can do nothing about it, but vow not to repeat a mistake."[10]

The Founding Fathers Go to the Movies

If the authors of the Constitution had taken a break to see a double feature, with *Drums along the Mohawk*, which depicted the struggle of Henry Fonda and Claudette Colbert as two newlyweds battling British loyalists and Indians at the outset of the Revolutionary War, followed by Sam Neill and Carmen Ejogo in the Thomas Jefferson biopic, *Sally Hemings: An American Scandal*, they'd probably have given a thumbs up to the first but been bothered by the second. Just a guess on my part. But much more than a guess on the part of the Supreme Court. Ten days before the release of *The Birth of a Nation*, the court ruled in *Mutual v. Ohio* that the authors of the Constitution would have agreed that states and local jurisdictions had the authority to censor films depicting stuff they didn't want others to see. The court declared that the First Amendment's guarantee of free speech did not apply to corporations, its ruling stating, "It cannot be put out of view that the exhibition of moving pictures is a business pure and simple, and conducted for profit . . . [and therefore] not to be regarded, nor intended to be regarded . . . as part of the press of the country or as organs of public opinion."[11] Or, in the reverse of more modern parlance, corporations are not people.

With this Supreme Court ruling giving the green light to government censorship of films, efforts to legislate official scissor-wielding commissions proliferated. In the next five years, such laws were proposed in twenty-four states. On the other hand, less than one-third of those states enacted those proposals.[12] A similar fate awaited a 1917 proposal in Congress to create a federal film censorship board. It too failed to pass. Apparently, various powers were at play in those days even when it came to sex and violence in films. Through the lens of views of vice, just who those conflicting powers were comes into focus.

Hollywood, with the industry's wealth, was one of those powers. While fearing federal censorship, film producers were far more concerned about state and local censorship laws, since they would then have to contend with the high costs entailed in making multiple versions of a film or accede to the strictest law among the localities, resulting in a less profitable product. To fend off such laws, Hollywood borrowed the vice device that boxing had recently devised: self-regulation. In 1917 the moguls' National Association of the Motion Picture Industry vowed to "lend its aid in the prosecution of any person or corporation which produces and causes to be exhibited any indecent or obscene motion picture or any motion pictures which tend to debase and corrupt morals."[13] And it worked.

Music up. Fade out. The end.

Except for a question. What did it mean: "lend its aid in the prosecution"? What aid might prosecutors need, given their power to subpoena witnesses and obtain search warrants—not to mention the fact that they would have as evidence the *filmus delicti*. Indeed, Hollywood had created, in keeping with the basis for its existence, an illusion. "Salacious Films Again," headlined a June 29, 1918, editorial in the *New York Times*, in which this normally sedate newspaper blew its stack: "The *Times* has never stood for the wild-eyed reformers.... It has even in the past taken up the cudgels for the film producers, insisting that they would voluntarily mend their ways. . . . But the reckless film producer has become more prevalent, more daring, more salacious as the days went on."

One might wonder which of those old flickering films that most Americans today would find quaint got that sophisticated newspaper so riled up? Salacious to many back then were films little remembered today, such as *Bestia* (later retitled *The Polish Dancer*) about a wild young girl who ran away from home; *The Sultan's Wife*, about a white girl forced into a harem; *A Strange Transgressor*, which depicted the lavish temptations of a kept woman; and the self-explanatory *Men Who Have Made Love to Me*—all released between the time the industry vowed to assist in policing salacious films and the publication of the *Times* editorial. While sexually tepid by today's standards, these films do contain elements that remain powerful. *Bestia / The Polish Dancer* examined parental power. *The Sultan's Wife* depicted a powerful Muslim. *A Strange Transgressor* challenged the power of husbands. And *Men Who Have Made Love to Me* questioned who controls women's wombs. It was for these reasons that the otherwise sophisticated *New York Times* went gaga. Gaga, in this instance, meaning using views of sexual vice in films to maintain those sources of power.

Soon after this editorial appeared, the effort to enact federal film censorship was revived. Faced with the failure of its ploy, Hollywood borrowed another vice device, this time from baseball, which had enthroned a commissioner (chosen by the team owners) in the wake of allegations that the 1919 World Series had been fixed by gambling racketeers.[14] Hollywood scrapped its discredited National Association of the Motion Picture Industry and created the Motion Picture Producers and Distributors of America (MPPDA), which would be overseen by a commissioner to assure that the films its member studios produced were not indecent, immoral, or obscene. To demonstrate their sincerity, the moguls hired Postmaster General Will Hays as their commissioner. Hays was widely known to Americans for the moral muscle he had demonstrated as postmaster general in his vigorous enforcement of the Comstock Act.[15]

Less clear was how Hays would enforce adherence to acceptable content—a fact that did not go unnoticed. "Will Hays is a Presbyterian elder and I am a Presbyterian preacher, but I cannot stand by him in his new role," declared Wilbur Crafts, one of a growing number of individuals now entering the ranks of professional reformer, in this case via his self-created National Bureau of Reforms. "We have evidence that the employment of Mr. Hays at a tremendous salary was deliberate and for a fixed purpose, that being to thwart those who would reform by government regulation moving pictures."[16] Hays's starting salary was $150,000, twice that of his former boss, the president of the United States. You can call Wilbur Crafts a prude, you can call him a zealot—but, as it soon became evident, you can't call him wrong.

"The principle of freedom upon which this nation was founded makes public censorship of the press, pulpit, film, or spoken word virtually impossible," Will Hays declared in his new capacity, going on to assert, "Statewide or nationwide censorship will fail."[17] During his tenure as Hollywood's film commissioner, its studios continued purveying what many viewed as vice. *Manslaughter* (1922) depicted orgies and a lesbian kiss. Violence and nudity helped pack movie theaters for *Ben Hur: A Tale of the Christ* (1925). *Flesh and Devil* (1926) pretty well speaks for itself—with, in this film, a soupçon of homosexual motivation.

Initially, Hollywood's shield held up. Legislation proposing federal film censorship was introduced in 1924 and once again failed. But a harbinger of change appeared during hearings over the bill, bringing into focus one of the critical divides in this crusade: "Mrs. Thomas A. McGoldrick, of the International Federation of Catholic Alumnae, assailed the proposed legislation as tending to 'over-Federalization,' while its passage was urged by Protestant minister C. J. Twombley."[18] Mrs. McGoldrick, along with many Catholic leaders, was wary of laws that could affect First Amendment guarantees in light of the long-standing effort to permit Bible study in public schools, the Bible to be studied being the Protestant version. Catholic leaders tended to urge a different approach: boycotts.

Following this latest legislative failure, Catholics were now in the best position to pick up the fallen weapons and lead the crusade. Indeed, their quest against film vice contributed to their becoming increasingly ensconced in America's power structure. Among the foremost of those Catholics rallying America to pursue this new direction in combating film vice was Father Daniel Lord. After consultation with other influential Catholics, he set to work on a motion picture code in 1929. It contained a far more specific list of dos and don'ts—and a mechanism for enforcement. If the code were accepted by the MPPDA, filmmakers agreed to pay a $25,000 fine for violating the commissioner's demand for revision based on the code. Will Hays, who was not averse to wielding power if he had it, was all for it, urging the MPPDA to adopt it.[19]

The studios could, of course, simply have told Hays to take a hike and take his Catholic friends with him—except that several elements of power had shifted. For one thing, telling the Catholics to stick their film code where no camera had yet dared to go was risky business, since Catholics now constituted nearly 20 percent of the population. And in urban areas, the primary source of Hollywood's revenues, Catholics constituted an even greater percentage of its population. Moreover, Hollywood's successes in fending off most efforts at censorship left Protestant moral reformers more willing to join the boycott ranks of Catholics. Hollywood's moguls had little choice but to sign on to this more enforceable and specific code.[20]

As they signed on the dotted line, however, their mogulian eyeball was on the code's provision for appeal if a producer believed the material deemed objectionable was within the guidelines of the code. The appeal would be heard by a special panel appointed for that purpose. And who would comprise the panel? The moguls' fellow movie producers. But the crusaders were smiling too, for they knew that clergy-led boycotts were yet a higher level of appeal.

A look at the specific film vices that this new film code prohibited reveals just whose power it sought to protect. Not surprisingly, it stated that members of the clergy "should not be used as comic characters or as villains." Joining together church and state cinematically—in lieu of constitutionally—the code declared, "The courts of the land should not be presented as unjust." Corrupt politicians or judges or cops were okay, provided they were shown to be the rare bad apple, but the nation's religious, political, and criminal justice systems "must not suffer as a result of this presentation."[21]

Still, what's salacious to some was bodacious to others, depending on whose power they were reflecting or seeking to impose. Among the first squabbles were films starring Mae West. Already renowned for her saucy wit in vaudeville and Broadway plays, West arrived in Hollywood following the advent of talkies, as it enabled her to bring her banter to film. Beginning with her starring role on the silver screen in *She Done Him Wrong* (1933), she became the nation's most popular naughty girl writ Woman due to her physical allure and titillating tropes, such as (from her second film in that year, *I'm No Angel*), "I used to be Snow White, but I drifted."

Will Hays was amused by her movies. Father Daniel Lord was not. No sooner had Hollywood released *She Done Him Wrong* than Father Lord declared that Catholics should boycott the film. Joined in his view by many offended Protestants, various sequences deemed too lewd were snipped out by local censors, and, in some jurisdictions, the entire film was banned.[22]

Why, however, did Mae West's roles evoke the wrath of moral reformers when "the lovely slut" depicted in Anna May Wong's films did not? Clearly it wasn't sexuality per se *but the way in which sexuality depicted power*. The Asian women portrayed by Wong had little power, whereas West played a woman in *She Done Him Wrong* who not only sings in a nightclub but owns it. Moreover, she is the one stringing along a bevy of lovers, going unpunished for using her sexuality to control suitors ranging from a criminal to a temperance advocate. Her character, and many others she portrayed, were self-empowered women, bound by—and judged by—no rules but those to which they consented.

Remember *Mary Lyndon*, the 1855 novel about a self-empowered woman that likewise caused reviewers to hit the roof? The vitriolic reaction to it and *She Done Him Wrong* reflected a kind of social physics: if one packs enough power into a container that's no longer strong enough to hold it, that container will explode. But the degree of the explosion depends on the strength of what is ultimately unable to contain it. In this sense, men, though they ultimately could not contain the power women were acquiring in the era of *Mary Lyndon*, exploded with far more vitriol in 1855, when they had far more power, than they did with *She Done Him Wrong* in 1933. By then, their power over women had decreased considerably due to the women's movement, which amassed its power, in no small part, through its use of views of vice and not-vice. Looking just at the 1930s, with the power of women slowly but steadily continuing to increase, we can detect that increase by the decreasing explosiveness in reactions to the soon-to-be-produced films in which performers such as Katharine

Hepburn, Joan Crawford, and Barbara Stanwyck portrayed powerful characters. There were little more than sparks after 1933—the year not only of *She Done Him Wrong* but also of Barbara Stanwyck in *Baby Face*. The character Stanwyck depicted, a woman using sex to rise in the corporate world, was brutally attacked in several states by censors wielding scissors. Money is another measure of this shift in the power of women being connected to a shift in views of female vice. *Mary Lyndon* was not a best seller. *She Done Him Wrong* garnered the highest box-office revenue of any film in 1933.[23]

Other films also sent Father Lord and his cohorts stomping up the aisles. Moviemakers not only continued to purvey violence, they eluded the Production Code's prohibition of disrespect for cops and courts by depicting criminals in ways that portrayed an understanding of their behavior—*Little Caesar* (1930) with Edward G. Robinson, *The Public Enemy* (1931) with James Cagney, and *Scarface* (1932) with Paul Muni.

With the Catholic Church now leading the crusade against vice in film, it upped the ante in 1933 by creating the Legion of Decency. Through rallies and sermons from pulpits, the organization recruited some seven million members who pledged not to attend films deemed indecent by the legion's leadership. With this movement sweeping the country and by no means limited to Catholics, its leaders demanded that Will Hays (whom the film moguls had ensconced in New York, three thousand miles from the studios he was hired to oversee) turn over control to Hollywood-based Joseph Breen, one of the original group who consulted with Daniel Lord in drafting the Production Code. Hollywood acceded to the demand, doing so for the simple reason that seven million potential ticket buyers, from Hollywood's point of view, beat rock, paper, or scissors.

Joseph Breen presided over film (and later television) content from 1934 to 1954. His red pencil revealed how the vices prohibited by these codes served the interests of those in power. For example, despite the fact that the Motion Picture Code (and later Television Code) stipulated that no picture should incite bigotry among people of different races, Breen did not view the depictions of African Americans as bigoted in the countless films and television shows in which they were often shown as simple-minded and content with their menial station in life. Nor did Breen view as vice in entertainment the countless instances of analogous stereotypes of Native Americans, Chinese, and other underempowered groups.

One of the most widely remembered artifacts of Breen's career was the dictum that husbands and wives could not share a double bed. In this instance, Breen did the opposite of ignoring stipulations as he did with racial stereotypes; he created them. The Production Code said nothing about bedroom furniture, only that a film or television program could not show a "man and woman in bed together."[24] In both cases, Breen imposed his views of vice to impose power. That this dictum was, in fact, Breen's doing can be seen by comparing the first two of Myrna Loy and William Powell's multisequeled box-office hit, *The Thin Man* (1934) and *After the Thin Man* (1936). In the initial film, produced and released before Breen had settled into his job, the husband and wife sleuths are shown chatting in their double bed. In the sequel, they have twin beds with a night table in between, representing Breen's view of a cinematic chaperone.

How did he pull this off, since the code did not prohibit double beds? In memos. One, for example, advised that "there be twin beds" by pointing to sexual mores in certain European markets (by which he likely meant, but did not say, many of the predominantly Catholic countries).[25] If that were truly his motive, it would be the only time Breen acted out of concern for Hollywood profits, as all his other pronouncements cut into the cash they could rake in by filming vice. Far more likely, Breen raised his finger at double beds, then pointed it at those markets, to misdirect moviemakers from his belief that twin beds were a useful approach to birth control, as viewed through his own particular Catholic lens.

Live Vice Onstage

Even as this new crusade brigade was deployed to watch Hollywood, other crusaders continued their watch on theatrical stages. They too revealed the groups for whom they sought to maintain power by virtue of what performances they deemed—as opposed to those they did not deem—as vice. Their successes and failures, in turn, brought into focus the current pecking order among the powers-that-be. In 1911, for example, Jesus appeared onstage as just another guy in a Broadway play, raising the hackles of enough religious advocates that police were sent in.[26] All the cops ended up doing, however, was applaud. Which is not what those cops' grandfathers would have done in their day. Though religious leaders were still powerful, they were far less influential than in the past, when America's demographics were less complex—and thus fewer groups vied for a grip on the levers of power.

But the past presents its own complexities. Consider this headline from Iowa's *Dubuque Herald* on July 1, 1869: "The Nude Drama: How Managers Coin Money by the Exhibition of Nudity."[27] Iowa, yes. And not a typo: 1869. Who knew that any of those women who look so upright and a bit blank in old tintypes were prancing in the buff to applauding farmers? But hold your britches. This ostensibly respectable newspaper report revealed itself to be intentionally sensational when, after several vice-enticing paragraphs on the "rage for nudity," it stated with as much shock as possible, "Stripped naked as she dare—and it seems there is little left when this is done—she becomes a prize to her manager, who knows that crowds will rush to see her." At the risk of being picky, *what little is left* makes all the difference in terms of nudity.

Language likewise obscured what, in this era, we consider nude in an 1895 *New York Times* article headlined "The Nude Onstage Denounced." It reported on a proposed law to make it a crime for a female performer to "expose her form or limbs in tights or in indecent attire." "Attire" and "nude," to our way of thinking today, are mutually exclusive.

The naked truth is that myths abound in the history of nudity onstage. And not just myths promulgated by moral reformers. In 1968 Hollywood released a star-studded film titled *The Night They Raided Minsky's*, centered around a legendary raid on April 25, 1925, of that famed New York burlesque theater. The key word being "legendary." If such a raid took place, no New York newspaper made mention of it.[28] The striptease dancer alleged to have crossed the line into indecency, one Mademoiselle Fifi (née Mary Dawson), denied that there was ever any such raid.[29] If, as it appears, the 1925 raid was a myth of immorality, what is not a myth is that it made a lot of money for a lot of people. Also not a myth is that Minsky's burlesque theaters (the four Minsky brothers operated several) were indeed raided from time to time, as were the theaters owned by their competitors.

Complicating the effort to hit the nail on the head in seeking to whack striptease was disagreement as to what constituted the nail. At what point is one illegally, even if not literally, stripped? In striptease, for example, the key word is "tease." The costumes, props, lighting, and manner in which the dancers disrobed were all designed to convince viewers that they had glimpsed what they actually had not seen. Indeed, in one 1924 arraignment, the producer of a burlesque show was charged not for what took place onstage but for the advertising displays in the theater's lobby and the street outside, which the prosecution contended fraudulently suggested that ticket buyers would see naked women when, in fact, they wouldn't.[30]

So when *did* female performers first appear on stage or screen completely naked? While not likely the first time, soon after motion pictures came into existence a cottage industry in pornographic films was well established by 1904.[31] The real deal. As for earlier eras, if we could remove the delicate veil that occludes written accounts from the past, most likely we'd discover that performances that included, in the parlance of present-day gentlemen's clubs, TOTALLY NUDE GIRLS date back to around the time prostitution began. A rough estimate being shortly after the invention of bartering for goods and services.

Some sense of the frequency of such performances in New York at the end of the nineteenth century can be gleaned from the fact that newspapers reported on three police raids of such events in a six-week stretch between 1896 and 1897. One raid was on a bachelor party at a swank New York restaurant called Sherry's. Acting on a tip, police found "four dancing women almost entirely naked." *Almost* meaning what? Had the cops' timing been better, might they have pounced when the girls were totally nude? To us today, that's what the captain leading the raid seems to have claimed when he stated that the girls "had been engaged to divest themselves of their clothes while they danced." A similar raid took place at a sumptuous "dinner with a Pompeiian flavoring" (suggesting we're all going to be buried under lava, so let's live it up?) at which the entertainment provided by the hired ladies was, in the words of the *Brooklyn Eagle*, "too vile for publication." Make of that what you will. Raid number three was at a Brooklyn hotel, where men paid $2.50 to attend a performance at which, the same newspaper reported, the dancing girls "might have been fashionable in the Garden of Eden."[32] Meaning fig leaf? In the buff?

Ambiguity, however, isn't what's most important. Most important is a difference that surfaced in these three raids. Police arrested the men who paid for the entertainment at the hotel in Brooklyn but only took down the names of the far wealthier men attending the same sort of event at Sherry's and the Pompeiian party. Indeed, one editorial on these events explicitly revealed views of vice being used to preserve the power of the upper class when it asserted, "What shall be done or said or sung in a home, a family, a club or private gathering . . . we unhesitatingly declare for liberty. . . . [But] what shall be done in a theater or other place to which the general public has admission, they [the police] have a large measure of public support and public respect."[33] Translation: if you've got enough loot to pay women to dance lewdly, that's not punishable vice, but if you're a working stiff who puts up a few bucks for such a show, put up your hands.

During these same years, theatrical producers began eluding the letter of the law prohibiting indecent exposure. In 1894 American audiences were introduced to the fan dance when Lola Yberri arrived from Spain to make her debut in the United States. The mesmerizing flow of Lola's folding and unfolding fans synchronized astonishingly well with the laws of New York. It was soon to become all the rage with erotic dance enthusiasts.

At the other end of the sexy ways to move spectrum, the law in New York (and elsewhere) did not deem indecent *standing still* onstage while exposed, since declaring it unlawful could create legal issues involving paintings and sculptures that well-heeled Americans did not view as vice. Hence producers in this era "educated" audiences (shades of eighteenth-century theatrical "lectures") by presenting well-known works of art using live actors. Not, however, well-known works such as Whistler's mother or even, despite her alluring smile, the unalluringly garbed Mona Lisa. Among the paintings presented as "living pictures" in one vaudeville theater in 1894 (the same year Lola Yberri arrived on the American stage) were *The Temptation of Tannhäuser*, *The Angelus*, and *The Queen of the Flowers*—works few remember today, what with newer and nuder acclaimed art having followed.[34]

So popular were these "living pictures" approaches to performances that they soon became fixtures in perennial Broadway revues, the most famous of which were Florenz Ziegfeld's *Follies*, Earl Carroll's *Vanities*, George White's *Scandals*, and, since the power of sex even trumps race, Lew Leslie's *Blackbirds*. Ziegfeld was the most skillful at cloaking in virtue minimally cloaked females. Billing his shows as "the glorification of the American girl," he presented her all-American breasts about to bust out with the boy next door or draped in sheer patriotism. "No 'Follies' was ever complete without a patriotic finale," a *New York Times* review noted two months after the United States entered World War I in 1917.[35] In that season's grand finale, the audience was canopied beneath a vast, mechanically unfurled flag as battleships, in the words of the review, "seemed to steam through the night up to the very breakwater of the footlights" under the protection of Lady Liberty. She stood unwavering (which legally is to say, not moving, lest she and Ziegfeld get arrested), her robe bespeaking our foundations in freedom, the beauty of which was enhanced by her unwavering display of one fully liberated breast. Truly a moment that made American men want to stand and salute Old Glory. Or old Ziegfeld.

Likewise, there were star performers in this genre of the performing arts. Among the most famous over the years were Sally Rand, Ann Corio, Josephine Baker, and Gypsy Rose Lee.

Josephine Baker was African American. And while sex has consistently trumped race in the realm of power, the power of race can nevertheless be seen in the varied ways Americans of different races viewed striptease. For all of Sally Rand's skill with fans and feathers, or the acting talent of Ann Corio, or the titillating wit of Gypsy Rose Lee, Josephine Baker was widely recognized as the greatest dancer in this group. And the lowest paid.[36]

In one respect, race made little difference. Most Americans, no matter their race, viewed striptease as a vice. But differences can be detected, and those differences reveal the use of a view of vice to maintain, or acquire, power. Syndicated columnist Paul Harrison, who was white, blamed the women who engaged in striptease when he wrote in 1935 of a stripper facing impending death from cancer: "To understand her, you should know her kind. The ambition of every performer is to originate a specialty, anything that is impregnable against the legions of imitators. . . . It was that way with Joanne Letournel. She has danced nude . . . [but] what she needed was a specialty. Then she thought of covering her body with radium paint. That was it—she'd be the original Radium Girl!"[37]

That same year, James Alsbrook, a columnist for an African American newspaper, expressed his view of black striptease dancers in a poem that questioned the degree to which the dancer consented in its lines,

But when she got her pay and went backstage
She wept alone in shame of wicked living.
Hers was a dance to placate hunger's rage,
So I believe her sin deserves forgiving.[38]

Undoubtedly there were whites with similarly sympathetic views about women who danced in the nude. But there was much more political motivation to express such views among blacks—and more poems about strippers by black writers than by white. African American poet Ray G. Dandridge wrote:

She danced, near nude, to tom-tom beat,
With swaying arms and flying feet,
'Mid swirling spangles, gauze and lace,
Her all was dancing—save her face.

. . . .

A body, marshalled by the will,
Kept dancing while a heart stood still:
And eyes obsessed with vacant stare,
Look over heads to empty air,
As though they sought to find therein
Redemption for a maiden sin.

. . . .

And then, to us, did it occur
That, though we saw—we saw not her.[39]

Likewise black poet Claude McKay, whose "Harlem Dancer" concluded:

Upon her swarthy neck black shiny curls
Luxuriant fell; and tossing coins in praise,
The wine-flushed, bold-eyed boys, and even the girls,
Devoured her shape with eager, passionate gaze;
But looking at her falsely-smiling face,
I knew her self was not in that strange place.[40]

Carl Sandburg, however, shared Paul Harrison's view of blaming the dancer, as in these lines from this renowned (white) poet's "Vaudeville Dancer":

The houses go wild when you finish the act shimmying a fast
shimmy to The Livery Stable Blues.
It is long ago, Elsie Flimmerwon, I saw your mother over a washtub in a grape arbor.

. . . .

It is long ago, Elsie, and now they spell your name with an electric sign.[41]

The underlying difference between Carl Sandburg's and Paul Harrison's view of nude dancing and that of James Alsbrook, Ray G. Dandridge, and Claude McKay regards consent. Sandburg and Harrison viewed nude dancers as having it, whereas the degree of consent is precisely what Alsbrook, Dandridge, and McKay questioned. And consent—or, rather, its absence—was a key element in many aspects of African Americans' quest for equality. Here, then, among African Americans, views of vice were being employed toward that end.[42]

On the other hand, white moral reformers employed this view of vice to maintain racial and social class status. In 1922 Chicago police raided the Entertainers' Café, a nightclub with an integrated clientele that featured black musicians and performers, including strippers. The strippers, not the white owners of the nightclub, were arrested and convicted. Quite different was the response of the authorities in cases involving only whites. When Chicago's branch of a group called the Church Federation demanded that the women in the 1924 touring production of George White's *Scandals* put on more garments, it was George White who was threatened with arrest.[43]

Not all efforts were so successful. Comparing those that were with those that weren't further brings into focus which groups were now the most powerful. When the New York Society for the Suppression of Vice prevailed upon police to raid the Minsky burlesque theaters in Harlem and the Lower East Side, the judges in both instances dismissed the case. But the vice-fighting society succeeded in getting the authorities to close Minsky's theater at Eighth Avenue and 28th Street in the neighborhood known as Chelsea. On Broadway, when New York's outpost of the Church Federation demanded more couture in Earl Carroll's *Vanities* in 1924, Carroll replied in a curtain speech, "I will not make a single alteration." And got busted. But got acquitted.[44]

This tangle of outcomes can be untangled by viewing views of vice as weapons for power. Let's begin with the judgment against Minsky's in Chelsea. In the 1920s Chelsea was a predominantly middle-class neighborhood. Which is to say its residents had just enough coin-of-the-realm-of-power to acquire the term coined for such people: "respectability." Many of its residents, therefore, joined with the New York Society for the Suppression of Vice in opposing the presence of a burlesque theater in their community. Minsky's theater on the Lower East Side, however, was located at Second Avenue and Houston Street, an intersection near neighborhoods of poor and working-class Jews and Italians, and its Harlem theater was in an African American neighborhood. Despite the fact that most of the residents in these neighborhoods also viewed such sexuality onstage as vice, even with the assistance of the New York Society for the Suppression of Vice they were unable to overcome the financial power of the Minskys when it was combined with those in power who feared their status ("respectability") would be undermined by sharing power with blacks and immigrants. Indeed, permitting these burlesque theaters to operate in Harlem and on the Lower East Side contributed to many Americans viewing it as a vice that blacks and immigrants found acceptable, thereby adding more disrespectability to these groups.

Well played, powers-that-be.

But power was shifting, which can also be detected in the tangle of outcomes in this crusade. Those efforts initiated by the New York Society for the Suppression of Vice were now less successful than those initiated by the local outposts of the newer Church Federation. The reason the federation's efforts to vacuum stage vice were more effective than the broom long used by the New York Society for the Suppression of Vice was that this vice-fighting Christian coalition included Catholics.[45] The society that Anthony Comstock formed was comprised of Protestants and remained predominantly Protestant, thus becoming more limited in its influence as Catholics increasingly acquired power.

As with efforts to combat vice in motion pictures, once Catholics had sufficient political clout, the battles began to tip in favor of the crusaders, who, likewise, increasingly fell into step with efforts led by Catholics. New York City was the main battleground, being both the theater capital of the nation and a city where Catholics comprised almost half the population during these years. "Cardinal Condemns Indecency on Stage," one 1925 *New York Times* headline declared, soon followed by another article headed "To Boycott Profane Plays," reporting on a proclamation from the Catholic Holy Name Society, which in 1926 included more than two million members. Filling the ranks behind this new leadership were not only many Protestant clergy and the New York Society for the Suppression of Vice but also a number of rabbis, such as Herbert S. Goldstein, president of the Union of Orthodox Jewish Congregations of America. Also in their ranks were groups whose goals were more economic than spiritual, most notably the Forty-Second Street Property Owners' Association.[46]

But sex is a powerful force, too. And because theater is a less centralized industry than film, fighting vice onstage presents far more challenges than its Hollywood equivalent, Whac-A-Mogul. Up to (and through) World War II, moral reformers bopped away at sex onstage in a crusade whose skirmishes—and their trend as the nation stockpiled social power in preparation for war—can be traced from headlines in the *New York Times*:

July 10, 1930: "Carroll's 'Vanities' Raided as Indecent"
August 13, 1930: "Clear Earl Carroll of Indecency in Play"
April 11, 1931: "Burlesque Show Raided"
September 20, 1932: "Prepare New Attack on Burlesque Shows— 42nd St. Owners Seek to Have Licenses Revoked, Indecency Charges Having Failed"
September 20, 1932: "Mckee Closes Two Burlesques in 42d St."
May 11, 1934: "12 Seized in Theatre Dismissed in Court"
November 17, 1934: "Nine Are Arrested in Raid on Burlesque"
December 27, 1934: "Policeman Dances for Court in Vain—200-Pound Gravely Imitates Hawaiian Manoeuvres, but 9 Are Freed in Burlesque Raid"
April 6, 1935: "Burlesque Show Raided"
April 7, 1935: "Court Upholds Nudity"
April 9, 1937: "'Strip Tease' Held Indecent by Court"

May 2, 1937: "Burlesque Shows of City Are Shut as Public Menace"
May 8, 1937: "Burlesque Bill Adopted—Would Give City Officials Broad Power to Close Shows"
April 12, 1942: "Moss Is Upheld on Burlesque Ban—No Evidence Is Found That Licensing Officials Abused Discretionary Power"

Unseen in these headlines is another powerful force that began hobbling burlesque around 1937. Ironically, it was not a group of moral reformers but the entertainment industry's new, so to speak, vice president.

Movies.

By 1937 the technology for motion pictures had advanced to the point that massive numbers of Americans now attended them. Adding to the attraction of film over live performance during these Depression years was that a movie ticket cost much less. Even without the moral crusader attacking burlesque, it—like its less risqué cousin, vaudeville—found itself on the ropes, pounded by sound and twenty-four flicking pictures per second. Burlesque and vaudeville both soon hit the mat, and the ten-count commenced as, unable to compete, movies began taking over their theaters.

Nudity in entertainment, however, had not thrown in the towel. Being nudity, it didn't have a towel. What it did have, being nudity, was unbeatable power. After World War II, as we'll see, it returned to the stage.

7

A New Power and New Views of Vice

On July 1, 1946, the United States conducted a test of a 23-kiloton atomic bomb on a tiny evacuated island in the South Pacific known as Bikini Atoll. The following year, a mechanical engineer in France named Louis Réard made a midcareer change to fashion design and a big splash with a little bathing suit he called the bikini. In its August 1947 issue, *Le monde illustré* noted that the name Réard had bestowed on this bathing suit was aptly akin to "l'explosion même correpondait" (the corresponding [atomic] explosion). Just as the bomb detonated at Bikini Atoll eviscerated so much of the landscape that whatever life was left in that depopulated place was destroyed, the article went on to say, so too did the bikini eviscerate so much of the cloth in bathing suits that whatever modesty was left was destroyed. But the connection was more profound than wordplay. Though few, then and now, fully understand Albert Einstein's Theory of Relativity, let alone how it contributed to the creation of the atomic bomb, most view the atomic bomb as confirming that relativity is a reality. And a very powerful one, at that. The fallout from that perception greatly affected views of vice.

In 1950, for example, when Milwaukee's chief of police sought guidance from the city attorney on whether a woman wearing a bikini in public constituted indecent exposure, that office responded, "The test must be how far the community has gone in the acceptance of [bikinis]. . . . In the absence of a statutory definition of the word 'obscene' we may assume that it must mean the present critical point in the compromise between candor and shame at which the community has arrived."[1] Obscenity, in other words, was relative.

Different as one may imagine a Milwaukee beach is compared to Laguna Beach in Southern California, there too one police officer lamented the relativity of vice when he stated, "There has to be a line drawn somewhere on these things, but we haven't had any specific instruction." Explaining why he'd issued no specific instructions, the Laguna Beach police chief echoed the question posed by Milwaukee's municipal authorities: "Who's to determine what outrages public decency?"[2]

How far had the public gone in the acceptance of skimpy bathing suits? In 1952 the *Long Island Star-Journal* sought out the views of residents in the borough of Queens. "Bikini bathing suits are immodest and I know that I would never wear one," one woman responded, as did a man who declared them "positively indecent and not the proper outfit for a public beach." Another resident declared them indecent and added, "I will go further by saying that they are also a bad influence."[3] Each of these views emanated from efforts that, as previously discussed, sought to control sexuality to maintain the power of particular groups. Still, an element of relativity surfaced not in what these people said but in what they didn't say. None of the individuals quoted in the article advocated a law banning bikinis. Evidently, they viewed their view as just that—their one view, as opposed to the one truth.

Still, there were Americans who warned of stern punishments to women who wore such minimal swimwear. One Catholic archbishop declared in 1949 that bikinis "violate the moral law and open the gates to the worst immorality"; he urged priests throughout the world to withhold absolution to those who persisted in this "sinful self-exhibition." Even in Alamogordo, New Mexico—the town nearest to where the atomic bomb was developed and first tested—Church of Christ minister Tice Elkins cited 1 Timothy 2:9 ("that women adorn themselves in modest apparel") in condemning "bathing suits . . . designed so as to put accent upon the physical appeal of the body." He then pointed to a recent incident in which a bikini-clad sunbather was raped and murdered as the basis for warning, "She paid for the disregard of decency with her life, and she must bear at least a large part of the guilt for the deed of the man who took her life."[4] That such a (to say the least) stern rebuke was voiced by a clergyman reflects the fact that religion is, understandably, resistant to the notion of a relatively Supreme Being.

Fewer Americans, however, now said amen to these men than in earlier eras when religious authorities competed with fewer groups for influence. Using the canary-in-the-coal-mine test of humor to gauge the degree to which the power of atomic energy was projecting relativity via views of vice, compare those 1952 (wo)man-in-the-street views to these from a 1959 *Chicago Tribune* feature asking the same bikini question: "Just picture all of the girls on the beach in bikinis—there would be too many auto accidents on Lake Shore Drive," one woman quipped. A man joked, "A bikini bathing suit is a must in this world. Everyone who is 110 pounds or under should have one—but anybody above it should stick to a mackinaw" (a mackinaw being a heavy raincoat). This individual then spoke directly to the relativity of vice when, dispensing with humor, he added, "Our Founding Fathers probably would have considered it indecent." More solid evidence of this relativity-based power blasting its way into the nation's inner Mount Rushmore via views of vice is the fact that no jurisdiction in the United States banned the bikini. Some places, however, did resist by engaging in a strategic retreat to deploy an increasingly used devicing device: zoning laws. A number of resort towns enacted ordinances prohibiting any kind of uncovered swimsuit to be worn in areas other than the beach.[5]

But there's more to the swimwear story. Or, more accurately, less. "Topless Swim Suit? Don't Try It Here" headlined a June 12, 1964, *Los Angeles Times* article. The *Chicago Tribune* joined in on July 9, announcing, "Fine for Wearing Topless Suit Is Increased," by which time a nationwide media chorus was in full throttle, ringing out headlines through the following year along the lines of "Uticans Have Mixed Reactions to Topless Suits," "What to Do about the Topless Problem," and—using this view of vice to impose patriotism during the Cold War—"Red View of Topless Bathing Suit." Once again test cases came before the courts, and once again judges found ways either to sidestep the issue or, in some instances, to rule against ordinances prohibiting topless suits for women. The most salient fact, however,

went unnoticed by those hurling these views of vice and those whacking gavels. Sales of topless bathing suits in the forty years extending
from 1960 to the end of the century totaled approximately three
thousand. Worldwide. Any which way you parse the numbers, the
percentage of women who bought topless bathing suits was infinites-
imal. The same can be said when looking ahead at behinds in thong
bathing suits, which caused much ado in the 1990s.[6]

Along with women wearing bikinis came taking off bikinis as nudity
in entertainment returned to American stages. But, as always in the
aftermath of war, the grip of those who'd held power had slipped
amid the upheaval. Groups such as the Church Federation, which
had come to acquire so much moral muscle in the years leading up to
the war, no longer packed as much punch. Despite having atrophied,
these forces still existed—though they'd have to regain strength if they
hoped to be able to wallop, as they once had, star-studded purveyors of nudity onstage. In 1951 police in Hollywood raided the famed
nightclub Ciro's on Sunset Strip for a strip being performed there by
Lili St. Cyr. Ms. St. Cyr was a highly successful performer in her field,
earning $5,000 a week at Ciro's, for which, in the testimony of one
police officer, she did "a couple of bumps and one grind . . . caressed
her body . . . unzipped her dress to below her buttocks . . . kick[ed]
her legs," and, to end her act, "took a bubble bath." In testimony less
erotic but in terms of its veracity equally eye-popping, another of the
officers claimed to have been too focused on observing the show to
notice any of the movie stars in attendance that night. At her trial,
Lili St. Cyr was acquitted.[7]

Less special people arrested for kicking their legs while dropping
their dresses below their buttocks were often less fortunate. "Convict
Two after Vice Squad Raid," a Maryland newspaper headlined after
a pair of striptease dancers were arrested while performing at a rural
venue at which, presumably, no movie stars were present. Indeed,
patrons without movie-star pedigrees were subject to leash laws on
morals, as evidenced in one Wisconsin headline, "270 Face Trial in
Big Raid on Club." On the other hand, an increasing number of judges
and juries were acquitting such defendants, viewing the morality of

nude dancing through a more relative lens. When, for example, one striptease dancer was put on trial in 1954, the judge asked the arresting officer if, when he saw her perform, he was personally offended. The police officer answered, "Well, no, your honor." To which his honor responded, "Case dismissed." Exposure that does not offend, this jurist maintained, is not indecent.[8]

Needless to say, not all Americans were onboard with a relativistic view of striptease dancers. One weapon used by moral crusaders to combat this new influence of relativity was that good old moral shotgun: myth. In 1954 Monsignor Joseph McCaffrey, pastor of the Holy Cross Church just off Times Square, spoke out against the peep shows and porn shops infesting the area by sharing his memories of the days when you could walk about Times Square and see shows like *Abie's Irish Rose* and wholesome performances by actors such as George M. Cohan. Which was true, but not the entire truth. Back in those same family-friendly days you could also see plenty of female flesh and get an earful of smut on Broadway at Minsky's Burlesque or, if inclined to more refined erotic performers, Earl Carroll's, George White's, Lew Leslie's, or Florenz Ziegfeld's revues. Conversely, even as Monsignor McCaffrey lamented the filth on the Great White Way in 1954, one could have stepped outside his church and bought a ticket to see a revival of *Abie's Irish Rose*—or taken the family to see Mary Martin in *Peter Pan*, or John Raitt and Shirley MacLaine in *The Pajama Game*, or a long list of other smut-free musicals and plays. What's more, twenty years earlier one could even have stepped back inside that same church and seen that same Joseph McCaffrey speaking out against the "vile conditions" on Broadway in good old 1934.[9]

By comparing his remarks in 1934 to those in 1954, we can get a rough assessment of how much the power of religious authorities had slipped in the wake of World War II. In 1934 McCaffrey's sermon was broadcast on radio; in 1954 it was not. In 1934, when the Church Federation was increasingly succeeding in its efforts to prohibit nudity onstage, McCaffrey's radio address also called upon city authorities to require bookstores to be licensed so that their business licenses could be revoked if they violated laws against obscenity. In 1954 he stuck with the Good Book and let the bad books be.

Whacking Gavels at Public Nudity

At a 1966 rally protesting the Vietnam War, nineteen-year-old David Paul O'Brien publicly burned his draft card and promptly got arrested, thereby setting in motion a new approach to making nude dancing a punishable vice—despite the fact that he was neither dancing nor nude. Bear with me as we wend our way through to the legal system to get to the bare part.

O'Brien's lawyers maintained that the conviction violated his freedom of speech. The case ended up before the Supreme Court, which ruled against O'Brien. Its basis was that the arrest and conviction were for the effect on the crowd caused by burning the draft card, not for publicly desecrating the content printed on the card. A fine line indeed, which the court recognized; therefore, its ruling included stipulations to distinguish expressions protected by the First Amendment from those that are not.

The stipulations, known as the O'Brien Test, were promptly applied to the question: Is dancing publicly in the nude protected by the First Amendment? Under the O'Brien Test, nude dance was not considered freedom of speech, provided that the following conditions were met:

1. The law prohibiting it is constitutional.

Duh. But when it comes to interpreting the Constitution, duh is debatable. Supreme Court justices have interpreted that document differently—via dissenting opinions—beginning with their first ruling on the constitutionality of a law, *Hylton v. United States*, in 1796.

2. The law must protect a "sufficiently important governmental interest."

Try to nail down that with a gavel.

3. Those important or substantial governmental interests must be "unrelated to the suppression of free expression."

Or that.

4. The law must be limited to that which is "essential to the furtherance of the governmental interest."[10]

Or that.

Rather than clarify, these rules resulted in gavels across America whacking this way and that when nude dancers defended their performances as expressions protected under the First Amendment. One such case commenced when the owners of the Kitty Kat Lounge filed suit to prevent police in South Bend, Indiana, from raiding their establishment if their dancers did not at least don pasties and G-strings. The Kitty Kat Lounge won. The federal judge who heard the case declared that Indiana's restrictions were not in compliance with all four guidelines in the O'Brien Test. Indiana authorities challenged that interpretation of the O'Brien Test before the U.S. Court of Appeals. This time *they* won. So the Kitty Kat loungers challenged the Court of Appeals interpretation, bringing the case before the U.S. Supreme Court in 1991.[11]

In that case, Justice Antonin Scalia maintained that indecency laws could be applied even to those who are not scandalized by voluntarily attending a public performance that includes viewing parts of the body possessed by only one sex. "If 60,000 fully consenting adults crowded into the Hoosierdome to display their genitals to one another," he maintained, it could be prohibited by law. In response, Justice Byron White wondered why, then, "those same 60,000 Hoosiers would be perfectly free to drive to their respective houses all across Indiana and, once there, cavort and revel in the nude."[12]

Five of the nine justices voted to uphold Indiana's law. But two of the five differed from the other three in their interpretation of the O'Brien Test and its interpretation of the Constitution.

Whack. Whack.

Not surprisingly, the Supreme Court had to take another whack at it not long after. When the city council in Erie, Pennsylvania, enacted an ordinance to restrict totally nude dancing, the corporation that owned a strip club called Kandyland challenged the law based on its interpretation of the O'Brien Test. And won. But when the city of Erie appealed the case, it won. But when Kandyland's owners then went to the Pennsylvania Supreme Court, they won. After which the U.S. Supreme Court overruled Pennsylvania's Supreme Court.[13]

Whack. Whack. Whack.

More important is what wasn't whacked. In the same year that the authorities in Erie were seeking to prohibit nude performances at places such as Kandyland, they took no action to prohibit performances in their town by Broadway touring productions of the musical *Hair* and the play *Equus*—both of which contained total nudity. When, soon after, legislators elsewhere enacted laws to justify the legality of such plays and the illegality of other nude performances, the use of views of vice on behalf of wealthier Americans was readily discernable. St. Louis, for example, adopted an ordinance prohibiting nude performances that entailed "touching, caressing, or fondling of the breasts, buttocks, or genitals . . . [unless] it occurs as a part of a performance at a place that has a seating capacity for patrons in excess of 950 persons, and which has annual ticket sales for admission thereto in excess of $750,000."[14]

Strippers, however, found a way around laws that prohibited them from touching themselves. "L.A. Council Approves Ban on Lap Dancing," the Associated Press reported on September 7, 2003. Yet again, however, moral reformers whacked in vain when their weapon was gavels. Even though a strip club producer could not compete financially with a Broadway producer, there were a lot more of them. As seen in the failure of Prohibition, lots of little pockets containing the element of consent add up to considerable power. In this instance, $400,000 worth of power, contributed by strip club owners to finance a signature-gathering campaign to force a referendum on the ordinance. "L.A. Council Retreating on Lap-Dance Ban," the *Los Angeles Times* reported soon after.[15]

Rather than combating nude dancing directly, moral reformers increasingly sought other avenues to combat it. Some jurisdictions prohibited the sale of alcoholic beverages at establishments that featured nude dancing. Proprietors of strip joints danced around that by allowing patrons to bring their own bottles.[16] Legislators whacked at that by prohibiting any consumption of alcohol at establishments featuring nude dancing. "Legal Challenges Have Yet to Squeeze Out Nude Juice Bar," Athens, Alabama's *News Courier* reported on February 3, 2005. While such battles would continue, the humor that fluttered in this headline was the omen indicating this war on nude dancing was lost.

At least for the time being. Because the powers-that-be are continually shifting. And because, when the "end" came in this crusade, it wasn't from surrender, it was from compromise. Both sides agreed to accept the use of zoning laws that stipulated where strip clubs could locate. In this way, those opposed to strip clubs and/or the rise of other groups, buttressed their power by vindicating this vice in areas of their choice, enabling them to ascribe this vice to the group that lived there, whether the majority of that group approved of nude dancing or not.

Just as movies undermined burlesque, a new technology similarly undermined strip clubs (though not, in this case, rendering them extinct). "Internet Has Replaced Brick-and-Mortar Sex Shops," Wisconsin's *Green Bay Gazette* reported on February 14, 2015. All across the country, much of the sex purveyed in porn shops and strip joints was increasingly being purveyed online. Hence, once again, moral crusaders donned their increasingly punctured armor.

In the early 1990s, when Internet access was becoming widespread, groups such as the Christian Coalition and the American Family Association devoted efforts to combating online pornography via legal restrictions and prohibitions. Senator James Exon proposed legislation that would prohibit sending material via the Internet that was deemed obscene. Others who had been down that road before— namely, anyone aware of the failures of the Comstock Act—expressed skepticism. Such as officials at the Justice Department. They noted that this kind of whackery (a phrase that may not do justice to the wording of their response) would be virtually impossible to enforce due to all the constitutional uncertainties that had gavels banging every which way. What *was* certain, the Justice Department stated, was that such a law would complicate its efforts to combat that aspect of obscenity purveyed on the Internet that was not consensual: child pornography. But most members of Congress preferred the moral myths of cowboys and crusaders and galloped off with Senator Exon, enacting the Communications Decency Act of 1996. It was promptly shot down in federal court, with the Supreme Court finishing off its one remaining provision soon after.[17]

"Clinton Vows to Work on Web Smut Safeguards," the *Washington Post* announced on July 17, 1997, less than a month after that Supreme Court decision. President Bill Clinton was indeed a man well versed in vice—as demonstrated, amid allegations of his having sexual relations with a young woman who was a White House intern, when he parsed the phrase "have sex" and the word "is." Though a major league avoider of moral whacks, even President Clinton could not use that talent to craft a whack that worked. The Child Online Protection Act, which he signed into law in 1998, was immediately derailed by a federal court injunction.

Meanwhile, Internet service providers, responding to these concerns among their customers—and indeed most, if not all, sharing these concerns—sought to address them (and enhance their competitive edge) by empowering their customers with the option of blocking access to objectionable websites and locking in that prohibition through the use of passwords. Calling these "parental controls," they were, in effect, a form of zoning.

Did it work? Since it's doubtful kids will give a truthful answer, let's look at what American history has told us (albeit not in schoolbooks) of boys and bosoms.

The November 1, 1896, edition of the highly regarded magazine *National Geographic* included a photo of an African tribeswoman in native dress—which is to say, with exposed breasts. American males, young and old, suddenly developed an avid interest in world cultures. Some might describe this interest as less educational than ejaculational, but the U.S. Postal Service did not. Never did it invoke the Comstock Act to block mail distribution of *National Geographic*, despite the publication being widely known for eliciting prurient interest. Nor did Congress or any other legislative body ever propose laws to prevent America's youth from getting their hormonal hands on it. After all, no white person's privates were shown in its photos, only those of Africans, Australian Aborigines, Pacific Islanders, and Latin Americans.[18] Thus was vice among middle-class and wealthy white males vindicated by those in power, since those in power were primarily comprised of—surprise!—middle-class and wealthy white males.

Needless to say, the same did not apply to the most well known magazine that featured photos of white women with bared breasts: *Playboy*. In December 1953 its first issue appeared on magazine stands. It featured a centerfold photo of Marilyn Monroe with her cinematically celebrated breasts fully revealed for all who wished to see. A stampede to newsstands worthy of anthropological coverage in *National Geographic* ensued.

Unlike *National Geographic*, however, *Playboy* faced a sustained effort by the post office to suppress it by rejecting the magazine's application for a second-class mail permit. While first-class mail is more constitutionally protected as to content, its additional cost would have bankrupted *Playboy* or any magazine. Lawyers for *Playboy* sued the postmaster general and, after lengthy legal dueling, got their second-class mail license in 1958—and, along the way, $100,000 in damages.[19] They succeeded because the government was unable to prove that the nude photographs were "utterly without redeeming social interest." More on the origin of that phrase shortly, but let's first keep looking at the magazine's photos—especially since President Ronald Reagan's attorney general, Edwin Meese, did.

In 1987 Meese did not dispute news reports that he had told a gathering of young lawyers that in his youth he'd thumbed through an issue or two of *Playboy*.[20] The attorney general's candor added considerable nuance and dimension to understanding crusades against vice since, during his years in the Reagan administration, Meese had stepped up efforts to enact legislation to clamp down on kids such as he once was by creating the Commission on Pornography. In its report, it cited *Playboy* among the publications it sought to curtail through the legislation it urged Congress to enact.

In response, those cads at *Playboy* sued the attorney general, since the federal government had never succeeded in deeming the magazine obscene under the law. Recognizing this First Amendment faux pas, the Justice Department quickly entered settlement talks, reportedly offering "to make statements to the effect that *Playboy* has never been found 'obscene.'"[21] Next thing you know, Ed Meese is talking guy-talk with young lawyers. Or, more accurately, tossing in the towel after a bout between very powerful forces.

While Attorney General Meese and the Reagan administration were viewed as conservative, opposition to magazines such as *Playboy* was by no means confined to that half of the political spectrum. Feminist Gloria Steinem (who also published a magazine, *Ms.*) attained national attention early in her career by going undercover—though not much cover—as a Playboy Bunny, the name given to the bunny-eared-and-tailed females who worked as cocktail waitresses at Playboy Clubs. Her account, pertly titled "A Bunny's Tale," appeared in the May and June 1963 issues of *Show* magazine. While her two-part article recognized that there was considerable "social interest" in this aspect of Hugh Hefner's *Playboy* enterprise, the notion of "redeeming" was notably absent from her account. Nevertheless, Steinem and her postwar feminist colleagues were imbued with the new power of relativity—as seen in the fact that they viewed such purveying of naked women as vice, although, unlike most of their predecessors, they did not view it as *punishable* vice.

Indeed, some protested *Playboy* in the nude. In 1969 five female and three male students at Grinnell College in Iowa staged a demonstration by removing their clothes when recruiters for *Playboy* arrived on campus. The nude protestors got busted. Like striptease dancers (whose purveying of female nudity they no doubt also opposed), the students maintained that their nudity was integral to their message and thus protected under the First Amendment. The judge at their trial disagreed, as did Iowa's Supreme Court.[22] The U.S. Supreme Court refused to hear the case.

Amazed or confused? Follow that era's brick-smashing-glass road to the powers-that-be.

At the time, many Americans had joined together to oppose college students protesting the Vietnam War. The violence often attendant upon antiwar protests contributed significantly to Richard Nixon winning the presidency in 1968, the first Republican to do so since 1956. Other Americans supported Richard Nixon in the hope that he would appoint more conservative justices to the Supreme Court, whose recent rulings on issues such as obscenity, they believed, undermined Right and Wrong. All in all, 1969 was not the ideal year for college kids to protest by taking off their clothes—even to protest what they too viewed as obscenity in *Playboy*.

Also in 1969 the executives at Eckerd Drug Stores, among the largest such national chains at the time, announced that their stores would no longer offer publications such as *Playboy*.[23] Most likely the company was responding to moral crusaders who had organized and brandished complaints by a sufficient number of customers. There were, however, many independent merchants who refused to sell *Playboy* because they themselves viewed it as indecent. Others, for personal or business reasons, opted to keep such stuff behind the counter so that kids couldn't thumb through it.

What merchants chose to do changed to what they *had* to do after 1973, when this shift in power led the Supreme Court to redefine obscenity yet again. This time, however, the court changed direction, ruling in a way that enabled a bigger net to be used to scoop up what those in power viewed as porn. In this case, *Miller v. California*, the court replaced the phrase "utterly without redeeming social interest" (and its 1966 incarnation from *Memoirs v. Massachusetts*, "redeeming social value") with "serious literary, artistic, political, or scientific value" to the average person, applying contemporary community standards.[24] While still imbued with relativity, the ruling was relatively different. Some communities promptly banned the sale of such publications, others opted for a form of zoning by requiring merchants to keep magazines such as *Playboy* behind a counter.

More Fallout from the War: Middle American Mutations

The Supreme Court case that enabled lawyers for *Playboy* to KO the post office in 1958 was *Roth v. United States*, handed down the year before. Remember Sam Roth? He who pirated James Joyce's esoteric novel *Ulysses*? More typical of the books he published were less esoteric works such as *Violations of the Child Marilyn Monroe* and *King Turd*. While *Roth v. United States* was a landmark case, redefining obscenity in 1957 by requiring that it be "utterly without redeeming social interest," often overlooked is that it also upheld Roth's conviction. To say it was a landmark case is not to say it was a game changer. What it marked was the fact that those empowered to play in the game had changed.

Emblematic of the increasing power of both middle-class and working-class Americans was the enactment in 1944 of the GI Bill. Even these initials were emblematic of their increasing power, since, in the era of World War I, the military used the initials GI in reference to *general issue* uniforms and equipment. During World War II, enlisted men began using it to refer to themselves. Laughter, bear in mind, is consensual, and the guffaws elicited by this dark joke revealed a powerful solidarity. Powerful enough to secure the GI Bill.

Among the benefits provided in this legislation were tuition and living expenses for those who opted to go to college. By 1956, the year before the Supreme Court redefined obscenity in *Roth v. United States*, more than two million veterans had availed themselves of that benefit.[25] While their higher education would not have made them more likely to read books such as *King Turd*, it very much made them more likely to read other works with sexually explicit content, such as *Lady Chatterley's Lover*, by British novelist D. H. Lawrence, or *Tropic of Cancer*, by our own home-grown transplant to France, Henry Miller. Both novels, however, had been banned in this country, despite the approval given in 1933 to *Ulysses*, with its far more obscure prose.[26] By the mid-1950s, however, with many millions more Americans having college educations (including but not limited to the two million veterans enrolled under the GI Bill), *Lady Chatterley's Lover* and *Tropic of Cancer* returned for a shoot-out at the What's OK Corral.

"In line after line and in sequence after sequence," the New York board tasked with censorship declared in 1956, *Lady Chatterley's Lover* "glorifies adultery and presents the same as desirable, as acceptable, and proper." What they were actually censoring was *L'amant de Lady Chatterley*, a film version of the novel produced in that longtime thorn in America's side of vice, France. That detail, however, reflects a larger fact: the battle over novels such as *Lady Chatterley's Lover* took place in the same years, and because of the same postwar shifts in power, as a parallel battle over the Motion Picture Code. Indeed, the American distributor for this film adaptation, Joseph Burstyn, had won a Supreme Court decision in 1952 that reversed its 1915 ruling that motion pictures, as a corporate product, were not protected by the First Amendment.[27] That earlier case had caused Hollywood to take cover by agreeing to the Motion Picture Code proffered on the lance of the Legion of Decency. But with film corporations now accorded the same First Amendment rights as people, it was the start of a whole new ballgame. And it opened with a rhubarb.

A court in New York subsequently overturned the board's decision to ban *L'amant de Lady Chatterley*. Then the state's highest court overturned the lower court. Then the U.S. Supreme Court overturned that court, clearing the way for the film to open on July 10, 1959.

To lukewarm reviews.

"Why the big fuss?" *Chicago Tribune* reviewer Mae Tinee wondered, summing up not only her reaction but also those of most of her colleagues.[28] The fuss wasn't about nudity, since the film contained none. Nor did it contain profanity. The fuss was about unpunished adultery. One can graph both the extent and rate of decline in the power of American religious authorities by comparing three points in time: (1) the punishments for adultery in the colonial era, (2) the prohibition of unpunished crime or sin in the prewar Motion Picture Production Code, and (3) the permission to show this film in 1959 along with the number of yawns in its audience.

Amid all the publicity generated by news coverage of the dust-up over the film, Grove Press announced that it would be publishing the original novel, unexpurgated. "It's time for a new crusade," Reverend Daniel Poling asserted in a national religious magazine. Having himself just read *Lady Chatterley's Lover*, he reported (not inaccurately), "In this book is page after page of sex—sex in the sun and rain, in the hut and forest, at all times and places, sex with what should be unprintable conversation, sex with nasty words that appear in public only on the walls of ill-kept outhouses."[29] One might question whether this description jives with his claim that he read it "sans all inherited or acquired Puritanical prejudices." While indeed his article did not advocate branding or wearing the letter *A*, it did advocate legal action.

Leading that battle was, once again, the U.S. Postal Service. Staggering back on its feet within a year of its losing bout with *Playboy*, its inspectors seized copies of *Lady Chatterley's Lover* being shipped through the mail. As expected, Grove Press went to court. And won. Which is not to say that the post office, and those powers on whose behalf it acted, lost. Rather, given the nature of this postwar rush for influence, the post office and its cohorts *relatively* lost. "I hold that, at this stage in the development of our society," Judge Frederick Bryan declared, "this major English novel does not exceed the outer limits of the tolerance which the community as a whole gives to writing about sex and sex relations."[30]

That same month (which was also when the film version of *Lady Chatterley's Lover* opened), Senator James Eastland proposed a constitutional amendment to ensure that "the right of each state to decide on the basis of its own public policy questions of decency and morality, and to enact legislation with respect thereto, shall not be abridged." Joining in this effort, Ohio senator Frank Lausche voiced the view of weakened—but by no means weak—religious leaders when he stated, "We believe in the Ten Commandments. We believe in the commandment, 'Thou shall not commit adultery.'"[31]

The proposed constitutional amendment failed to pass. But the effort pointed the way to the next stage of the battle: "the average person, applying contemporary community standards," in the previously cited words of the Supreme Court. Or in words that courts would be reticent to use: the local powers-that-be. Hence, when Henry Miller's *Tropic of Cancer* was published unexpurgated in 1961, moral reformers confined their crusades to the state and local levels, securing prohibitions of the book in Boston, Hartford, Cleveland, Milwaukee, Chicago, Sarasota, Dallas, and Los Angeles and throughout Rhode Island, New York, and New Jersey. Still, their power was not as powerful as the power residing in more than two million people in the United States who, by the time these state and local battles piled high enough to reach the Supreme Court in 1964, had consented to purchase *Tropic of Cancer*. The numbers represented what was, by then, "the average person, applying contemporary community standards." The Supreme Court had little choice but to deem the book not obscene. Bear in mind, however, that four of the five justices maintained that *Tropic of Cancer*—despite its popularity among so many "average" Americans—was punishably obscene.

Loving v. Law

On February 23, 1962, police in Miami Beach arrested Connie Hoffman, a white woman, and Dewey McLaughlin, a black man (technically Honduran, but apparently dark enough), for sharing an apartment in which, presumably, they engaged in sex. Probably an accurate assumption. Unfortunately for them, Florida was one of eighteen states that still prohibited interracial sex. For which they were promptly convicted.[32]

The fact that, by 1962, an avalanche of scientific evidence indicated no ill effects from interracial sexual reproduction shows us that the power of scientists in the United States, for all that it had expanded, still had limits. On the other hand, the fact that Hoffman and McLaughlin's conviction was overturned by a unanimous decision by the U.S. Supreme Court, which thereby declared all such laws unconstitutional, shows us that the power of white supremacists was now more limited than it had been in the past.

The war over interracial love, however, was not over. Also in the courts at the time was an appeal of a case from 1958, when police in

Caroline County, Virginia, had burst into the home of Richard and Mildred Loving at two o'clock in the morning, charging them with the crime of marriage. Richard Loving was white; Mildred Jeter Loving was African American (and part Native American and part white—but it would be many more years before race was viewed as relative). Interracial marriage was illegal in thirty states at the close of World War II. Nor did Virginia recognize interracial marriages performed elsewhere, such as the District of Columbia, where Mildred Jeter and Richard Loving had been legally wed.

"Almighty God created the races white, black, yellow, Malay, and red, and he placed them on separate continents," Judge Leon M. Bazile said in declaring Mr. and Mrs. Loving guilty, thereby demonstrating views of vice being used in Virginia to impose the power of some religious groups.[33] Similarly using views of vice in the service of white power, the judge enlisted God when he stated, "The fact that He separated the races shows that He did not intend for the races to mix." Judge Bazile then sentenced the Lovings to one year in prison, offering to suspend the sentence if they left Virginia and did not return for at least twenty-five years.[34]

For nearly a decade, the Lovings' case battled its way through the judicial system. That statistic alone provides a measure of how powerful white supremacists remained. But the fact that the Lovings' legal challenge was able to stagger its way through the courts also provides a glimpse into that part of the postwar melee for power that entailed African Americans. Right up to the war, court rulings had upheld state bans on interracial marriage. In the free-for-all for influence that followed the war, African Americans rushed in, too. Here, too, we're talking about more than a la-di-da metaphor. The melee was all too often literal, and all too often entailed death and horrific violence to African Americans. But among the levers on which prewar grips had slipped and would not be regained was the one that declared interracial marriage a punishable vice. Most state laws prohibiting it fell by the wayside. And in 1967 the U.S. Supreme Court ruled unanimously, in *Loving v. Virginia*, that laws prohibiting interracial marriage are unconstitutional.[35]

While it was white supremacists who sought to impose their power through the view that love between people of different races was a punishable vice, what group or groups sought influence by viewing love between people of the same sex as punishable vice? One such group, as we have seen, consisted of religious authorities, justifying their opposition by citing strictures in Leviticus against homosexuality. Still, also as previously discussed, far fewer of those religious leaders were as adamant about identical strictures in Leviticus against adultery. Moreover, far fewer women in the United States were prosecuted for gay sex than men—which makes sense when one considers that there was less need to suppress same-sex love among women since what were viewed as other female vices did a splendid job keeping all women under men's—let's say "thumbs."

Powerful as heterosexual American men have been, they never have been powerful enough to overcome the power packed into the element of consent, especially when combined with the power of sex. Consequently, adherence to laws prohibiting homosexual acts by consenting adults was rare. Even after President Dwight D. Eisenhower issued Executive Order 10450 in 1953, barring homosexuals from employment in the federal government, so many government workers continued to engage in gay sex that President Lyndon Johnson sought to reinvigorate enforcement in 1964 by directing Oval Office aide Walter Jenkins to remind all federal departments and agencies to have the FBI check out the sexual proclivities of prospective employees prior to their appointment.[36]

Still, while heterosexual American men may not have had sufficient power to curtail same-sex relationships, their power was sufficient to force virtually all Americans who engaged in these relationships to do so in secret. Walter Jenkins, for example, was arrested in a YMCA bathroom on what the news media delicately termed a "morals charge" one month after he had issued President Johnson's warning that government employees must be screened for gaiety, as it were, prior to their appointment.[37]

That these presidential efforts began in 1953 suggests that gay Americans were part of the postwar fracas for influence. Indeed, in

1951 a group of gay men officially formed the Mattachine Society, whose mission was to support its members collectively and to advocate publicly for gay rights. FBI director J. Edgar Hoover deployed federal agents to investigate the group—a particularly striking example of views of vice being used for purposes of power, since a mountain of subsequent evidence has indicated that Hoover himself was secretly gay.[38] Employing this view of vice, however, enabled Hoover to keep his hands on the levers of power, provided he kept secret other levers his hands may have gripped.

The fact that the postwar free-for-all for influence that took place amidst fallout that caused many Americans' views of sexuality to mutate into a more relativistic outlook is evidenced by, among other events, reactions to the arrest of Walter Jenkins. In its aftermath, the *Washington Post* reported that his neighbors "have quietly and willingly volunteered their time to help the family during a troubled time." Alongside statements of outrage by politicians, the article quoted those who lived on his block echoing the sentiments of the neighbor who said, "They are good people. . . . He was a dedicated and hardworking man."[39]

This more relativistic view of sex expressed by these neighbors was a particle from a viewpoint that detonated shortly after World War II and sent shockwaves through the nation. In 1948 Alfred Kinsey, a professor of biology at Indiana University, published a report on male sexuality in the United States, including the prevalence of homosexuality. Hot stuff for newspapers, many of which were more turned on (or assumed—probably correctly—that their readers would be more turned on) by lurid reporting than lucid wording. "Kinsey says ninety-five per cent have at some time or other been involved in activities which are illegal," the *Austin Daily Texan* told readers. Well, not exactly—or, more accurately, not even close—since Kinsey's statistic included a variety of homoerotic acts that might be considered foreplay but were not illegal. Still, even scholarly colleagues were taken aback by many of Kinsey's claims—though few disputed his claim that sexuality was too relativistic for fixed labels. Psychiatrist Robert W.

Laidlaw, for example, questioned Kinsey's findings but agreed with Kinsey that "the terms 'homosexual,' 'bi-sexual,' and 'heterosexual' are very unsatisfactory."[40]

Not all psychologists agreed more relative views were needed. In 1949, one year after Alfred Kinsey published his first report, psychiatrist George Crane wrote of five fixed sexual stages in "emotional growth." After summing up the first two, he went on to say that stage three was "the 'gang' or truly homosexual phase where boys have no use for girls and little girls consider boys as simply inevitable evils." I would have used the term "cootie phase," but admittedly that tag lacks gravitas. And it does not adequately capture Dr. Crane's professional observation: "Adults who remain fixated at this level are called pansies, fairies, etc." One can only guess which of the influences in Dr. Crane's life he was projecting through this view of vice. But it can be an educated guess. For more than thirty-five years, he taught Bible classes at the Chicago Methodist Temple.[41]

Religious leaders and heterosexual supremacists remained sufficiently influential after the war and for the next half-century that the vast majority of Americans continued to view same-sex love as a vice, with most of them believing it should be prohibited, at the very least, in certain realms such as teachers or troop leaders in Boy Scouts. At the same time, even in 1949 we find evidence that gay Americans were beginning to get their toes in the door to the tower of power. "Anti-loitering legislation aimed at homosexuals, degenerates, and other lewd characters set off a flurry of debate in the city council and resulted in another postponement of the touchy subject," California's *Van Nuys News* reported, noting that its opponents "objected that the proposal would give proprietors the power to pass moral judgment on patrons."[42]

Maybe not surprising to those who consider Californians kooky but even in straitlaced Salt Lake City in 1949, residents were opening newspapers to book reviewer Maude Robinson telling them, "Once the word homosexual was whispered—today it is as casually mentioned as diphtheria or a cold in the head, recognized as a mark of human disability for which no moral blame can attach to the unhappy individuals."⁴³ That she believed, albeit sympathetically, that homosexuals were sick (and perhaps, by implication, contagious) reveals that scientists and physicians were one of the most powerful groups in the United States. At the same time, one can detect the incipient rise of gay power in the fact that same-sex love was the subject of the book she was reviewing, *Stranger in the Land* by Ward Thomas, and how little that power still was in the fact that Ward Thomas was a pseudonym for an author who chose to remain unknown.

Other gays, however, were starting to go public in ever so slightly increasing numbers. "Homosexuality Discussion Set," headlined a 1958 news item in Walnut Creek, California, announcing that a local radio station, "in response to unprecedented public demand, will re-broadcast its informative inquiry and discussion of the problems facing the homosexual individual and the legal and social problems posed for society by homosexuality."⁴⁴ Among the participants in the broadcast was the editor of the *Mattachine Review*.

As gays continued to exit the closet and knock at the doors to power, those opposed to their passing through those doors deployed larger-gauged views of vice. "There used to be a town called Sodom," syndicated columnist George Sokolsky wrote in 1962, "which the Lord in his eternal wisdom destroyed." Sokolsky then went nuclear. "Society battles self-destruction, which homosexuality obviously is. The time has come, in our civilization, when we think of physical survival to consider also moral survival."⁴⁵

Sokolsky's argument pretty much bombed. But another bombshell did detonate on June 28, 1969, when police raided a gay bar in Greenwich Village called the Stonewall Inn. When the men in the bar unexpectedly fought back, the police had to retreat to the street, where they were confronted by hundreds of enraged gay men descending on the scene. Those who thought the incident some oddball occurrence were disabused of that view when, the following night, some four hundred gay men gathered in Greenwich Village to face off with the cops again. And again, night after night, into July. Similar militant acts spread throughout the country, along with nonviolent flank attacks, such as a successful lawsuit against the police department in the District of Columbia for arrests of gay men engaging in "consensual sex in the privacy of their homes."[46]

Also coming out of the closet were gay Americans who were members of powerful groups, openly applying their influence in those groups. In 1974, for example, the American Psychiatric Association removed homosexuality from its list of mental disorders. That same year, the city councils of Minneapolis and the District of Columbia joined a growing list of jurisdictions banning discrimination against gays in employment, housing, and public accommodations.[47]

By 1977 the "closets" were virtually emptied as tens of thousands of gay men and women gathered in cities across America for nationwide demonstrations demanding equal rights.[48] And on March 31, 1986, the U.S. Supreme Court heard arguments urging it to strike down laws that declared it illegal for gay adults to have consensual sex.

To which the court said: No.

We can plot another "headline graph" here, this one providing as good a measure as any of the rate and extent to which gay Americans continued to acquire power. The starting point on this "graph" is Bowers v. Hardwick, the 1986 Supreme Court decision that upheld state laws prohibiting homosexual acts. The end point is the Supreme Court's 2003 decision, Lawrence v. Texas, which overturned Bowers by striking down state laws prohibiting homosexual acts.[49] Headlines from the Washington Post during these intervening years reveal what changed the prevailing view among the justices on the court. And a good deal more. Just from the headlines we can see which bastions of power were shifting their views in order to maintain power as a result of being besieged by so many gays coming out of the closet—including many who were members of those bastions of power:

July 2, 1987: "[Congressman] Barney Frank, Out of Closet"[50]
October 11, 1987: "2000 Gay Couples Exchange Vows in Ceremony of Rights"
October 12, 1987: "Hundreds of Thousands March for Gay Rights"

June 5, 1991: "Episcopalians to Ordain Gay Woman"

June 19, 1992: "Hill Study Challenges Military's Exclusion of Gays"

July 20, 1993: "President Opens Military to Gays"

August 1, 1996: "Rep. Kolbe Announces He Is Gay"

December 4, 1996: "Gay Marriage Is Allowed by Hawaii Court"

October 1, 1997: "U.S. Catholic Bishops Urge Acceptance of Gay Orientation"

November 9, 1997: "Clinton Equates Gay Rights, Civil Rights"

March 14, 1998: "Jury Acquits Pastor Who Performed Gay Marriage"

Am I suggesting that the legal reasoning expressed in Supreme Court rulings is little more than rationalizations that endorse the views of groups prevailing in power at the time? Yes. Or, rather, as a product of my era: relatively yes.

As to the yes: the court expended 5,415 words in *Lawrence v. Texas* (not including those in the appended opinions that concurred or dissented), with all but 23 of those 5,415 words interpreting the Constitution in a way that conformed with the shift in the power revealed in those 23 words: "The Court in *Bowers* was making the broader point that for centuries there have been powerful voices to condemn homosexual conduct as immoral." One could as well say that the court in *Lawrence* was making the broader point that many powerful voices now do not condemn homosexual conduct as immoral.[51]

As to the "relatively." Those Americans in this era who began to view sexuality through a relativistic lens found that it actually brought "homosexual" into sharper focus. For them, the notion of being lesbian, gay, or bisexual became more accurately understood by recognizing relative aspects such as transgender and queer (or questioning). As this more relativistic view began to become widespread, its initialism, LGBTQ, entered the lexicon.

In addition, those with a more relativistic view were more likely to spot in headlines such as those listed above something else that was relative to themselves. Those headlines reveal that what the LGBTQ community wanted was the right to be religious, the right to fight for their country, the right to form families, and the right to participate in democracy.

Sixteen Candles . . . Make a Helluva Fight

In Gem County, Idaho, located nearby nowhere, seven unwed teenagers became pregnant in 1996. To curtail such teen pregnancies, the sheriff arrested the seven girls and the young (or not so young) men who impregnated them, charging them all with fornication.[52] As often with old statutes that have fallen into disuse, it was still on the books.

No other jurisdictions in the United States picked up on this new/old approach, most likely because no reports ever appeared indicating that teen pregnancy rates declined in Gem County, Idaho. Plenty of other reports on teen pregnancy, however, expressed alarm over the rate of teen pregnancy. More than seventy articles in regard to the topic were published that year in the *Washington Post*.

What made this issue such an important concern in 1996? Nothing. It was always a major concern. "Unplanned Parenthood among Teenagers" had headlined a *Washington Post* column on March 12, 1975. "1100 D.C. Teenagers Became Mothers in '64," the same paper announced on March 31, 1965, despite having trumpeted on November 22, 1963, "Unwed Pregnancy Rise Is Seen as Misleading"—perhaps in response to its numerous articles along the lines of "Illegitimacies Double Here in 10 Years" on January 23, 1958, and "War Blamed for Rise in Illegitimacy Here" on August 7, 1942.

Even two hundred years earlier, Americans had expressed concern over the number of girls engaging in what most adults, then and now, view as the vice of (choose the word you prefer) sinful or irresponsible sex. In this century, far more would opt for "irresponsible" than back in the day when religious leaders had more sway, as reflected back then in a biblical reference in the title of an 1832 book on young unwed mothers, *Magdalen Facts*.[53] It discussed in considerable depth case studies involving an orphan, a young girl in a big city, a minister's daughter, and a college girl.

In the 1890s one of the now more secularly named groups seeking to combat teen pregnancy was the Little Mothers' Association. In the early twentieth century, social scientists began measuring the extent of unwed motherhood. In Minneapolis, for example, 4.6 percent of births in 1915 involved unmarried females.[54] By comparison, the census of 2010 revealed that the annual percentage of births by unwed mothers was 4.0 percent.

More detailed statistics collected after World War II indicate that the peak year for teenage pregnancy in the United States was 1957. Not a typo. Not the present day. Not the late 1960s, with its free-love hippies. Those hippie girls had greater access to birth control (as do teens today) than their bobby-soxer counterparts who became their mothers and grandmothers. This 1957 peak was reached via the return of the nation's heroic—horny but heroic—soldiers after World War II, followed by those returning from the Korean War, and joined by teenage boys (that era's proverbial rebels without a cause) asserting their adolescent can-do spirit to compete for beautifully budding, but often naive, teenage girls.[55] Put it all together and boom goes the name of the next generation: the baby boomers.

Given this nation's long tradition of hand-wringing over its unfounded belief that unwed motherhood is worse than ever, one can imagine the response when in fact it *was* worse than ever. Most notable, however, as Americans ran to their armories to get vice fighting weapons, are the various armories to which they ran. For this wasn't just a war on unwed pregnancy. It was, rather, a battle in a larger war for power.

"We are in a period when reaction to the unrealistic and un-Christian prudery of puritanism has given way to the equally un-Christian shamelessness of hedonistic Epicureanism," Catholic priest Joseph Haley declared in 1950. Father Haley was joined by a Greek Orthodox priest, Demetrius Manousos, who called for a moral crusade: "If there is a conspiracy against chastity, our strongest armor against it is a correct attitude toward sex."[56]

No evidence existed that teenage boys and returning GIs had met and conspired. Nevertheless, other evidence revealed that there was indeed such a conspiracy, and its leader had now been identified. Gonads. This longtime nemesis of religious leaders and parents was yet again invading with legions of Hormones who ambushed unsuspecting teens. Metaphors aside, those are facts. But facts often gum up one of the most effective weapons in such crusades: moral myths. Consequently, that same year, a conference of American Catholic bishops declared their opposition to facts (in the form of sex education in the public schools), asserting that such matters ought to be solely the province of parents and pastors. Few if any Americans disagreed about the primary role of parents regarding moral views, but, given the rate of teen pregnancies, clearly many parents weren't up to the task of imparting facts. Seeking to acquire greater influence for teachers, one educator said at the time, "The public school system was organized to prepare students for life, and it certainly cannot omit sex."[57]

A third group that joined this particular fray during the postwar power grab illustrates even more strikingly how views of vice are employed for purposes of power, that group being the John Birch Society. Established in 1958 for the purpose of fighting Communism, one of its offshoots was a subgroup called the Christian Crusade. It produced a documentary film, *Pavlov's Children*, which asserted that sex education in the public schools was a Communist plot. The Pavlov in the film's title referred to a Russian, Ivan Pavlov, one of the world's most prominent psychologists—who was indeed adored by Communists (despite the fact that he abhorred them).[58] Pavlov acquired fame around the turn of the century by demonstrating that if he rang a bell whenever he fed a dog, in time he could make the dog salivate simply by ringing the bell. His research led some to believe he had found an avenue for brainwashing—an avenue that suggested schools were ideal places for brainwashing.

"Birch Head Sees Sex Education as Red Plot" headlined a January 19, 1969, article in the *Washington Post*. The plot to which Robert Welch, the founder of the John Birch Society, referred was "uncovered" by Baptist minister Jack Hyles, who described it in a pamphlet that spoke volumes about views of vice and power. Among its claims was that Isadore Rubin, the treasurer of the Sex Information and Education Council of the United States (SIECUS), which Reverend Hyles described as "the organization that is behind the sex education program . . . in school systems across this great nation," was a Communist. As proof that the ultimate aim of SIECUS was to instill Communism in American children, Hyles pointed to the fact that Rubin had refused to cooperate when called before the House Un-American Activities Committee.[59] He then quoted (without citation) sex education advocate Lester Kirkendall, a sociologist at Oregon State University, as urging SIECUS "to just sneak it in." At which point in his pamphlet, Hyles went on to demonstrate very explicitly views of vice in the service of power. Interweaving commentary with Kirkendall quotes, he wrote:

[Kirkendall] said, "Just sneak it in." What? Sex education. "Go to the PTA. That is where the power lies." And, by the way, let me say a word about them. There is a magazine called *The PTA Magazine* that is going to answer to God for a lot of the rot in America. "Go to the PTA. There is where the power lies." . . . Then Kirkendall advised [SIECUS] to get a group of leading businessmen, doctors, lawyers—and form a committee. Get them to endorse it, then you can sneak it in better.[60]

The point isn't that Reverend Hyles was an anti-Communist kook. Whether he was or wasn't, the man knew the groups in which power resided—in this instance, the PTA, local businessmen, doctors, lawyers. While he may have been wrong about the Communists and sex ed., he wasn't wrong about the ways groups can use views of vice for purposes of power. Indeed, we will be visiting remarks virtually identical to his again—except in reverse. Keep him in mind when we encounter others citing the PTA not as a purveyor of vice but as a combatant against it, and when we encounter a call to organize businessmen, doctors, lawyers, and those in Jack Hyles's profession, the clergy, to combat, of all things, teen pregnancy.

As for Pavlov, it has been said that in his later years every time Pavlov saw a dog salivate, he rang a bell. Those who said it were psych majors telling each other jokes, but the quip echoes an important question regarding those who fight to suppress vice. That question was asked in a 1946 interview of John S. Sumner, the man who followed Anthony Comstock as the head of the New York Society for the Suppression of Vice: "Has reading so many books of this type [pornography] harmed you?" To which Sumner answered, "I don't think they have done me any good."[61] Sumner was half right and half wrong. Dirty books had done him a great deal of good by providing him with a career as a moral crusader. On the other hand, they do not appear to have done any harm to his morals. Despite all the prurient prose that his brain drained day after day, there was never a whiff of suspicion that John Sumner (or Anthony Comstock) ever crossed the boundaries of sexual propriety by any standard. What did he think made him but not others immune to sexual information? He never said—at least, not publicly. But others, whom we'll encounter ahead, will provide insight into why some are, in verifiable fact, more susceptible than others to vice as a gateway to crime.

To the extent that there was any increase in premarital sex at the time so many young Americans began protesting war, smoking pot, and turning into hippies, it was not because of Communists, pornography, bikinis, or rock and roll; it was because the longtime team of science and industry developed and purveyed the birth control pill.

When the FDA approved the use of the birth control pill in 1960, it too was seized upon as a proxy for power by those both pro and con. By 1965 the postwar dust-ups had sufficiently settled to reveal that the starting lineup of the nation's power players now included more women seeking to control their own wombs. In that year, the Supreme Court struck down state laws that prohibited husbands and wives from using birth control devices. As more women continued to get a place on the starting lineup, the justices swung for the fences in 1972, applying the ruling to unmarried couples as well.

While crusaders against contraceptives had been forced to retreat, they were far from defeated. They regrouped with a drive to modify sex education courses in ways that would promote sexual abstinence for teens. Those efforts bore fruit in 2001, when the administration of President George W. Bush altered its policies regarding sex education courses and programs to prevent teen pregnancy by shifting the bulk of federal financial support to those that advocated abstinence, *and only abstinence*, as the means for birth control—thereby privileging those programs that excluded information on access or use of contraceptives. But prohibition (in this case of information) did not work. A government-sponsored assessment of the first five years of these "abstinence only" programs found they did not reduce the rate of teen pregnancy.[62] Recognizing that combatting teen pregnancy required coping with, rather than trying to bop, the power of sex, the administration of President Bush's successor, Barack Obama, undid these changes.

Nevertheless, those who remained in this crusade continued to engage in periodic battles that were still winnable. They filed more than sixty lawsuits challenging a requirement in the 2010 Affordable Care Act that employer-provided health insurance had to include coverage for birth control. Coalescing around one such challenge brought by the company Hobby Lobby, they used this view of vice to assert the constitutional right of employers whose religious faith opposed contraception to opt out of including it in their company health care plans. In 2013 four of the justices on the Supreme Court disagreed. But five did not, resulting in Hobby Lobby and its supporters succeeding in imposing their view of vice. Power had ever so slightly, but critically, shifted again.

Cracking Drugs

"Nixon emphasized that you have to face the fact that the whole problem is really the blacks. The key is to devise a system that recognizes this while not appearing to do so." Presidential aide H. R. Haldeman wrote those words in his diary following a confidential meeting with President Richard Nixon in 1969.[63] Not confidential, however, was that unequal treatment of African Americans did not end with integrated schools or, a decade after that Supreme Court decision, the

1964 Civil Rights Act. White power continued, though increasingly in ways "not appearing to do so." One of which—even if not consciously for some—was via views of vice.

Shortly after President Nixon shared his racial insight with Haldeman, his administration proposed a sweeping revision of the federal government's drug laws. Congress then duly enacted the Comprehensive Drug Abuse Prevention and Control Act of 1970. While it increased penalties for those convicted of selling illegal drugs, it eliminated mandatory sentences for those convicted of possession. That certainly doesn't appear to be racist; indeed, it appears to be open-minded. And was—for impartial judges. But it enabled other judges to hand down sentences influenced by racial preconceptions.

And they did. Again, consciously or not. For example, we often (judges included—and, in this example, judges especially) form our views based on what a person wears. Indeed, some of America's most powerful moral myths involve clothing—most notably in this example, the power-projecting myth that the robes worn by judges invest them with wisdom. (For the Brits, the myth of a white powdered wig to top off judicial attire adds to the awe—whereas in the United States, a judge in a wig of any kind would elicit hand-hidden snickers.) As for views based on race, after the enactment of Nixon's 1970 drug law, data gathered by the government's own National Institute on Drug Abuse and, separately, by the Justice Department revealed that African Americans were more than three times more likely than whites to be arrested on drug charges even though the percentage of African Americans who used illegal drugs was found to be equal to that of white Americans. FBI data found that, after those arrests, the jail terms imposed by judges were 49 percent longer for African Americans than for whites.[64] Contributing to this discrepancy was the option, dating back to our colonial inheritance from England, of monetary fines in lieu of jail, which has always contributed to the ability of wealthier defendants to elude prison.

As a consequence of such convictions, these predominantly black Americans could legally be denied employment, access to housing, and—they didn't call him Tricky Dick for nothing—the right to vote.

Nixon's 1970 drug law became the foundation of, in the words that entitled an article by law professor Michelle Alexander, "The War on Drugs and the New Jim Crow."[65]

Blacks were not the only Americans Nixon sought to keep in their place through views of vice. All those white kids who'd turned into antiwar hippies, some of whom went so far as to question capitalism, drove Nixon (and many others) nuts. Yet for all their countercultural do-your-own-thingedness, they too—like so many unhip businessmen with their Scotch-on-the-rocks or housewives with their Valium—had their own drugs of choice: marijuana and, for the truly hip, the recently concocted hallucinogen LSD. Thus Nixon's 1970 law used a view of vice to take aim at a group he despised by listing LSD on Schedule I—those drugs that were the most punishable, such as heroin, despite the fact that LSD was not addictive. More revealingly, his law moved marijuana up in the list of prohibited drugs to Schedule I. Also revealingly, opium, that one-time Chinese threat to our morals, and cocaine—both addictive and long illegal—were just Schedule II stuff in Nixon's law, thereby deeming them less dangerous than pot or LSD. The Comprehensive Drug Abuse Prevention and Control Act of 1970 could indeed be called the Power According to Nixon Act.

While marijuana was previously viewed as a Mexican vice when those in power feared the influx of Mexicans, heroin was *not* viewed as a (in the lexicon of the past) Negro vice until after World War II, when the African American quest for equality reached critical mass and became the civil rights movement. Thus back in 1926, a full-page *Los Angeles Times* feature headlined "Stamping Out the Drug Habit" told readers, "Heroin and morphine are the most expensive and would be called the rich man's drug, while marijuana's the cheapest and is used by Mexicans, Negroes, and other addicts when they have not the means of procuring their regular drug." Back then, the drug most feared as the gateway to heroin for white people was not pot. Rather, it was that era's public enemy number one drug: booze. "The chagrin which overwhelms the drinker in his lucid moments," physician William Brady wrote in 1923, "when he realizes that he hasn't the strength to leave it alone, prompts him to venture further and try a sniff, a whiff, or a jab of heroin."[66]

By 1951, however, the civil rights movement was commencing, and with it the shift in power. And it could be witnessed in those opposed to the shift expressing a different view of heroin. For them, it was not a rich man's drug; it was a gateway to negritude. "A pretty blonde from Cincinnati" were the words the Associated Press used in reporting that year on the testimony of one young addict before a Senate hearing on drugs. Similarly, it told readers, "An 18-year-old Chicago Negro told of white girls as young as fifteen engaging in prostitution for drug money, sometimes with Negroes—'there is no segregation in the use of dope.'"[67] That same year, Congress enacted the Boggs Act, not only imposing stiffer penalties for drug possession but also, for the first time, making those sentences mandatory. With judges required to impose these sentences, race could not be a factor in how long those convicted were sent to jail.

Though it could be a factor in who got convicted.

Or, right from the judicial get-go, arrested.

These lessons were not lost on a newly elected senator from California named Richard Nixon.

Nor, years later, on another Californian, Ronald Reagan. "We've taken down the surrender flag and run up the battle flag," President Reagan declared in 1982, "and we're going to win the war on drugs." Echoing not only Nixon's call for a "war on drugs" but also crusades using precisely that phrase back in 1972, 1954, 1945, and 1921, President Reagan went on to tell how "few things in my life have frightened me as much as the drug epidemic among our children."[68]

Drug addiction truly is frightening and, when it afflicts young people, heartbreaking. The epidemic, however, was a moral myth. In this regard, the data separately collected from the National Institute on Drug Abuse and the Justice Department showed that the level of drug abuse had remained constant for more than a decade. Still, there was reason for renewed concern in the 1980s. A new form of cocaine had recently been introduced. Known as "crack," it was a crystallized form of cocaine that proved to be a more cost-effective way to get high. And it was more quickly addictive. The human ruin and crime resulting from crack addiction was appalling. So let's give another listen to what President Reagan was saying about drugs:

> The revolution out of which our liberty was conceived signaled an historical call to an entire world seeking hope. Each new arrival of immigrants rode the crest of that hope. They came, millions seeking a safe harbor from the oppression of cruel regimes. They came, to escape starvation and disease. They came, those surviving the Holocaust and the Soviet gulags. They came, the boat people, chancing death for even a glimmer of hope that they could have a new life. They all came to taste the air redolent and rich with the freedom that is ours. What an insult it will be to what we are and whence we came if we do not rise up together in defiance against this cancer of drugs.[69]

Without appearing to do so (to paraphrase President Nixon), notice anyone missing from this call to arms for a war on drugs?

Such as black people?

It's a curious omission from the president's list. All those African Americans who arrived on these shores enslaved, and after slavery their descendants, had struggled against the variety of chains that bound them—they too thirsted for freedom. And some of them were likewise enslaved to drugs, along with the many descendants of the groups the president saluted. Why weren't African Americans included in his list?

Because a lot of them, as anyone who followed the news knew, were doing crack. "Anybody can buy it and anybody can smoke it," the Associated Press reported, adding, "Cocaine is no longer a rich man's drug." Nor were such reports isolated. The *Chicago Tribune* told readers, "As crack grows in popularity and the pattern of cocaine abuse continues, the stereotype of the coke addict as a Porsche-driving advertising executive is becoming, if not a myth, then just one chapter in the cocaine story." This article went on to cite a study from Illinois's Department of Alcohol and Substance Abuse, which found that crack "began increasing among inner-city drug users a few years ago, while at the same time its popularity among more affluent users was declining."[70]

President Reagan and Congress responded by enacting a new/old drug law—new, in that it was newly enacted; old, in that it returned to the use of mandatory sentences. But with a difference, given the prevalence of crack among predominantly black users. The 1986 legislation stipulated a mandatory minimum sentence that was one hundred times more punitive for crack than for a comparable amount of traditional cocaine.

Clang went the doors of prisons. By 2014 the population in federal prisons had grown by 800 percent, largely due to mandatory sentencing for drug offenders—these figures not from some loosey-goosey liberal group but from the Edwin Meese Center for Legal and Judicial Studies. Despite the fact that the per capita use of powdered cocaine among blacks was virtually equal to its use among whites, police arrested and courts convicted over 50 percent more blacks than whites for its possession. As for crack, nearly 80 percent of those arrested were African American.[71]

Sounds bad, but let's not get too teary-eyed without asking: Did mandatory minimum sentencing whack crack? "The substantially greater sentences for those who are involved with crack cocaine do not appear to have any greater deterrent impact than that achieved by the lower powder cocaine penalties," twenty-six federal judges declared in a 1997 letter to the Senate and House Judiciary Committees. Nevertheless, by the time these judges spoke out, the use of crack was declining. So noticeable was this change by 1993 that prize-winning author (in his days as a journalist) Malcolm Gladwell set out to discover why. "The teenagers have seen what happened to their parents and their friends," one former crack addict told him, echoing similar explanations from numerous others in that city. Heroin, those interviewed told Gladwell, "was a sustainable addiction that could be maintained for many years; crack, in contrast, produces a much more powerful and crippling high." Gladwell's inquiry did not find that drug use was declining, simply that crack cocaine was on the outs. "Teenagers and adults have turned from destructive use of a single drug to occasional dabbling in a variety of substances," he wrote, "smoking 'blunts,' or cigars stuffed with marijuana and a sprinkling of cocaine, and increased alcohol use." Data later collected by social scientists confirmed this anecdotal evidence.[72]

The failure of mandatory minimum sentencing may account for changes in views regarding punishment of drug users. As governor of Florida from 1999 to 2007, Jeb Bush advocated and signed into law tougher minimum sentences for a variety of drug users. But when seeking the Republican presidential nomination in 2016, he spoke of the need for "an alternative to the punishment system, so that nonviolent drug offenders obtain treatment and recovery support."[73] Possibly, Bush changed his views of this vice less because of the statistical failure of jail time than because of the unfortunate fact that one of his children had fallen prey to drug use and landed in jail. His views may also have been altered when, as a consequence of the mandatory sentencing legislation he'd signed into law, a Floridian whose doctor prescribed pain pills following an accident that destroyed one of his eyes was sentenced to a mandatory twenty-five years in prison for providing some of the pills to a new friend claiming to be in pain but actually being an undercover cop. Or perhaps Bush revised his views because this man's extraordinarily harsh incarceration became the subject of a nationally discussed article in the *Atlantic*.[74] Or perhaps it became a nationally discussed story in the *Atlantic* because this unfortunate fellow was white.

This last aspect gains traction when one realizes that Jeb Bush was not the only Republican to spout new views of this vice. "Several GOP presidential contenders have advocated treating the nation's growing heroin epidemic as a health crisis, not a criminal one," the *Washington Post* observed during the run-up to the 2016 election, going on to add, "But most stop short of advocating the same approach to other drug laws, most notably those involving marijuana and crack cocaine, which disproportionately affect African Americans."[75]

Among the Republicans cited in the article as stopping short of this racial line was New Jersey governor Chris Christie. But in this instance the *Washington Post* was wrong—or very less than correct. As far back as 2012, Christie declared to his state's legislature, "Let us reclaim the lives of those drug offenders who have not committed a violent crime by investing in drug treatment—in an in-house, secure facility—rather than putting them in prison."[76] Though Governor Christie is a Republican, his constituents are predominantly Democrats, as evidenced by New Jersey having favored Democratic presidential candidates every year since 1992. What this instance demonstrates is that views of vice provide a more accurate lens to perceive who rules in a particular realm than does the lens of political party.

And not just for the more conservative Republican Party. For the best example among 2016's Democratic presidential contenders, let's set aside heroin use and take up sexual harassment. "Every survivor of sexual assault deserves to be heard, believed, and supported," Hillary Clinton tweeted in November 2015.[77] Her assertion is undeniably true—since "survivor of sexual assault" presupposes the existence of the assault. Saying any *accuser* of sexual assault deserves to be heard and supported may more accurately approach her meaning.

When she was First Lady, however, Hillary Clinton was anything but believing and supportive of Paula Jones. Jones asserted that when she had been an Arkansas state employee, then-governor Bill Clinton had state troopers bring her to a hotel room, where he exposed himself and sought sexual gratification. Hillary Clinton assigned this and other allegations of sexual misconduct by her husband to a right-wing conspiracy. Of accuser Gennifer Flowers, rather than believe and support her, the then First Lady branded her claims unsubstantiated and declared that if she could ever cross-examine Flowers in a courtroom, "I would crucify her."[78] A rather gruesome form of "support." And (though not likely what Hillary Clinton intended to convey) a form of punishment closely associated with the imposition of power.

It is important to keep in mind, however, that there is often a distinction in what one views as punishable vice in public versus what one views as punishable vice in private. Previously, this distinction was discussed regarding nudity. In this instance, we can catch a glimpse of another key aspect of this distinction. "I could have wrung his neck," Hillary Clinton publicly revealed in 2003 when asked about her husband's sexual misconduct.[79] And in so saying, in that year, in those words, the role of power in forming views of punishable vice is thrice demonstrated. During her husband's presidency, Hillary Clinton publicly viewed the accusations against him as a threat to his (and, with public speculation already rife regarding her own ambitions, her) power. Within one's private life, however, power is often configured differently. While Hillary Clinton apparently did not wring her husband's neck, her choice of words indicates that, within their private sphere, she wanted him to be punished. Her publicly expressing this view in 2003, when Bill Clinton was no longer the president and she was now a senator from New York, suggests that Hillary Clinton viewed women, at this point in her career, as critical to her quest for power in the form of the presidency.

All told, when various vices are used as lenses, it becomes clear that what we consider to be punishable vice takes the shape of the powers-that-be at particular times and places in each of our lives.

Newer Vice but the Same Old Shape

Currently wreaking havoc among many drug users are synthetic drugs—sometimes called "designer drugs," the most notorious being synthetic forms of marijuana. "Just what parents don't need," columnist Colbert King wrote in 2012, "another way for their kids to get high, or worse . . . and it's available at your local store."[80] King went on to cite the brand names of products that contain a synthesized variant of tetrahydrocannabinol (THC), the active ingredient in marijuana.

Synthetic pot was not new. In 1967 scientists synthesized a variant of THC in order to better understand how it affects the brain. It didn't take long for armchair chemists to catch on. One year later, a University of Wisconsin student was arrested for possession of a shipment of synthetic marijuana—but released, since no law banned the substance created to replicate the effects of smoking pot. Synthetic marijuana sprouted far more fully in the early decades of the twenty-first century, largely due to advances in technology. After its ingredients were included in a 2012 adjustment to federal drug laws, those who produced it were able to use computer-generated molecular models to create alternatives. Lawmakers have found themselves confronted with, in a sense, Whac-A-Mole on steroids. But users of synthetic pot have been finding themselves confronted with new drugs whose full effects and side effects are unknown. In 2015 emergency rooms in and around Syracuse, New York, treated 179 people in a one-month period for what appeared to be overdoses of a substance they ingested from synthetic marijuana. Similar reports were appearing across the country. Because of the rapidity with which producers of synthetic pot can alter the active ingredient(s), its detection often eludes traditional drug tests. Physicians and other scientists have had to scramble to devise methods of diagnosis—with lawmakers and law enforcement and, most heartbreaking, parents breathing down their necks.

The effort to create synthetic drugs to get high is not new. In 1950, word was widespread in this country that mixing Coca Cola with aspirin could get you high. Myth, as it turned out. Which didn't stop kids from mixing Coke with other stuff, including ammonia, and claiming it would carbonate their brains. Which, in fact, it didn't.

But later concoctions did. After the Controlled Substances Act of 1970 was passed under President Nixon, its tighter restrictions on amphetamines and methamphetamines (both of which are synthetic drugs that pharmaceutical companies had been producing for many years), a new market was created for the illegal drug industry. Particularly in Latin America, one of the frontlines in the War on Drugs where large tracts of marijuana and facilities illegally producing cocaine were being wiped out, drug traffickers turned to making "meth."[81] Its production was less detectable because its ingredients were easily and legally obtainable, so much so that a cottage industry also emerged in the United States when brilliant but brainless armchair chemists figured out how to make it in their own homes—though a number of those homes blew up, since (herein the brainless) its production requires such highly flammable products as benzene (found in gasoline) and acetone (found in things like paint remover) used to process lithium (found in battery acid) and ephedrine or pseudoephedrine (extracted from over-the-counter cold or asthma medications).

As with crack cocaine, the effects of ingesting methamphetamine were often far more addictive than the user had bargained for. Also as with crack, the risks entailed in using meth were so great that its use declined. Data collected by the National Institute on Drug Abuse found that the number of meth users in 2013 was a fraction of what it had been during its peak years in the 1990s and opening decade of the twenty-first century. Those taking it had either quit or (more often) found other substances to get high; plus, with this greater awareness, there were fewer new users.[82] Also as with crack, a surge in homicides and other violent crimes took place during the epidemic of meth use. So, too, with the more recent popularity of synthetic marijuana, crime rates have risen in many jurisdictions. But the same data, when examined beyond headlines, have shown there to be more factors involved in these spikes in crime. While drugs are clearly a factor, other factors more consistently correlated with crime suggest that drugs function more as a catalyst than a cause.[83]

Among some, however, headlines are enough—with the result that, for them, there is no learning curve. Just as, in the nineteenth and early twentieth centuries, there was more than met the eye in reports of the hideous effects of cocaine on blacks, marijuana on Mexicans, and opium on Chinese, so too is there reason for skepticism in regard to the reports, such as this one in the *New York Post* on August 4, 2015: "Synthetic Marijuana Gives People Abnormal Strength, Makes Them Dangerous: NYPD." Consequently, these Americans continue to whack-on, so to speak, for no other reason than that it makes them feel good. Along with the previously mentioned federal legislation, numerous laws aimed at stomping out these synthetic drugs have been enacted at the state and local levels. As in the past, such legislation is likely to have little effect. In addition to the preponderance of empirical evidence indicating that laws do little to deter drug use, there is also another key indicator, if humor truly is a canary-in-the-coal-mine on views of vice, that being a headline from the satirical newspaper the *Onion*: "Drugs Win Drug War."

Most likely, as we saw with most users of crack and meth, most users of synthetic marijuana will turn to more reliable substances for getting high or, if conditions are right, turn away altogether from drug use. Those conditions will be examined in the next chapter by stepping back to further examine the entire slice of vice through American history. For now, however, many of these drugs present an issue of more immediate concern: addiction.

Be it crack, or meth, or heroin, or any other physically addictive substance, once a user becomes addicted, by definition the element of consent is essentially eliminated. Is not, then, this absence of consent justification for laws prohibiting such drugs, in the same way that we justify other laws involving a perpetrator and a victim?

The answer is yes.

And the answer is no, since all the evidence indicates that such laws are ineffective. One reason they are ineffective is that, in the case of drug addiction, one of the perpetrators *is* the victim. Plus there's another bummer regarding power and this vice. Substance abuse is itself often an effort for empowerment by self-medicating personal problems, such as anger or depression or other behavioral difficulties. One effect of prohibitory legislation is to add both a layer of legal complication and a layer of stigmatization to what are already profound and complex problems.

Not a happy prognosis. To paraphrase from the film *Chinatown*: Forget it, Jake; it's Whac-a-Mole. Still, in the final analysis there is reason for hope. But it requires that we think twice about vice.

Think Twice about Vice

In 1987 an American artist named Andres Serrano peed in a jar, then dropped a crucifix into the jar, then took a photograph of it. He went on to win for his photo a $15,000 award, a portion of which came from the National Endowment for the Arts. Not surprisingly, many Americans were, one could say, "pissed off," but out of respect, let's just say "offended." "No one I know has ever said . . . Serrano should not be free to produce the trash they call art," Congressman Dick Armey declared, "but the working men and women of America should not be forced to pay for it."[1] Even though unpunishable under the First Amendment, Serrano's *Piss Christ*, as he called it, was not only obscene but, to a Christian, blasphemous.

Or was it?

"I thought he was saying, in a rather simplistic, magazine-y type of way, that this is what we are doing to Christ," the widely respected art historian—and Catholic nun—Sister Wendy Beckett said of the work. "We are not treating Him with reverence. His great sacrifice is not used. We live very vulgar lives. We put Christ in a bottle of urine—in practice."[2] Sister Wendy's insight went far beyond this particular taxpayer debate over this particular photo. Her response to it teaches us to think twice about vice.

But thinking twice works both ways. Might pornography contribute to nonconsensual sexual acts? Might violence in film, television, and video games contribute to violence in society? Might marijuana lead some of its users to addictive drugs? Is there nothing we can achieve by enacting laws to prohibit these and other vices?

Picture this in your TV room. Two video gamers at the controls of semi-automatic firearms, shotguns, explosives, and knives enter a high school and proceed to mow down students, teachers, and staff, staving off rapid-response law enforcement until they go down in a dual suicidal finale. Game over. Except, as many readers may have recognized, it wasn't a game. It occurred on April 20, 1999, when eighteen-year-old Eric Harris and seventeen-year-old Dylan Klebold entered Columbine High School in Colorado and, before indeed killing themselves, left behind twelve dead students, a dead teacher, and twenty-four others badly injured.

Needless to say, pretty much everyone in this shocked nation had something to say. Among them were many, such as Jeff Bartlow, a school counselor in Walla Walla, Washington, who put considerable blame on violent video games. An article in that town's *Union-Bulletin* stated that Bartlow believed "troubled students are finding it increasingly more difficult to express their anger and hatred in nonviolent ways, because every night they see violence on television or spend time 'killing' people in the video games." Not everyone agreed, even in the immediate shock of Columbine. Most succinctly voicing an opposing view was journalist Tom Maurstad, whose columns on entertainment and culture appeared in newspapers nationwide. "If violent entertainment were the cause of such tragic effects," he wrote, "why is it happening here in America rather than, say, Japan, a country with an even bloodier pop culture?"[3]

Whatever the answer, violent video games do differ from previous forms of violence in entertainment because the viewer participates in the violence. Six years before the killings at Columbine, psychology professor Ed Donnerstein said of this participatory element, "Theoretically, that tells me the effects [of violence on the player] could be heightened."[4]

While video games present us with this new—and possibly very significant—element of participation, reactions to them provide us with connections to previous views of vice and, more importantly, insight into how and why many of those views have changed while others have not. For starters, one word that was used by school counselor Jeff Bartlow revealed the relativistic shift in the way many Americans have come to view vice since World War II. In his instance, that word was "troubled." It conveyed a view that violent video games are not a gateway to actual violence for all youth, only "troubled" youth. The article, written in the immediate aftermath of the massacre at Columbine High School, was not a forum for exploring what constitutes and causes "troubled" youth, but, the implication that variable factors result in "troubled" youth makes Bartlow's view of video games as a vice relativistic.

But are relativistic views always more accurate? Not according to data compiled by one of the foremost researchers into violent video games, psychologist Craig Anderson, who holds a PhD from Stanford University and has studied the issue since 1986, thirteen years before Columbine. His findings, even on those now seemingly quaint early video games, led him to warn that those in his test groups who played the higher-aggression game came away "significantly more anxious than either those who played the mild-aggression game or those who played no game." His research continued through ensuing years as video graphics and sounds grew more realistic. In 2005 he and co-researcher Nicholas Carnagey concluded, "Rewarding violent game actions increased hostile emotions, aggressive thinking, and aggressive behavior." Using a different experimental configuration, Anderson arrived at the same conclusion in 2007.[5]

Similarly, though for even longer, others have been studying the effects of violence in film and television. A team of six psychologists stated in a 2001 assessment of that research: "The consensus among most social scientists who have reviewed this literature is that there is a causal relation between viewing violence and aggressive behavior."

The same view was also voiced by a group of New York judges who reported that they saw a connection between the number of criminal cases brought before them and the kinds of movies increasingly being shown. That was in 1925. Violence and immorality in films were getting more prevalent and, according to those judges, accounted for a 3 percent increase in convictions of people under twenty-one years of age between 1923 and 1924.[6] Hard to imagine today that silent films such as *Within the Law* with Norma Talmadge, *Souls for Sale* with Richard Dix, or Anna May Wong in *The Thief of Bagdad* could lure youth into a life of crime.

Might the judges have been wrong? Maybe they were, but, bear in mind, they weren't the first to warn of the effects of violence in entertainment. In 1888 an educator wrote an article in a professional journal that told of how, when she was young, the violence she so frequently found when reading fiction "filled me with such horror." The genre of fiction she was discussing was fairy tales. She went on to say that when she read fairy tales to her little sister, "I altered every one, instinctively feeling that what was so dreadful to me must be kept from her." Call her a nineteenth-century biddy if you want, but in 1908 an organized campaign in New Jersey sought to ban violent fairy tales from schools, and as late as 1935 syndicated columnist Brooke Peters Church wrote of parents he knew who "did not believe in fairy tales . . . [because] their cruelty either encouraged callousness or gave bad dreams."[7] This column, however, went on to offer an opposing view, thereby urging its readers to reconsider the view of these parents that fairy tale violence is vice.

Which brings us back to violent video games. In 2011 the Supreme Court struck down a California law that banned the sale of violent video games to anyone under the age of eighteen. In writing the majority opinion for the 7–2 decision, Justice Antonin Scalia made this connection when he stated, "Grimm's Fairy Tales, for example, are grim indeed. As her just deserts for trying to poison Snow White, the wicked queen is made to dance in red hot slippers 'till she fell dead on the floor.' . . . Cinderella's evil stepsisters have their eyes plucked out by doves. . . . And Hansel and Gretel (children!) kill their captor by baking her in an oven."[8]

Justice Scalia was not alone in looking at fairy tales when questioning the effects of violent video games. In an opinion piece headlined "Fact Is, There's Nothing Wrong with Video Games," the managing editor of Texas's *Paris News* asked, "Have we thought maybe children who are predisposed to violence are drawn to video games, instead of video games being the cause of the violent behavior? Who is to say that taking aggression out in a video games doesn't keep that violence from taking a physical form?"[9]

Psychiatrist Bruno Bettelheim did say so. In 1976 he published *The Uses of Enchantment: The Meaning and Importance of Fairy Tales*. Still in print, it stands as a marker of the vast influence not only of scientists but also of their far less empirically based colleagues, psychoanalysts. Bettelheim's book viewed violence in fairy tales as a way to address children's profound anxieties without belittling them. Through these fantasies, he argued, the child is provided with imaginative ways to gain mastery over them.

Bettelheim was, by then, a veteran in the realm of violence in entertainment. As a young clinician in the 1950s, he reviewed a book that, in that era, stood as a highly influential view of the subject by a prominent psychiatrist: Frederic Wertham's *Seduction of the Innocent*. Wertham was writing about comic books. Not *Superman* and *Archie* and *Little Lulu*—Wertham was concerned about comic books along the lines of *Tales of the Crypt*, *Weird Terror*, and *Crime Suspense Stories*, whose gory graphics, he declared, result "in a blunting of the finer feelings of consciences, or mercy, of sympathy for other people's suffering, and of respect for women as women and not merely as sex objects to be bandied around as luxury prizes or fought over."[10] One thing we can conclude is that Wertham was not a pig or prig. One thing Wertham concluded was that violent comic books should be banned or restricted by law.

Wertham and other members of his profession were not the only group seeking to expand their influence (indeed, by urging legislation, seeking to impose their power) through this view of vice. The horror-enhancing graphics of these comic books enhanced the call to arms, heard anywhere in America where there was a drugstore with a comic book rack. Among the many groups joining in this crusade were rural Americans, whose influence had been, for so long, so steadily in decline. In a 1948 syndicated column called "Farmer's Diary," Calvin Byers called upon the teenagers in his readers' families to combat "the comic book menace" when he wrote, "Why not a high school age group to clean up the town?" That same year in

Spencer, West Virginia, the PTA organized a public burning of some two thousand comic books.[11]

Parents—be they rural, urban, or suburban—were, and remain, a key group in this issue of violent entertainment as vice. But let's not lose perspective—seeking to influence the behavior of their children is what parents do. It's what the word *parenting* means. And, as all parents know, their influence becomes more difficult to assert when their children become teenagers.

It is not quite the same, however, when parents form an organized group. In those instances, if the group expresses a view of vice, it does so in an effort to impose the group's power. And despite whatever name these parents give to their group—such as Parent Teacher Association (PTA) or Mothers Against Drunk Driving (MADD)—it isn't parental power per se they're seeking to impose; it's that of the powers-that-be within the group. Take, for example, the PTA leaders in the industrial town of Binghamton, New York. In 1948 they too commenced a crusade against violent comic books. Among those addressing some five hundred people at a PTA-sponsored rally was Father Charles C. Smith, director of a diocese division of what the Catholic Church called the National Legion for Wholesome Literature. His address led to 560 students overseeing a public burning of violent comic books. Other efforts against violent comic books were led by representatives of the Episcopal Church and the Federation of Women's Clubs.[12]

Just as notable in terms of views of vice and power are certain groups that didn't join this crusade against violent comic books. Where was the Chamber of Commerce? Where was the American Medical Association, the American Bar Association, or the group representing those who best knew the horrors of violence, the Veterans of Foreign Wars? In power is where they were. Sufficiently in power that they didn't need a ban on violent comic books to maintain their power.

Still, there's one group yet to be mentioned, that being those in what is, by definition, a power-imposing group: politicians. Where were they?

They were like moths on a lightbulb. Senator Estes Kefauver convened hearings to investigate violence in comic books, resulting in nationwide headlines—but no federal legislation. New York, however, passed a law prohibiting the publication or sale of any printed matter devoted to "stories of deeds of bloodshed, lust, or crime." But the Supreme Court quickly ruled it a violation of the First Amendment. If the horror-filled comic books had come before the court in the early years of this nation, quite likely the justices would have issued a different verdict. But as we have seen, the powers-that-were now had to share the bench with a lot of others.

Nevertheless, the Founding Forces were still suited up. Shaking off this blow as if the fight itself were a comic book bout, the Council of State Governments returned to the fray with new legislative language, which many states adopted, prohibiting the sale of violent comic books to anyone under eighteen years of age. With two exceptions. Biblical and historical comic books were exempt.[13] Views of vice serving sources of power doesn't get any clearer than that.

Though it does get more complicated. These laws, too, were overturned in court, despite the fact that the courts had upheld many other antivice laws that limit their restrictions to youth. What accounted for the sometimes thumbs up, sometimes thumbs down? The rising power of scientists. The 1959 ruling that marked the undoing of these anti–violent comic book laws stated, "No showing has been made of a clear and present danger of a substantive evil justifying suppression of the constitutional guarantee."[14] Which is to say, data showing that violent comic books led to violent behavior did not exist. Not at the time, anyway.

As for more recent studies indicating that violence in film, television, and video games do lead to violent or callous behavior, here too there are reasons to squint before deciding to swallow. Bruno Bettelheim provided one in his 1955 review of Frederic Wertham's book. Bettelheim disagreed that violent comic books should be banned or restricted, arguing that the desire to read them "springs from inner motives, which are the real problem." Viewing them as a prohibit-able vice, he wrote, "attacks the symptom rather than the underlying disease."[15]

Those inclined to do backflips of joy for Bettelheim should bear in mind that he too was seeking, in his way, to assert the power of psychiatry by using a view, in this case, of not-punishable vice.

The opposing views of Bettelheim and Wertham are particularly pertinent when one considers the way in which these acts of random slaughter have come to bear an uncanny resemblance to video games involving mass slaughter. Adding to this connection of such mass killings in video games and actual mass murders is the fact that such video games first surfaced not long before Columbine, when technological advances enabled major enhancements in graphics and the interactive aspects of the games.[16] Though the work of both Wertham and Bettelheim predated video games, it was Wertham's conclusions that were backed by data. In his career as a psychiatrist, some of his work was with New York's prisons, and in that capacity he conducted studies of violent offenders, both adult and juvenile.

On the other hand, in 2012 a researcher studying the effects of violence in entertainment reviewed Wertham's raw figures and discovered that the numbers were cooked. Which is not to say Wertham made them up; just that he had arranged them for statistical analysis in a very particular way.[17] It was not the first time nor the last that scientific data were organized in a way that led to a desired destination. Scientists, like all the rest of us, are susceptible to the influences in their lives. When those moral lenses become part of their mental microscopes, however, defective assessments can result. Which is, in effect, *mythinformation.*

Mythinformation

Personally, I have a high regard for scientists—as, obviously, do many (indeed most) other people. To the extent that we hold them in high regard, however, we are vulnerable to instances in which their research generates, intentionally or not, mythinformation. Is there a way for those of us without their scientific expertise to assess their views of vice? Sort of. Which is to say, it isn't easy, but maybe.

Let's take a glimpse at the findings of twentieth-century physicians and other scientists in regard to smoking and drugs, keeping an eye out for *consistency*:

Previously cited from the *Medical Standard*, 1914: "Dr. [Edward H.] Williams declares that the negro who has become a cocaine-dope taker is a constant menace to his community.... Peaceable negroes become quarrelsome.... An ordinary bullet will not stop an individual who is crazed with this drug."

From the *Medical Summary*, 1919: "[Through] the consumption of tobacco, especially in the form of cigarettes ... many have since become 'fiends' in their insistent demand for this particular brand of poison ... the results of which are evidenced in ... nicotine addiction."

From the *American Journal of Nursing*, 1936: "In the narcotic world, [marijuana] is well known as the 'murderous' narcotic—a well-deserved caption, for it is known that in the Orient bands of men under its influence have run amuck and perpetrated the most heinous crimes."

From the *New York Times*, 1940: "An assertion that the increase in the smoking of cigarettes was a cause of the rise in recent years of cancer of the lung ... was made by Dr. Alton Oschner."

From a report by physicians at the Medical College of Virginia (a tobacco-growing state), 1945: "There is seemingly no correlation between the number of cigarettes smoked daily and the degree to which nicotine becomes a factor."

From the *Journal of the American Statistical Association*, 1955: "The increase in lung cancer mortality has been generally parallel to an increase in cigarette consumption.... [R]esults of two population studies indicate higher mortality from lung cancer among smokers than among non-smokers and a still higher mortality among heavy smokers."

From the *Washington Post*, 1967: "Dr. Joel Fort ... a former drug consultant for the World Health Organization made these

points: Marijuana is not a narcotic; it is not addictive; it does
not cause mental illness."

From a report by the cigarette industry's Tobacco Institute,
1971: "Scientists have been trying for nearly thirty years to
induce human-type lung cancer in animals by having them
inhale cigarette smoke. . . . They have consistently failed. No
research demonstrates that any ingredient as found in cigarette smoke causes cancer."

From the *American Journal of Nursing*, 1977: "A well-controlled
study, funded by the National Institute of Mental Health,
found no brain damage in thirty Jamaicans who smoked
ganja, much stronger than U.S. marijuana, for an average of
17.5 years."

From a report by the surgeon general of the United States, 1988:
"Cigarettes and other forms of tobacco are addicting. Nicotine is the drug in tobacco that causes addiction. . . . Tens of
thousands of studies have documented that smoking causes
lung cancer."[18]

When viewed together in one big scientific stew, the scum that rises
to the surface is composed of unscientific influences. Valid research
stays in the broth.

Which brings us back, once again, to violent video games. How is
it that, despite extensive research by Craig Anderson, many Americans remain unconvinced that violent video games can lead to actual
violence? Short answer: because most Americans don't read *Cognitive
Technology* or the *Personality and Social Psychology Bulletin*. Longer, and
more important, answer: because many Americans who have contem-
plated prohibitions on violent video games have thought twice about
vice—including, perhaps, those who do know of Anderson's studies.
In them, the measure he used to gauge the effects of video game
violence was the General Aggression Model, an interactive series of
questions. One way to understand how this measure works is to look
into the research that created it to see how well it predicted actual
violence on a random sample of people. Its creator, lo and behold,

was Craig Anderson. And, no and behold, he never published data correlating results on his test with actual violence.[19]

Troublingly, it is indeed as likely today as in the past that unscientific influences (if, in fact, such turns out to be the case with Professor Anderson's research) periodically produce mythinformation. More troublingly, this risk does not just apply to scientists with whom one disagrees. Starting around 1967, for example to readers who see little if any harm in smoking pot, scientific evidence increasingly shifted from concluding that marijuana was an addictive drug that can cause its users to run amok to finding it was not addictive, not brain damaging, and not amok inducing. Why was that era the tipping point in scientific views? Maybe because this more recent research was, in fact, valid. Still, let's think twice. Or, in this case, thrice. (1) Was there some breakthrough in scientific procedures enabling more accurate analysis? (2) Was there a change in the group using pot? (3) Was there a change among those in power?

Yes, yes, and yes.

Yes, the development of CAT scans and other medical devices yielded more detailed and accurate assessments of changes to the brain.

Yes, a new group was smoking pot in the era around 1967. Much as (though in the opposite way) abstaining from alcohol became a patriotic act among Native Americans during Pontiac's Rebellion, smoking pot became a "countercultural patriotic" act among many of those youth opposed to the Vietnam War. This group was far from peripheral, being largely comprised of the "baby boom," a population spike that ensued when the nation's soldiers returned from World War II. In and around 1967 baby boomers were both reaching voting age and beginning to become financially self-sufficient—a one-two power punch. In 1969 cigarette executives at Philip Morris began contemplating how they might enter the marijuana market if and when these no-longer-babies acquired enough boom to make marijuana legal.[20] Their tobacco industry competitors were soon doing likewise.

And yes, there was a shift in those who ruled. To continue the Native American comparison, as the "elder chiefs" of the United

States elded away, the pipe of power fell into the hands of now adult baby boomers as they started to become the scientists, lawmakers, and members of other influential groups. Not long after, Americans began to sniff a new view of an old vice wafting over the land. In 2012 the states of Colorado and Washington legalized marijuana. Alaskans did likewise in 2014, followed by Oregon and the District of Columbia in 2015. Aptly summed up by comic news commentator Stephen Colbert, "The market has spoken, and the market is tokin'."

Still, there have been some curmudgeons in the sciences who don't care if they're the turd in the punch bowl. In 2003 a team of six medical researchers reported that marijuana affects the body's ability to synthesize nitric oxide and may thereby diminish the ability of white blood cells to kill tumor cells. In 2006 research by a team of four epidemiologists indicated that marijuana use by women one to three months before conception or during pregnancy might be associated with childhood cancers in that offspring.[21]

Should we, then, return to its original ban? On the other hand, how well did that law work the first time? Maybe the best thing for now is just to sit back, have a drink and a cigarette, and think about it. Or, more usefully, think about why the sentence before this one was weird but once upon a time would not have been.

V.V. for Victories over Vice

Chances are you don't smoke. Some years ago, chances would have been much more likely that you did. In 1965 42 percent of American adults smoked cigarettes, after which the rate began to decline to the extent that by 2011 only 17 percent of American adults smoked cigarettes.[22] Such impressive vice-fighting results are well worth a closer look.

In the years following World War II, the percentage of Americans who smoked cigarettes was essentially the same as in 1965. The turning point followed a report in 1964 from a committee created by Surgeon General Luther Terry that concluded that smoking is a cause of cancer and other respiratory diseases.[23] The report made headlines—and not just in the likes of the *Washington Post* or the

New York Times but all across America, appearing on the front pages of newspapers such as Big Spring, Texas's *Daily Herald*, Petersburg, Virginia's *Progress-Index*, Florence, South Carolina's *Morning News*, and virtually every other newspaper in the nation.

Why was this news? Back in the days of James I they were aware that tobacco was bad for the lungs, and by the mid-nineteenth century nicotine was known to be both a key substance in tobacco and toxic.[24] This report was, however, from high-ranking health officials in the federal government, boldly and unequivocally declaring for the first time what other high-ranking officials had been saying for three hundred years.

Why, for so long, had the top health officials in the federal government tap danced around what they knew to be true? Same reason as in the days of James I. Though he hated tobacco and, as we saw, spoke out against its dangers to health, he later vindicated the vice because he needed the revenue it garnered in taxes. Money, after all, is power, and power forms views of vice. Likewise with the federal government. In the early 1960s, for example, it raked in some two billion bucks a year in taxes on tobacco. Not to mention what government officials garnered from tobacco industry lobbyists. In addition, during these years some forty thousand Americans were employed in the tobacco industry.[25]

But messing up the satisfaction of power groups puffing financial smoke rings was that increasingly powerful group, scientists. The only deviation in their views came from those associated with the tobacco industry.[26] By the time of the 1964 surgeon general's report, however, physicians and scientists had acquired sufficient power to tip the scales.

But only slightly tip them. "Even if there is a drop in sales, I don't think it will be but for a few weeks," the manager of a cigarette vending machine company stated.[27] As he and his colleagues in the tobacco industry knew, most addicted smokers could be counted on to remain steady customers, even if they attempted to quit.

Nevertheless, as the industry soon learned, it would have to do more to recruit new users. By 1987 the percentage of Americans who smoked had declined to under 30 percent. Thus in that year, R. J. Reynolds tobacco company commenced an ad campaign featuring a cartoon character, Joe Camel. For the next ten years, Americans in general—and younger ones in specific—gazed upon the always super-cool dude Joe, with a cigarette dangling from his lips as he shot a round of pool, leaned against his sports car, made the scene at Vegas, tuxed up for a night on the town, leathered down on his Harley, and you get the picture. Or rather, lots of pictures, since, as one advertising expert noted in regard to the success of this campaign, "Adolescents are continuously seeking to define themselves as individuals and trying on various images." Between 1987 and 1997 (the year of Joe Camel's advertising demise), smoking among American high school students rose from just under 28 percent to 36 percent, despite the fact that state laws prohibiting the sale of cigarettes to teens had been on the books since the nineteenth century.[28]

Joe Camel did not die a natural death. He got run over, as we'll soon see, when the crusade against cigarettes changed its route. After the surgeon general was finally allowed to blow the government's bugle, only a small contingent of crusaders pursued the old route of prohibition. In 1970 this contingent succeeded in getting Congress to enact a law prohibiting cigarette advertising in television and radio. Its effectiveness turned out to be dubious, at best, given that the percentage of Americans who smoked increased for a few years after the ban was implemented. Moreover, at the time the law was passed, the tobacco companies were already significantly reducing the number of cigarette commercials on television and radio—and not because the industry saw this law in the offing.[29] Rather, they retreated from that field to cope with attacks from other routes.[30]

One such route directly affected advertising. It successfully sought laws and government agency regulations that required health warnings in cigarette ads and on packages of cigarettes, which were also required to list their ingredients. This route recognized the power of consent in vice and availed itself of that power by requiring that it be more informed consent.

Another route with which cigarette manufacturers now had to contend was the relatively recent "zoning" approach to fighting vice. Increasingly, government buildings, restaurants, airplanes, and other public accommodations were being designated No Smoking areas. But in this instance these policies and government regulations were not solely directed at fighting vice. They arose in response to research revealing the dangers of tobacco smoke inhaled by others in its vicinity. For those people, their inhaling smoke was not a consensual act.

Yet another route that detoured around traditional prohibition was lawsuits. Not an entirely new route; we saw it tried back in the nineteenth century to combat the use of laudanum. Back then, even though those lawsuits sometimes succeeded, their impact was limited. With cigarettes in the twentieth century, such lawsuits didn't even succeed—at first—since the plaintiffs could not prove their lung cancer or emphysema was caused by having smoked cigarettes. In 1966, however, an attorney named John F. Banzhaf III tried a different path to the courthouse. Banzhaf asked a New York City television station to donate time for public service ads on the dangers of smoking. When the station told him (as he expected) to get lost, he did anything but. Rather, he followed the letter of the law to the Federal Communications Commission (FCC), where he argued that cigarettes were sufficiently controversial as to come under the Fairness Doctrine, thereby requiring television stations to donate equal time for the opposing view. The FCC agreed about the need for the opposing view, but *equal time*—do you know how much television time (spelled $$$$) was devoted to cigarette ads? Here's a hint for the mid-1960s: pick a number between $2.8 million and $2.9 million a year. Thanking Banzhaf for his interest, blah-blah-blah, sincerely yours, the FCC hoped he'd get the message. He did. And delivered it to a federal court. And won.[31] After which the brawl went on to the U.S. Court of Appeals, where Banzhaf won again. He and the FCC, joined by the television and tobacco industries, then punched and clawed their way to the Supreme Court, where, in 1969, Banzhaf won again. With the Fairness Doctrine now applied to cigarette ads on television and radio, tobacco companies decided to shift their ad dollars to print media, rather than have public service announcements providing viewers—particularly younger ones—with information the companies did not want them to know. And in so doing, they gave birth to Joe Camel.

Soon, however, the path established by Banzhaf became a highway. With increasingly precise scientific data on the health effects of cigarettes, state governments began going to court, seeking to recover Medicaid costs attributable to smoking. Individuals joined in class-action suits. By the late 1990s, the tobacco industry had pulled to the side of this highway and raised its hands not in surrender but in hopes of negotiating a deal. During that "highway" negotiation, Joe Camel got flattened. The four largest tobacco companies signed the Tobacco Master Settlement Agreement, under which they committed their industry to vast financial compensations along with specified contributions to groups that produced antismoking programs, and they vowed to cease practices aimed at inducing young people to smoke.

Victory over a vice. Or about as close to victory as one can hope to come.

But not the only such victory. Indeed, there have been others, equally significant, and adding up to the point that moral reformers, of whatever stripe, should take heart.

For example, who hears any longer of Chinese Americans smoking opium? Doubtless some Americans of Chinese descent have fallen prey to drug addictions, but as Chinese Americans have gained greater access to the levers of power via increased educational and economic opportunities, many of the reasons for the drug dependency of their ancestors (even accounting for its exaggeration as a moral myth) dissipated and ultimately disappeared.

By the same token, how often do we now hear about laudanum addiction among housewives? Or, for that matter, any similar form of drug addiction among middle-class women? Not too long ago, however, we did—as, for example, in the 1966 song by the Rolling Stones, "Mother's Little Helper," the helper being a "little yellow pill" (presumably tranquilizers widely prescribed at the time, such as Miltown and Librium) to which she went "running to the shelter." While antidepressants remain widely prescribed, their use is no longer associated with housewives in particular. Here too, the victory over vice was achieved not by prohibition and punishment for its violation but by what is a founding cornerstone of the United States: equality of opportunity. Or, more soberly and, alas, accurately, less *unequal* opportunity.

Less unequal opportunity has also led to a significant decrease in another vice, particularly among white women (who have benefited from more "less unequal" opportunity): prostitution. While data, past and present, must be viewed as approximate (being as difficult to obtain as an effective definition of what constitutes a prostitute), one large-scale report from 2014 estimated that about 17 percent of female prostitutes in the United States were white.[32] Even in the absence of reliable data from the past, clearly more than 17 percent of American prostitutes were white in the years prior to the political and social gains of white women in the early decades of the twentieth century. Undoubtedly, a comparable decrease has taken place among women of all races in this nation, to the extent that they too have been accorded more economic opportunities.

Nevertheless, one of the few sources of power in this nation that, over the years, has not had to cede any influence is sex. Not so surprisingly, then, most researchers have estimated that prostitution has remained about as widespread today as in the past. What has changed, amid the shifts among those who rule, are the demographics of prostitutes and, with that shift, views of prostitution. As white women in the late nineteenth and early twentieth centuries were acquiring more power (and, with it, more career opportunities), the spotlight on views of this vice widened to encompass not only the proprietors of whorehouses and those responsible for enticing or forcing women into prostitution but also the prostitutes themselves. Why, Americans increasingly began to wonder, would a woman be a prostitute? Raising the wattage on that spotlight was the diminishing wattage of religious leaders, dimming the view of prostitutes as "fallen women" more sinned against than sinning. While street prostitutes had always been viewed as subject to arrest, police raids on whorehouses now included round-ups of the prostitutes as well as the proprietors.[33]

And, indeed, there's no avoiding the fact that the number of brothels did decline in this era, an achievement for which moral reformers took credit.[34] However, the decline in the number of whorehouses was more the result of an industrial development in these years: the telephone. This handy-dandy device gave birth to the term *call girl*. And that form of prostitution has remained far more difficult for moral reformers to bop.

This newer view of prostitutes as culpable shifted again in the years ahead, again reflecting changes among those gripping society's steering wheel when hookers asked drivers who pulled over if they were looking for some fun. The first of these shifts can be seen in a 1914 *Chicago Tribune* article that began, "Scientific methods for the suppression of vice [and] the rescue of fallen women . . . were urged yesterday upon representatives of the city council." In furtherance of this scientific vein of thought, psychiatrist Walter Treadway published a study of prostitutes in 1920 that arrived at the conclusion that prostitutes were dominated by three particular traits: "exaggerated estimate of self . . . diminution of contact with the cares and pursuits of others . . . [and] a lack of tenderness"—all of which, he pointed out, are "characteristic of the neurotic and psychopathic constitution."[35]

Thanks, Doc.

If you follow my drift. Which is the drift in the influence of science in general and psychiatry in particular. While their power was growing back then and would continue to do so, a measure of the limit of that power can be obtained by the number of people today who, after reading Dr. Treadway's analysis, have an urge to say sarcastically, "Thanks, Doc."

Views of prostitution shifted again in the Great Depression, reflecting yet another way in which that economic collapse diminished the ability of industrialists to project power through views of vice. "Prostitution is a contractual relation [that] . . . is naturally connected with the entire system of economic forces," sociologist Kingsley Davis wrote in 1937. Which was just the tip of the shifting iceberg, as Davis went on to say, "We cannot, however, define prostitution simply as the use of sexual responses for an ulterior purpose ... [since] it would include marriage, for example, wherein women trade their sexual favors for an economic and social status supplied by men. It would include the employment of pretty girls in stores, cafes, charity drives, advertisements. ... The employment of sex for non-sexual ends ... characterizes not simply prostitution itself but all of our institutions in which sex is involved."[36]

What, then, is this vice we call prostitution? Davis defined it as being that economic aspect of sex that those in power, at any given time, need it to be. In this respect, a relativistic view pervaded his view, despite the fact that in 1937 the atomic bomb had yet to explode. Einstein's theory, however, had been in the wind since the beginning of the century. While Davis may have been ahead of his time in viewing marriage and other economic remunerations to women because of their sex appeal as sharing "contractual" characteristics with prostitution, he did not dismiss the value of punishable prostitution, even with his relativistic lens. "The institutional control of sex," he said, ". . . [is] indispensable to the continuance of a given social system."[37]

After World War II, views of prostitution increasingly reflected relativistic perspectives. Criminology professor Valerie Jenness aptly described this shift in the title of her article, "From Sex as Sin to Sex as Work," in which she observed that "a new image of prostitution has emerged to challenge traditional views of prostitutes as social misfits, sexual slaves, victims of pimps and drug addiction, and tools of organized crime." Jenness went on to describe an effort among prostitutes to acquire greater political power by expressing a view of not-vice through an organization called COYOTE (an acronym for Call Off Your Old Tired Ethics). In addition to conventions at which resolutions were passed calling for changes in the laws against prostitution, COYOTE also sponsored an annual Hookers' Film Festival and Hookers' Ball. By joining together to voice this view of not-vice, these women influenced many Americans who now had more relativistic views of vice. In 1972 a judge in Washington DC dismissed charges against five women arrested for prostitution on the basis of the law violating their right to privacy without a "compelling state interest" to justify this incursion into constitutional safeguards. The impact of this ruling, however, was limited to that case. However, as of this writing in 2015, the District of Columbia is considering legislation that would decriminalize prostitution.[38]

Still, one view involving prostitution has never shifted, since it is rooted in the absence of consent. Kidnapping and trafficking of females (almost exclusively today of girls from less empowered nations) will continue to be viewed as punishable for all involved other than those kidnapped and coerced. Similarly, many who view prostitution as a punishable vice do not view teenage prostitutes as sufficiently consenting to be punished under the law. Along the same lines, for some the issue of consent is the fulcrum regarding whether or not to punish prostitutes who are addicted to drugs, since addiction can be viewed as undermining consent—though many Americans, including a number of physicians and neuroscientists, do not dismiss consent in addiction.[39]

The rise of women as a political power has led not only to numerous views of vice falling into disuse but also to views of vices that in the past were not punishable but are today. Sexual harassment in the workplace, for example, used to be considered par for the course. The prevailing view was along the lines of a phrase in a 1935 book, the title of which itself reflected women expanding their place in society, *She Strives to Conquer: Business Behavior, Opportunities and Job Requirements for Women*. "She had better learn to paddle her own canoe," author Frances Maule, herself a woman's rights leader, declared in regard to male workplace behavior that was unwanted by women or that demeaned them. By the mid-1970s, Title VII of the 1964 Civil Rights Act came to be viewed in the courts as prohibiting those acts of sexual harassment that contribute to workplace discrimination. But, as with other laws and regulations that whack at vice, no matter how well intentioned, their impact is negligible. "Finding Meager Help in a Sex-Complaint System," headlined a November 27, 1992, article in the *New York Times*, detailing the ineffectiveness of efforts to combat sexual harassment in the workplace through lawsuits or filings with the Equal Employment Opportunity Commission.[40]

Along the same lines, though these power lines have a lot more jolt, are changes in views of wife abuse. It too was viewed in the past as not punishable vice (provided the husband didn't murder his wife or injure her to the degree that constituted felony assault), and, as previously discussed, more than a few viewed it as imposing virtue. But when women in the mid-nineteenth century commenced to organize their quest for more power, the handwriting was on the wall regarding this view of vice. In its June 20, 1868, issue, *Harper's Bazaar* published an article, neither pro nor con, but nevertheless entitled "Abuse of Women." In 1885 the *Maine Farmer* published a letter from a woman who declared, "The man that will abuse the wife . . . is the most mean and contemptible being on earth." Notably, however, even then this woman had little hope that attitudes would change. "The Lord knoweth all things, and I feel that a just retribution will be meted out in season to every man that abuses his wife," she wrote.[41]

Sadly, she held out little hope for good reason. One law book from 1889 cited six recent cases in which American courts had upheld the right of men "to use toward the wife such a degree of force as is necessary to control an unruly temper or make her behave herself." So accepted was this view that, between 1930 and 1965, no fewer than twenty-five Hollywood films included scenes of their story's ostensible good guys spanking their wives or the women they were romancing. Television shows were no different. Even Lucille Ball, the enormously popular star (and producer) of the classic sit-com *I Love Lucy*, got spanked in one episode by her TV (and real-life) husband, Desi Arnaz.[42]

By the 1970s, however, women were acquiring enough power to begin joining together in voicing the view that hitting one's wife was, at a minimum, an unacceptable vice. "Feminists Getting Mad" was the subhead to one 1975 newspaper report on the issue in which the headline above it ended with revealing punctuation in regard to this shift in power: "Wife Beating: Major Social Ill?"[43] Still, the trend in reporting was toward headlines such as "Abused Wives: The Hidden Ordeal," an April 8, 1976, article in Uniontown, Pennsylvania's *Morning Herald*, which told of new legislation in that state designed to provide more immediate safety for battered wives through state-funded shelters. Other states, too, were now following suit.

Most notable is that these new laws did not seek to combat wife abuse by increased prohibitions or penalties but by increased empowerment of women. They provided abused women with more avenues to pursue. Protection in shelters was one such new avenue. Often added to those shelters were staff members trained to point out available avenues for untangling personal issues in which consent and refusal are often tied in psychological knots. Women were further empowered by laws that enabled them to seek recourse other than charging their husband (or unmarried mate) with felony assault. Too often that legal sledge hammer risked putting the family's main source of income in prison.[44]

There have also been regional victories in recent years in combating teen pregnancy. In this realm, moral reformers have fought other moral reformers regarding the availability of birth control devices to teens. While birth control devices can reduce the number of teen pregnancies, they are also considered by some to be a gateway to promiscuity. Pointing to an avenue that gets beyond this disagreement, author Joan Arehart-Treichel suggested, "Probably the best solution to the teen pregnancy epidemic is the strengthening of American family life."[45] Setting aside the moral myth that teen pregnancy has reached "epidemic" proportions, she was right in pointing to the value of strong families in combating this vice.

But, unfortunately, not sufficiently right. Even strong families are all too often unable to win battles against irresponsible sex or, for that matter, other vices among their youth. Native Americans, for example, whose tribal families succeeded so well in preventing self-destructive vices up to the point when they were no longer the dominant culture, now struggle to combat alcohol and drug addiction. Likewise, many modern-day families are faced with the struggle to impart moral views that are at odds with more dominant views in the community. Even teens who wish to adhere to their parents' moral views must struggle when those views are at odds with the powers-that-be within *their* worlds. Or, for short, peer pressure.

While most teen pregnancy prevention programs have recognized these hurdles, some have *incorporated* them—and in so doing, their efforts have achieved greater success. Regarding the relationship between views of vice and power, a key phrase surfaced in the report of one such program when it noted that all its components were designed to enhance its participants' "chances for valued participation" in society.[46] This seemingly simple phrase not only is connected to empowerment but very much resonates with the underlying reason for the diminishment of prostitution among white women in the United States, the diminishment of laudanum addiction and other drug dependency among middle-class housewives, and the diminishment of opium smoking among Chinese Americans.

Those components, in the words of a similar program with similarly successful outcomes, consisted of "acquiring support from community representatives, i.e., parents, religious leaders, teachers and school administrators, and other interested community members [whose] representatives were involved in program planning from the beginning of the project."[47] Who those representatives represented were the local powers-that-be. Which is also to say, those best positioned to provide "chances for valued participation" in the community.

Easier said than done, however, and not done overnight—as those previous successes with Chinese and housewives and hookers from middle-class families also did not occur overnight. As pointedly noted by Barbara Goldberg, a principal evaluator of many philanthropic and federally funded projects in teen pregnancy, "Whenever we'd interview teachers for the evaluation, they'd say how they hated the two-year wonders—the programs that would come into the schools for two or three years and then vanish."[48]

In recent years, many who have engaged in combating teen pregnancy have honed in on those components that have repeatedly proven their importance to the success of such programs. "Successful

Community Engagement: Laying the Foundation for Effective Teen Pregnancy Prevention" is the title of one of several such studies that urged not only recognition of each community's "core values" but also the inclusion of those views—which is to say, finding common ground with the powers-that-be.[49]

But There's a Hitch: Vice as Empowerment

Despite all this high-fiving, it is still a tall order to get anyone to change their behavior. In addition to which, there is a hitch in vice that can trip up even the savviest of moral reformers from across the spectrum. That sad fact is that vice itself is often employed to assert power. Teenagers, for example, remain under the thumb of adults even though in many ways they are adults. Thus what parents and others in positions of power often view as teenage rebellion might more usefully be viewed as teens' efforts (often self-destructive) to empower themselves by doing what is opposed by those seeking to control them.

From this perspective, those teens who, in addition, have little hope for a future in which they can achieve "valued participation" (to borrow that previously cited phrase from teen pregnancy prevention) would understandably be all the more susceptible to vices that are self-empowering, despite the risks and harms that often accompany those vices. Nor is this form of self-empowerment through vice confined to teens. The same can be said of many, if not most, instances of drug addiction among African Americans and alcoholism among Native Americans—just as, in the past, the same applied to opium smoking among Chinese Americans and laudanum addiction among housewives.

To return to a question cited in the opening chapter: "What to do? What to do?" If the answers were easy, these problems would have been solved some time ago. Clearly the answers require us to think, at a minimum, twice. Even then, successfully combating vice is a tall order, all the taller in regard to those who live under conditions to which they do not consent or in which views of vice are employed by empowered people to keep other people unempowered.

Disproportionate punishments for vice have also long been meted out to Native Americans. Those with drug or alcohol addictions have their children placed in foster homes far more frequently than other groups. In addition, Native American parents have far more often been denied access to their custody hearings, some of which lasted only sixty seconds. So often have such instances occurred that both the Oglala Sioux and Rosebud Sioux filed a class-action suit.[50]

In a vivid illustration from 2013 of imposing power through the use of this view of vice, two children of a Crow Creek mother accused of drug abuse were placed in a white foster home one hundred miles away, despite the fact that the woman's mother, a college graduate with a degree in nursing, lived close by and begged for her grandchildren to be put in her care—as did other relatives who offered to care for the children—until the matter could be straightened out. Straightened out, in this instance, meant verifying whether or not her daughter had, in fact, misused drugs—which the daughter denied, and charges were never brought. Nor was she allowed to see the complaint, which, it turned out, was based on a rumor emanating from a neighbor who did not like her. Before this situation was remedied, her children had been gone well over a year, during which time she had been permitted to see them only once.[51] So frequently has there been such disproportionate (and, at times, totally unwarranted) punishment for vice, a headline regarding such cases had already appeared on October 29, 2011, and boldly put it in the context of power: "Mass Confiscation of Native American Children Hasn't Gone Away." That is how clear it was in Dublin's *Irish Times*.

And there's more that makes combating vice a tall order. Another aspect of the hitch in which vice is used, even self-destructively, for self-empowerment can be seen in individuals who will do things for no other reason than to rebel against those who tell them they can't do those things or to flummox those who claim they can predict our behavior. Indeed, all of us opt at times to be unpredictable for purposes of empowerment. In sports, being unpredictable is often a game-winning behavior. In war, and sometimes in the everyday world, unpredictability can be life-saving. It is an essential, perhaps instinctual, skill in human behavior.

Both the power of unpredictability and the power of consent are no small matters in the realm of human behavior. Moral reformers of all stripes would do well to take note. Those who seek the day when this or that vice has been eliminated can eliminate a lot of unnecessary misery in this world by thinking twice about vice.

Notes

Introduction

1. Brigham Young's tenth wife, Eliza Roxcy Snow, expressed adoration for him in *The Personal Writings of Eliza Roxcy Snow*. Young's nineteenth wife, Ann Eliza Young, viewed his polygamous sexuality as base, as she expressed in *Wife No. 19, or The True Story of a Life in Bondage, Being a Complete Exposé of Mormonism*.

2. Hedda Hopper, "Yvette Mimieux to Do 'Summer Affair'—Changes in Motion Picture Code Decried by Rock Hudson," syndicated column in the *Los Angeles Times*, February 23, 1962, C16. The change was this revision, as stated by Eric Johnston, then president of the Motion Picture Producers and Distributors of America: "It is permissible under the Code for the Production Code Administration to consider approving reference in motion pictures to the subject of sex aberrations, provided any references are treated with care, discretion, and restraint." See also "Hollywood Changes Film Code Subject of Sex Deviation Okayed by Movie Group," *Corpus Christi (TX) Caller-Times*, October 4, 1961, 6B.

3. "Media Influences Are Powerful and Real," *New York Times*, May 16, 1991, A22.

4. Ray Richmond, "Monitor: Most Children's Programming Is on Cable, Survey Indicates," syndicated column in *Orange County (CA) Register*, October 9, 1991, F3.

5. Richard Christiansen, "Curb TV Violence, but Don't Censor It," *Chicago Tribune*, November 7, 1993, C2.

6. Jacobellis v. Ohio, 378 U.S. 184 (1984).

7. "Grandmother's Sex Book Held Obscene," *Washington Post*, April 24, 1929, 9.

8. Kendrick, *Observations Civil and Canonical*, unnumbered "Advertisement" page.

9. "Posies from Wedding Rings," *Littell's Living Age*, February 23, 1856, 484. Punishment of wives in the nineteenth century is more fully explored in Noble, *The Masochistic Pleasures of Sentimental Literature*.

10. "Santorum Knows Best," *Beaver County (PA) Times*, April 24, 2003, http://www.timesonline.com/santorum-knows-best/article_cb9de194-e883-5c6c-ad50-5b3013fe4eca.html.

11. "Violence and Video Games," *Video Game Addiction*, http://www.video
-game-addiction.org/violence.html (accessed February 8, 2014).

1. Inheritance

1. 1606 Charter of Virginia, in MacDonald, *Documentary Source Book*, 2.
2. Raleigh had been a favorite of James I's predecessor, Queen Elizabeth, who
had not much cared for James's mother, Mary, Queen of Scots. Back then,
one whom a monarch disliked or distrusted ran the risk of ending up in
prison—which, albeit in grand style, is where Elizabeth hosted her cousin
queen, Mary, for nearly nineteen years before ordering her beheading. After
Elizabeth died childless, Raleigh did his best to smile as Mary's son, James,
ascended to England's throne. But James I never fully trusted Raleigh's loy-
alty. James had him executed in 1618.
3. Philaretes [pseud.], *Work for Chimney-sweepers: or A Warning for Tobacconists*
(1602), cited in Arbor, "On the Introduction and Early Use of Tobacco," 94.
4. Charlton, "Tobacco or Health 1602," 101–11.
5. James I, *A Counter-Blaste to Tobacco*, 30, 26, 12, 9; Best, "Economic Interests," 173.
6. Best, "Economic Interests," 171–82; Faroqhi, *Subjects of the Sultan*, 217.
7. *The Book of the General Lauues and Libertyes*, 38, 75; *The General Laws and
Liberties of New Plimoth Colony*, 10.
8. Webb, *Office and Authority of a Justice of the Peace*, 349.
9. Example of itinerants as seducers of women in "To the Venerable Father
Janus," *New England Courant* (Boston), January 22, 1726, 1. Example of itinerants as con artists in "Letter from Capt. Summers to Capt. Smith," *Boston
Evening Post*, February 11, 1765, 2.
10. Glanvil, *Saddicismus Triumphatus*, 13–14.
11. Ford, "Mather-Calef Paper on Witchcraft," 47:255.
12. Mather, *Magnalia Christi Americana*, 2:400. See also Bragdon, "Crime and
Punishment," 23–32.
13. Philips, "African Smoking and Pipes," 303–19; Bofman, *A New and Accurate
Description*, 306.
14. "Narrative of the Sufferings and Surpizing [*sic*] Deliverance of William and
Elizabeth Fleming," *New York Mercury*, March 8, 1756, 2.
15. Mather, *Magnalia Christi Americana*, 2:400; "To the Venerable Father
Janus," *New England Courant* (Boston), February 19–26, 1726, 1.
16. "New York," *Providence (RI) Gazette*, November 8, 1766, 3.
17. May, "Explanations of Native American Drinking," 223–32; Holmes and
Antell, "The Social Construction of American Drinking," 151–73; James and

Jameson, *Journal of Jasper Danckaerts*, 179-80, cited in Trenk, "Religious Uses of Alcohol," 73-86.

18. *Records of the Court of Assistants*; Mather, *Magnalia Christi Americana*, 2:665.

19. Greenberg, *Crime and Law Enforcement*, 38-39.

20. "God Save the King—the Following Is Inserted by Order of the Magistrates of This City," *New York Gazette*, October 23, 1769, 2.

21. One of the literally dirtiest secrets of prison life, punishing prisoners by forcing them to drink some form of oil to induce diarrhea—typically combined with confinement in a small space, and typically a punishment reserved for African American prisoners—continued in this nation until the mid-1930s, when Alabama and Florida finally ended its use. See Kinshasa, *The Man from Scottsboro*, 80; "Prisoners Never Had It So Bad after '32," *Florida Times-Union* (Jacksonville), July 12, 1998, B1.

22. Hauptman and Knapp, "Dutch-Aboriginal Interaction," 170; Dailey, "The Role of Alcohol," 46; Falk, "Forts, Rum, Slaves," 228.

23. Hunter, "The Delaware Nativist Revival," 39-49.

24. *The Book of the General Lauues and Libertyes*, 33.

25. Assembly of New York, *Laws of New York*, 355; Burns, *The History of the Poor Laws*, 17.

26. *Acts of the Assembly of the Province of Pennsylvania*, 144.

27. Assembly of Virginia, *Acts of the Assembly Passed in the Colony of Virginia*, 1:181; attributed to Allestreet, *The Whole Duty of Man*, 19, 76, 79, 80, 81, 83, 84, 94.

28. A widely reported American boxing match took place in 1760 when William Rodwell and Jonas Dawson disagreed, in the words of one news report, "about their skill in dancing a jig." Rodwell suggested they resolve the issue by boxing. The match ended when Dawson conceded Rodwell's superior skill, though whether he meant boxing or dancing a jig was unspecified. They shook hands and sat down to drinks, and minutes later Dawson keeled over and died. The degree of injury that often resulted was largely due to the fact that boxing in this era was bare-knuckled. The rules did not require padded gloves, because boxing did not yet have rules. For the victor, however, the jig was up. Rodwell turned himself in to face charges of manslaughter. See "Annapolis, in Maryland," *New Hampshire Gazette* (Portsmouth), October 3, 1760, 1.

29. Conant, *Alexander Hamilton*, 139. See also Freeman, "Dueling as Politics," 289-318.

30. Not all states had laws specifically prohibiting duels, since laws against manslaughter or assault—neither of which is affected by the element of consent—could be invoked. South Carolina is often cited as the last state to prohibit duels. While it may have been the last state that fully enforced its

prohibition, dueling was prohibited in South Carolina in 1812. See Nott and M'Cord, *Cases Determined*, 2:181–83.

31. Morton, *New English Canaan*, 153–54; Johansen, *The Encyclopedia of Native American Legal Tradition*, 55.

32. In what is today southern Ethiopia and part of South Sudan, boys in the Surma tribe played at combat by dueling with sticks. The Congolese depicted duels with spears in certain of their theatrical traditions. The closest thing to a duel as we tend to think of it were verbal duels that often emanated from disputes. The weapons were insults, and the winner was the man or woman adjudged by onlookers as the wittiest. It was this form of duel that Africans brought with them to America when enslaved. Such verbal duels came to be known as "The Dozens." See Graham-White, "Ritual and Drama in Africa," 339–49; Abbink, "Violence, Ritual, and Reproduction," 227–42; Lefever, "'Playing the Dozens,'" 73–85.

33. Cotton, *Abstract of the Lawes of New England*, 12–14.

34. Raynor quoted in Bradford, *History of Plymouth Plantation*, 2:316; Hutchinson, *History of the Colony*, 441.

35. Records indicate that at least one man and woman were executed in Massachusetts for adultery in 1644, and in non-Puritan Virginia, records show a man was executed for sodomy and another for rape. See Flaherty, "Laws and the Enforcement of Morals," 214; Scott, *Criminal Law in Colonial Virginia*, 154–60, 314–18; 1731 punishment in "Boston," *New England Weekly Journal* (Boston), March 8, 1731, 2; letter *A* punishment in "Boston," *New York Gazette*, October 16, 1752, 2. Tougher still, though still not death, was Connecticut's penalty imposed on philanderers Nathanael Richards and Sarah Leffingwell, who likewise got the cart, the rope, the sit, the whip, and the *A*—but theirs were branded on their foreheads. See "New London," *Boston Gazette*, June 28, 1743, 3.

36. Flaherty, "Laws and the Enforcement of Morals," 243.

37. Cunningham, *A New and Complete Law-Dictionary*, 2:142 (pages are unnumbered); Noble, *Records of the Court of Assistants*, 2:89, 93.

38. Assembly of Virginia, *Acts of the Assembly Passed in the Colony of Virginia*, 308–9.

39. *The Charter Granted by their Majesties*, 151–52.

40. I. Mather, *An Arrow against Profane and Promiscuous Dancing*.

41. Howe, *The Puritan Republic of Massachusetts Bay*, 98, 99; Goodman, "Blue Laws," 663–73; Felt, "Collections Relating to Fashions," 5:124.

42. Gouge, *Of Domesticall Duties*, 82. The divorce rulings may have emanated from the belief expressed by numerous seventeenth-century medical experts that both male and female orgasm were necessary in order for conception to take place. See Foster, "Deficient Husbands," 727.

43. "Boston," *Boston Gazette*, May 8, 1753, 3.

44. Mather, *Diary of Cotton Mather*, 8:229.

45. "Records of the Suffolk County Court, 1671–1680"; "Records of the Company of the Massachusetts Bay," 3:232; McManus, *Law and Liberty in Early New England*, 166, 169.

46. Bradford, *History of Plymouth Plantation*, 2:48.

47. The new name for the settlement entailed more than one pun, when one discovers that Bradford got the name wrong. Morton actually renamed it Ma-re Mount, additionally suggestive of sodomy with a horse and of honoring—or dishonoring—the mother of Jesus. See Major, "William Bradford versus Thomas Morton," 1–13; Heath, "Thomas Morton," 135–68.

48. Bradford, *History of Plymouth Plantation*, 2:49; Morton, *New English Canaan*, 279–80.

49. Morton, *New English Canaan*, 320.

50. Morton, *New English Canaan*, 311.

51. Morton, *New English Canaan*, 145, 161, 167, 137, 138. Bradford claimed that Morton's success was due to his illegally trading in guns to the Native Americans, a claim one historian disputes. See Major, "William Bradford versus Thomas Morton," 2.

52. "The American Whig," *New York Gazette*, April 4, 1768, 1.

53. Flaherty, "Laws and the Enforcement of Morals," 5:222.

54. Gillingham, "Lotteries in Philadelphia," 77–100; Ezell, "The Lottery in Colonial America," 185–200; Watson, "The Lottery in Early North Carolina," 365–87.

55. Ezell, "When Massachusetts Played the Lottery," 316–35.

56. "Some indeed plead as an excuse that persons may . . . gain as much advantage from a play as from hearing a sermon," a letter to the editor of Rhode Island's *Providence Gazette* declared on April 23, 1774.

57. Advertisement, *Boston News-Letter*, December 14, 1775, 2.

58. Play advertisement, "For the Benefit of the Orphans and Widows of Soldiers," *New York Gazette*, March 10, 1777, 3; play advertisement, "For the Benefit of the Widows and Orphans of the Army," *Pennsylvania Ledger* (Philadelphia), January 17, 1778, 3; play advertisement, "Theatre Royal," *Royal Gazette* (New York City), February 6, 1779, 2; play advertisement, "By Permission," *Royal Georgia Gazette* (Savannah), September 20, 1781, 2.

2. A "Virtue-ly" New Nation

1. Randolph, *Memoirs, Correspondence, and Private Papers of Thomas Jefferson*, 1:123, 127–28.

2. Alexander Hamilton, "Message to House of Representatives, March 6, 1792," in Hamilton, *The Works of Alexander Hamilton*, 3:316.

3. The carriage tax led to a Supreme Court decision, Hylton v. United States, 3 U.S. 171 (1796), upholding the right of the federal government to impose an excise tax. The larger significance of this decision was its establishing the right of the Supreme Court to rule on the constitutionality of legislation, thereby staking out its realm of power in the new republic. Seven years after *Hylton*, the Supreme Court issued the more widely known ruling Marbury v. Madison, 5 U.S. 137 (1803), in which it asserted its authority to *overturn* legislation it deemed unconstitutional.

4. "New York—from a Correspondent," *City Gazette and Advertiser* (Charleston SC), March 17, 1796, 3.

5. [No headline], *Boston Gazette*, February 4, 1793, 3.

6. "Review of Jefferson's Administration," *Columbian Centennial* (Boston), July 11, 1804, 1.

7. "New Orleans," *Alexandria Gazette* article reprinted in *Poulson's American Daily* (Philadelphia), October 10, 1812, 3.

8. Millward, "'The Relics of Slavery,'" 22–30; Lachance, "The Formation of a Three-Caste Society," 211–42.

9. Turner, "Mardi Gras Indians," 124–56.

10. "Idolatry and Quackery," *National Intelligencer* (Washington DC), September 13, 1820, 1.

11. [No headline], *Boston Gazette*, February 4, 1793, 3.

12. Along with the First Amendment prohibition of Congress establishing an official religion, benefit of clergy had been expunged from the nation's laws on the basis of being unconstitutional. See Sawyer, "'Benefit of Clergy,'" 65.

13. "Eli Hamilton," *Vermont Centinel* (Burlington), February 10, 1808, 1.

14. "The Methodist Church in New Orleans," 1:161–62; "Triumph of Infidelity!!!," *Norwich (CT) Courier*, April 6, 1814, 1.

15. "Philadelphia—Proceedings of the First Session of the Tenth General Assembly," *Carlisle (PA) Gazette*, December 21, 1785, 1.

16. "For the Connecticut Courant," *Connecticut Courant* (Hartford), March 9, 1795, 1.

17. "From a Correspondent," *National Gazette* (Philadelphia), March 6, 1793, 147.

18. "For the New York Packet," *New York Packet*, January 19, 1786, 2.

19. Play advertisement, "A Lecture on Heads," *Pennsylvania Packet* (Philadelphia), March 30, 1784, 1; play advertisement, "Darby and Patrick" and "Harlequin's Frolics," *Pennsylvania Packet* (Philadelphia), January 30, 1787, 3; play advertisement, "Feats of Activities . . . Harlequin Doctor," *Columbian Centinel* (Boston), August 25, 1792, 191.

20. "Theatrical Defeat," *Weekly Recorder* (Chillicothe OH), November 27, 1816, 142; "Thespian Corps," *Weekly Recorder* (Chillicothe OH), November 27,

1816, 142; "Cincinnati Theatre," *Weekly Recorder* (Chillicothe OH), April 23, 1819, 294; "Lexington Theatre," *Baltimore (MD) Patriot*, April 29, 1819, 4; "Six Newspapers," *Independent Chronicle* (Boston), December 7, 1825, 1.

21. [No headline, editorial], *Weekly Recorder* (Chillicothe OH), January 5, 1815, 210.

22. "Addison County Society for the Suppression of Vice and the Promotion of Good Morals," *Columbian Patriot* (Middlebury VT), March 8, 1815, 3; "Society for the Suppression of Vice and Immorality," *Weekly Recorder* (Chillicothe OH), January 26, 1815, 237; "State of Religion in Connecticut," *Boston Recorder*, July 10, 1816, 110; "Extracts from a Late Interesting Report of the Society in Portland for the Suppression of Vice and Immorality," *Farmer's Cabinet*, July 20, 1816, 1; "Revivals of Religion," *Christian Messenger* (Middlebury VT), January 15, 1817, 130; "At a Meeting of the Moral Society," *Northern Post* (Salem NY), July 24, 1817, 2; "Moral Society," *Christian Messenger*, July 29, 1818, 3; "Suppression of Vice," *Essex (MA) Patriot*, December 26, 1818, 3; "Observance of the Sabbath," *New Hampshire Gazette* (Portsmouth), September 16, 1828, 1; "Rev. John Leland," *New Hampshire Gazette*, May 11, 1830, 1. See also Bernard, "Between Religion and Reform," 1-38.

23. "To the Editors," 301.

24. "Suppression of Vice," *Essex Patriot* (Haverhill MA), December 26, 1818, 3.

25. *Venus School Mistress, or, Birchen Sports*, by R. Birch [pseud.], "translator" of "Manon's Memoirs" (London, 1808-10), 35-36, cited in Sigel, "Name Your Pleasure," 395-419.

26. Chester, *Knowledge and Holiness*, 21-22.

27. "Observations on Prostitution," *Massachusetts Gazette*, June 13, 1788, 1.

28. De Cunzo, "Reform, Respite, Ritual," 1-168.

29. "For the Herald of Freedom—an extract from a Manuscript Volume not yet published," *Herald of Freedom* (Boston), July 7, 1789, 129.

30. "Portland," *Rhode Island American*, July 1, 1823, 2.

31. *The Public Statute Laws of the State of Connecticut*, 483.

32. Gould, *A Digest of the Statutes of Arkansas*, 335.

33. "Charge of Libel," *Rhode Island Republican*, January 16, 1839, 3. Regarding awareness of Adeline Miller's brothel, see Gilfoyle, "Strumpets and Misogynists," 44-65.

34. "Destruction of the National Theatre," *Hudson River Chronicle* (Ossining NY), June 1, 1841, 3.

35. Regarding awareness of Julia Brown as the operator of a brothel, see Gilfoyle, "Strumpets and Misogynists," 60.

36. "Mentioned in Mobile Advertiser," *Times-Picayune* (New Orleans), April 13, 1837, 2.

37. "Riot in Portland," *Newport (RI) Mercury*, November 19, 1825, 3.

38. "Law," *Essex Gazette* (Haverhill MA), September 27, 1827, 1.

39. "From Our Buffalo Correspondent," *Frederick Douglass Paper* (Rochester NY), February 1, 1856, 3.

40. *Laws of the State of New York*, 1:123–24.

41. John C. Calhoun, letter to the House of Representatives dated January 15, 1820, in *American State Papers*, 200–201.

42. *The Statutes at Large and Treaties of the United States of America*, 9:203.

43. Ishii, "Alcohol and Politics in the Cherokee Nation before Removal," 671–95.

44. Evarts, *Essays on the Present Crisis*, 29.

45. Tuttle, *Letters and Conversations on the Cherokee Mission*, 115, 171.

46. Considerable scholarly research and debate have been devoted to what Western white culture calls "homosexuality," which most closely corresponds to what is called "berdache" in Native American culture. Among the notable studies are Lurie, "Winnebago Berdache," 708–12; Forgey, "The Institution of Berdache," 1–15; Thayer, "The Berdache of the Northern Plains," 287–93; Callender et al., "The North American Berdache," 443–70; Hauser, "The Berdache and the Illinois Indian Tribe," 45–65; Schnarch, "Neither Man nor Woman," 105–21; Woodsum, "Gender and Sexuality in Native American Societies," 527–54; Trexler, "Making the American Berdache," 613–36.

47. Tanner, *A Narrative of the Captivity and Adventures of John Tanner*, 105.

48. "The Senator from Texas," *Farmer's Cabinet* (Amherst NH), March 1, 1855, 2. "A Western Locofoco paper, in speaking of the next President, says that 'Sam Houston may yet be the next President of the United States,'" [no headline], *Hudson River Chronicle* (Ossining NY), August 12, 1845, 1; Williams, *Sam Houston*, 282, 288–301.

49. Williams, *Sam Houston and the War of Independence in Texas*, 19–20, 28–29, 35, 44–45, 50, 393; Broyles, "Behind the Lines," 5.

50. Burnap, *Lectures to Young Men*, 110.

51. Burnap, *Lectures to Young Men*, 110, 113, 111.

52. Cary, *Letters on Female Character*, 97, 101.

53. Cary, *Letters on Female Character*, 112, 193.

54. Cary, *Letters on Female Character*, 102.

55. Smith, "'Some Perilous Stuff,'" 135–43.

56. Fowler and Fowler, *Phrenology*, 60.

57. "The Author of 'Mary Lyndon,'" *Sandusky (OH) Register*, August 14, 1855, 3; "Mary Lyndon," *Milwaukee (WI) Sentinel*, October 2, 1855, 2; "New York Times—Mary Lyndon," *Newport (RI) Mercury*, October 6, 1855, 2.

58. Spurlock, "The Free Love Network," 765–79.

59. Wollstonecraft, *A Vindication of the Rights of Woman*, 151–52; Fordyce, *Sermons to Young Women*.

60. "The Marriage Institution," *Lily*, July 15, 1855, 82.

61. "The 'Free Love' Iniquity—from the Sandusky Register," *New York Times*, July 27, 1858, 2.

62. "Herding in Cities," *Weekly Eagle* (Brattleboro VT), June 24, 1852, 4.

63. Lofaro, "The Many Lives of Daniel Boone," 488–511.

64. Nathaniel Hawthorne, "Sketches from Memory," in *The Dolliver Romance, and Other Pieces*, reprinted in Hawthorne, *The Works of Nathaniel Hawthorne*, 11:68–69.

65. Nathaniel Hawthorne, *Passages from the American Notebooks of Nathaniel Hawthorne*, reprinted in Hawthorne, *The Works of Nathaniel Hawthorne*, 9:53–54. Eviction of the Irish in this community in Singer, "Hawthorne and the 'Wild Irish,'" 425–32.

66. Hawthorne, *Passages from the American Notebooks*, 62.

67. Hawthorne, *Passages from the American Notebooks*, 61–62.

68. "Miscellany," *Salem (MA) Gazette*, May 20, 1831, 1.

69. "Religious-Temptations to Which Young Men Are Exposed," *Farmer's Cabinet* (Amherst NH), July 12, 1833, 1.

70. Cary, *Letters on Female Character*, 24, 128.

71. Brownson, "The Laboring Classes," 358–95.

72. "The Temperance Cause," *Hudson River Chronicle* (Ossining NY), January 11, 1842, 3.

73. Jeffrey, "Reform, Renewal, and Vindication," 407–31.

74. "Interesting Incident," *Portsmouth Journal*, July 18, 1840, 4.

75. Malcolm, "The Catholic Church," 1–16. In the realm of "what a small world," Bishop Daniel O'Connell was one of the bishops with whom Orestes Brownson clashed—over an entirely different issue—after his conversion to Catholicism.

76. Stowe, *Uncle Tom's Cabin*, 10.

77. Hentz, *The Planter's Northern Bride*, 1:27–28.

3. "Free at Last"

1. Hoffman, *Race Traits and Tendencies*, 94.

2. Advertisement, *American Economic Association Publications* 4, no. 2 (May 1904): 18.

3. Hammond, "The Cotton Industry," 3–382.

4. Du Bois, "Review of *Race Traits and Tendencies*," 127–33.

5. Du Bois, *Souls of Black Folk*, 117, 100.

6. Bennett, "Hygiene in the Higher Education of Women," 522–23, 526.

7. *Acts and Laws of the State of Connecticut*, 288.

8. Eskridge, *Gaylaw*, 338–39.

9. "From the Cincinnati Times, the Turkish Dress," *Pittsfield (MA) Sun*, July 10, 1851, 2.

10. Workingmen's Party, *Chinatown Declared a Nuisance!*, 12.

11. Typical medical views of leprosy in the United States were White, "Leprosy in America," 196–200; Jeffries, "Leprosy of the Bible," 246–49.

12. Testimony of Benjamin S. Brooks, *Report of the Special Joint Committee to Investigate Chinese Immigration*, 44th Cong., 2nd sess., Senate Report 689 (Washington DC: Government Printing Office, 1877), 58–60.

13. "The Opium Dens—Action of the Board of Supervisors," *San Francisco Chronicle*, November 16, 1875, 3; *Statutes of California, 33rd Session of the Legislature, 1899*, 4–5.

14. "Latest Telegrams," *Los Angeles Herald*, December 7, 1875, 1.

15. "The Opium Disease," *Farmer's Cabinet* (Amherst NH), March 12, 1878, 1.

16. Capp, *The Church and Chinese Immigration*, 14.

17. Shoemaker, "The Abuse of Drugs," 1405–8.

18. "Samuel Taylor Coleridge," *Salem (MA) Gazette*, October 17, 1834; "Peculiarities of Noted People," *Elevator* (San Francisco), August 20, 1869; Platizky, "'Like Dull Narcotics Numbing Pain,'" 209–15.

19. Collins, *The Moonstone*, 191.

20. Booth, *The Doctor and the Detective*, 150.

21. "Use of Cocaine among Negroes," *Atlanta Constitution*, October 28, 1902, 4.

22. Williams, *The Question of Alcohol*, 14.

23. Williams, *The Question of Alcohol*, 15–16.

24. Examples include "The Use of Narcotic Drugs in the South," 127–28; Viereck, "An Object Lesson in Prohibition," 77; "Negro Cocaine 'Fiends' New Southern Menace," *New York Times*, February 8, 1914, SM12.

25. Kolb and Du Mez, "The Prevalence and Trend of Drug Addiction," 161–73; Courtwright, "The Hidden Epidemic," 57–72.

26. W. Whalley, "Confessions of a Laudanum Drinker," *Lancet*, July 14, 1866, reprinted in "Medical Jurisprudence and Toxicology," *New York Medical Journal* 4, no. 11 (November 1867): 140.

27. Crothers, *Morphinism and Narcomanias from Other Drugs*, 87–88.

28. Hoard v. Peck, 56 Barb. 202; Holleman v. Harvard, 119 N.C. 150, 34 L.R.A. 803, both cited in Browne, "The Lawyer's Easy Chair," 281.

29. J. J. McCarthy, "How the Drug Habit Grips the Unwary," *Pearson's Magazine*, August 1910, 176.

30. Harrison Narcotics Act, 1914, in *U.S. Government, Internal Revenue Regulations No. 35*, 3.

31. Wiedman, "Upholding Indigenous Freedoms and Medicine," 215–46.

32. "Law Says the Medicine Man Must Go," *Chicago Tribune*, April 2, 1899, D3.

33. Known at the time was that the ritual's messianic vision was adapted from Christianity and also included faith in nonviolence. See Mooney, "The Ghost Dance Religion and the Sioux Outbreak of 1890," reprinted in Mooney, *The Ghost Dance*, 139–53.

34. DeMontravel, "General Nelson A. Miles," 23–44; Lookingbill, "The Killing Fields of Wounded Knee," 379–86.

35. "Those Indian Dances," *Washington Post*, December 28, 1890, 16.

36. "Those Indian Dances," 16.

37. "Indian Snake Dance Is Fake," *Bicknell (IN) Daily News*, October 29, 1923, 7.

38. Clemmer, "'A Carnival of Promiscuous Carnal Indulgence,'" 60.

39. "Indian Snake Dance Is Fake," 7.

40. "Report of the Secretary of the Interior," 651.

41. The fact that polygamy has come to be viewed as a punishable vice throughout more and more of the world itself reveals a shift in the powers-that-be throughout the world. This tectonic shift, both comparably slow and significant, is the increasing power of women. Regarding polygamy as vice has altered the primary power entailed in marriage: the power of consent—a power now explicitly represented in Western culture by the demand for the public statement "I do." Because this shift occurred among Europeans long before they discovered the "New World," viewing polygamy as a punishable vice was part of America's moral inheritance.

42. *Remarks of the Hon. Stephen A. Douglas*, 13.

43. *The Compiled Laws of Nevada in Force from 1861 to 1900*, 962. Some municipalities in Nevada enacted ordinances prohibiting prostitution.

44. Bullard, "Abraham Lincoln and the Statehood of Nevada," 210–13, 236; Elliot and Rowley, *History of Nevada*, 69–89.

4. Careers in Vice

1. "An Act Relating to the Postal Laws, 13 Stat. 504, March 3, 1865," in *Statutes at Large*, 38th Cong., 2nd sess., chap. 89; Bates, *Weeder in the Garden of the Lord*, 9, 52–60.

2. Horowitz, "Victoria Woodhull," 403–34.

3. Victoria Woodhull, "The Beecher-Tilton Case," *Woodhull & Claflin's Weekly*, November 2, 1872, reprinted in Woodhull, *Complete and Detailed Version*, 12.

4. Woodhull, *Complete and Detailed Version*, 13.

5. "Woodhull Matters," *Chicago Tribune*, November 25, 1872, 8.

6. "Woodhull Matters," 8.

7. *Report of the Postmaster General*, 43rd Cong., 2nd sess. (Washington DC: Government Printing Office, 1874), 282; *Report of the Postmaster General*, 44th Cong., 1st sess. (Washington DC: Government Printing Office, 1875), 233; Long, *Wages and Earning in the United States, 1860-1890*, 42; "An Act for the Suppression of Trade in, and Circulation of Obscene Literature and Articles of Immoral Use, 17 Stat. 598, May 3, 1873," in *Statutes at Large*, 42nd Cong., 3rd sess., chap. 258.

8. "Act of Incorporation, Passed May 16, 1873," reprinted in *The New York Society for the Suppression of Vice*, 23; "Social Self-Protection," *New York Times*, April 21, 1875, 6.

9. "Prevention of Vice—Important Arrest by Mr. Anthony Comstock," *New York Times*, November 26, 1876, 2; "Lottery Agents Arrested—Anthony Comstock's Raid," *New York Times*, November 11, 1879, 8; "Pool Sellers Arrested—the Hunter's Point Dens Raided by Anthony Comstock," *New York Times*, October 10, 1882, 2; "Raid by Anthony Comstock—Improper Songs Given in Phonographs," *New York Times*, October 14, 1897, 3; "Comstock's Western Raid," *New York Times*, November 17, 1876, 8; "Anthony Comstock on Art—He Establishes a Branch Association in Baltimore," *New York Times*, December 20, 1887, 1.

10. "Comstock at It Again—Warns Arnold Daly against Playing 'Mrs. Warren's Profession,'" *New York Times*, October 25, 1905, 1; "Shaw's Play Unfit; the Critics Unanimous—Police Called to Handle Crush at 'Mrs. Warren's Profession,'" *New York Times*, October 31, 1905, 9.

11. Joyce, *Ulysses*, 641, 642, 643, 644.

12. Manifesto included in full in "War on Censorship Opens on Big Scale," *New York Times*, August 13, 1922, 14.

13. Munson, "Our Post-War Novel," 141; Alec Waugh, "The Post-War Novel," *Independent*, September 27, 1924, 194; H. C. Harwood, "The Post-War Novel in England," *Living Age*, July 1, 1927, 67; William Soskin, "A Bird's-Eye View of What the War Has Done to Contemporary European Literature," *New York Evening Post*, March 28, 1929, 10; DeBruyne and Leland, "American War and Military Operations Casualties," 2.

14. Manifesto, 14.

15. "Topics of the Times," *New York Times*, February 23, 1921, 12.

16. "Some of the Literature on Sale at the Rand School of Social Science," *Brooklyn Eagle*, October 12, 1919, 2; "Mr. Sumner Is Shocked Again," *New York Tribune*, February 16, 1921, 8.

17. "Morality on the Rampage and Those Who Censor Our Literature," reprinted from the *Freeman* in the *Call Magazine* (Saturday supplement to the *Evening Call*, New York City), September 27, 1922, 9.

18. Collins, "Sex in Literature."

19. "The Book Column," *Capital (WI) Times*, November 21, 1923, 14; "Bedside Criticism of Current Novels and Short Stories," *New York Times*, May 27, 1923, BR10. Other articles devoted to the book were "Neurologist Not Only Analyzes Books but Also Peers into Writers' Souls," *Ogden (UT) Standard-Examiner*, June 17, 1923, 3; "Purity and Pornography," 49; Collins, "Sex in Literature," 129–33.

20. "Printing of 'Ulysses' Here Causes Protest—160 Literary Men Abroad Call Publication of Joyce Book Invasion of Rights," *New York Times*, February 18, 1927, 21; "U.S. Mail Charge Jails Samuel Roth," *New York Evening Post*, January 4, 1928, 1.

21. "Ban on 'Ulysses' to Be Fought Again," *New York Times*, June 24, 1933, 14.

22. Lader, *The Margaret Sanger Story*, 5.

23. "'Woman Rebel' Editor Indicted," *Philadelphia Inquirer*, August 26, 1914, 16; "Birth Control in the Sanger Trial—Author Accused of Sending Obscene Matter through Mails," *Saratogian* (Saratoga NY), January 17, 1916, 8; "Clash over Birth Control," *Washington Post*, July 2, 1916, ES8; "Spread Birth Control," *Washington Post*, October 22, 1916, 9; "Congress against 'Birth Control,'" *Washington Post*, January 28, 1917, 3.

24. See "Arrest Margaret Sanger," *Washington Post*, November 14, 1921, 3; "Margaret Sanger Held," *Creston (IA) Daily Advertiser*, November 21, 1921, 1; "Control of Birth Activities Scored," *Daily Herald* (Biloxi MS), November 23, 1921, 8.

25. Tobin-Schlesinger, "The Changing American City," 67–85; *Washington Post*, December 16, 1935, 6.

26. Sanger, "National Security and Birth Control," 139. For a fuller exploration of Sanger's views, see Borell, "Biologists and the Promotion of Birth Control Research," 51–87.

27. The first state constitutions of New Hampshire, New Jersey, North Carolina, South Carolina, and Georgia limited public office to Protestants.

28. United States v. Dennett, 39 F.2nd, 564 (1939). For more on Mary Ware Dennett's career and trial, see Craig, "'The Sex Side of Life,'" 145–66; United States v. One Package of Japanese Pessaries, 86 F.2nd 737 (2nd Cir. 1936).

29. "Wrecks in the Name of Law," *Chicago Tribune*, December 28, 1900, 1.

30. "The Prohibitory Amendment," *Emporia (KS) News*, December 31, 1880, 1; Lockington, "Prohibition in the State of Maine," 286–94; "Prohibition in

Maine," *Independent*, September 21, 1911, 658; "What Is Confiscation?,"
Dodge City (KS) Times, December 22, 1887, 1. For examples of efforts to outlaw the sale of drug paraphernalia, see "Carter Seeks Drug Paraphernalia
Ban," *Washington Post*, October 5, 1979, A4; "Florida Bans Sale of Drug Paraphernalia," *Los Angeles Times*, May 22, 1980, B4; Taylor, *Kansas Criminal Law
and Practice*, 1:280.

31. Straub, *Straub's Manual of Mixed Drinks*, 5–7.

32. "For Your Medicine Chest," ad for the Falstaff Saloon, *Hayti (MO) Herald*,
June 28, 1917, 9.

33. Advertisement, *Goodwin's Weekly* (Salt Lake City UT), June 12, 1915, 14.

34. Sanger, "The Woman Spirit and the Better Day," 17–18; Baumgarten, "Margaret Sanger," 612.

35. Tyrrell, "Temperance, Feminism, and the WCTU," 27–36.

36. McKay, "Alcoholic Drink and the Immigrant," 205–6; Wilson, "Alcohol the
Barrier to Patriotism," 211; Stoddard, "The Drink Curve and the Immigration Curve," 214–15.

37. Pickett, *The Cyclopedia of Temperance*, 216.

38. Dow and Lewis, "Prohibition and Persuasion," 185.

39. Dow and Lewis, "Prohibition and Persuasion," 187–88.

40. "Negro Dive Raided—Thirteen Black Men Dressed as Women Surprised at
Dinner and Arrested," *Washington Post*, April 13, 1888, 3.

41. Jelliffe, "Homosexuality and the Law," 95–96. Attorney Alfred W. Herzog
amplified this view in "Homosexuality and the Law," 11–12; "Curing Crime
with Conversation," *Ironwood (MI) Times*, June 11, 1926, 1.

42. "M'Donald Sentenced to Ten Years in Pen," *Bismarck Weekly Tribune*, September 15, 1911, 8; *The Consolidated Laws of New York*, 29:246.

43. Million, "Enforceability of Prize Fight Statutes," 152–68; "Another Disgrace-
ful Prize Fight—McCool the Victor," *Baltimore Sun*, September 2, 1867, 1.

44. Burns, *The Smoke of the God*, 129; *Oxford English Dictionary*.

45. "Women and the Cigarette," *Harper's Bazaar*, March 26, 1887, 214.

46. "Women and the Cigarette," 214.

47. "Boldness in Young Girls," *Youth's Companion*, January 8, 1885, 12.

48. "The Use of Tobacco by Boys," *Christian Union*, June 1, 1881, 514; Goodman,
"Blue Laws," 663–73; Advisory Commission on Intergovernmental Relations, *State-Federal Overlapping in Cigarette Taxes*, 12. Among the numerous
studies providing empirical evidence regarding brain development in youth
are Keverne, "Understanding Well-Being," 1349–58; Lenroot and Giedd,
"Brain Development in Children and Adolescents," 718–29; Kuhn, "Do Cognitive Changes Accompany Developments in the Adolescent Brain?," 59–67.

49. LaHood, "Huck Finn's Search for Identity," 11–24; Laird, "Consuming Smoke," 96–104.

5. Vices That Roared

1. "Convicted of Profanity—Maine Court Finds Man Guilty Who Blasphemed," *Press and Banner* (Abbeville SC), October 5, 1921, 7; State v. Mockus, 120 Me. 84, 113 A. 39 (1921).
2. Weber, "Silk Stockings," 81.
3. Weber, "Silk Stockings," 81.
4. William C. Allen, "Our Debt to Darkest Africa," *Herald of Gospel Liberty*, November 17, 1927, 1072.
5. "Plans to Get Better Music," *Baltimore Sun*, February 1, 1921, 9.
6. Allen, "Our Debt to Darkest Africa," 1072; "The Charleston," *Independent*, April 17, 1926, 437.
7. Du Bois, "The Superior Race," 55–60.
8. Letter from Harold Ickes in *Conferring Jurisdiction on United States District Courts over Osage Indian Drug and Liquor Addicts*, House of Representatives, 74th Cong., 1st sess., Report 740 (April 19, 1935), 2.
9. "Dipsomania," *Littell's Living Age*, May 15, 1858, 557–58.
10. *See* Hays, *The Trend of the Races*, 38–39; Gaudet, Harris, and St. John, "Individual Differences in Sentencing Tendencies of Judges," 811–18; Hobbs, "Criminality in Philadelphia," 198–202.
11. Bureau of the Census, *Prisoners and Juvenile Delinquents*, 87–91.
12. Trice, "Alcoholics Anonymous," 108–16.
13. Among these laws were the Chinese Exclusion Act of 1882, the Emergency Quota Act of 1921, and the National Origins Acts of 1924 and 1929.
14. "Arrests Bare Sale of Dope to Gary Students," *Chicago Tribune*, December 19, 1927, 15.
15. See "Fighting Weed Vendor Gets Stiff Jolt," *Weekly Journal-Miner* (Prescott AZ), April 16, 1919, 2; "Some Mexican Slayings That Were Hushed Up," *Chicago Tribune*, September 17, 1919, 10; "'Diez-Y-Seis' Is Observed," *San Antonio News*, September 17, 1919, 7; "Oh, You Topers if You Knew," *Oxnard (CA) Daily Courier*, November 24, 1920, 1.
16. Ad for cannabis, *Pittsfield (MA) Sun*, December 31, 1857, 3.
17. Along with young Mexican American men, white musicians also quickly picked it up. For example, the members of acclaimed drummer Gene Krupa's dance band wore zoot suits. Krupa was of Polish and Pennsylvanian descent. See "Zoot Suit Riots Held Anarchy; Probe Widened—Musicians Mistakenly Beaten," *Chicago Tribune*, June 11, 1943, 2.

18. "Zoot Suit Riots Held Anarchy—Probe Widened," *Chicago Tribune*, June 11, 1943, 2.

19. "Ban on Freak Suits Studied by Councilmen," *Los Angeles Times*, June 10, 1943, A; "Magistrate 'Unfrocks' Pair of Zoot Suiters," *Los Angeles Times*, March 7, 1943, A1; "Flowing Locks Given Up to Obtain Liberty," *Los Angeles Times*, June 11, 1943, A; Westbrook Pegler, "Fair Enough," *Los Angeles Times*, June 14, 1943, A.

20. Foote, *Plain Home Talk*, 114. In addition to being an advocate for medical science, Dr. Foote spoke out on behalf of voting rights for women, birth control, free speech, and free love. See Wood, "Prescription for a Periodical," 26–44; Wood, *The Struggle for Free Speech*.

21. "The Emancipation of Woman," 70.

22. Foote, *Plain Home Talk*, 115.

23. "Arrested for Wearing Bloomers," *Jamestown (NY) Journal*, June 29, 1866, 2.

24. See "Indecent Apparel," *Bolivar (TN) Bulletin*, August 30, 1895, 1; "Against Bloomers," *Daily Astorian* (Astoria OR), December 24, 1895, 2; "Ruled Out the Bloomers," *Baxter Springs (TX) News*, March 14, 1896, 3.

25. "Items of General News," *Maine Farmer*, August 20, 1891, 3.

26. "Bathing Suits for Water," *Los Angeles Times*, July 22, 1908, II.

27. "Women May Swim in Bloomer Suits," *Chicago Tribune*, July 29, 1913, 1.

28. "Lincoln Beaches Ban Newest in Paris Scanties," *Chicago Tribune*, July 19, 1931, C3; "Study Race Relations in Contacts," *Chicago Defender*, October 28, 1922, 14.

29. "It's a Dark Day for Sunbathing; Mayor Says 'No,'" *Chicago Tribune*, March 22, 1932, 4.

30. "Police Raid Home of Sun Bathers," *Chicago Tribune*, June 27, 1911, 9. Among the many news accounts of nudist colonies springing up in these years are "Cult of Nudity Stirs Honolulu," *Chicago Tribune*, January 15, 1933, 6; "Nudist Apostle Tells of Camp near Chicago," *Chicago Tribune*, September 15, 1933, 3; "Nudists Frolic in Indiana Camp," *Chicago Tribune*, September 18, 1933, 11; "10 New York Nudists Freed," *Washington Post*, December 15, 1931, 2; "Just a Bare Fact: Maryland Picked for Nudist Camp," *Washington Post*, April 5, 1934, 3; "Nudists Call on America to Take Off Its Clothes," *Chicago Tribune*, August 26, 1936, 3.

31. "Allegan Nudist Trial Open to Capacity House," *Chicago Tribune*, October 24, 1933, 3; "Nudist Camp Leaders Move to Fight Case," *Chicago Tribune*, September 10, 1933, 3; "Michigan Jury Trying Nudist," *Los Angeles Times*, October 24, 1933, 11.

32. Literally interpreted, this wording, adopted in other states as well, rather gallantly let women off the hook by referring only to a person who exposes

his private parts. Possibly "his" was meant to include all humanity, but it is also possible that those who enacted the law viewed women's participation in nudist gatherings as being of questionable consent—much as laws against brothels were aimed at their proprietors, not the women who worked there. Nevertheless, there remained laws against indecent exposure, and some female nudists were arrested under them.

33. People v. Ring, 267 Mich. 657, 255 N.W. 373, 93 A.L.R. 993 (1934); Nevitt, "Legal Aspects of Nudism," 57–61; "Kentucky House Votes Nudist Colony Curb," *Washington Post*, March 11, 1934, 8; "Fairfax Board Bans Proposed Nudist Colony," *Washington Post*, October 5, 1933, 12; "Nudists Given Cold Shoulder in New Laws," *Washington Post*, April, 1934, 9; "Life Term for Nudists Asked in Oklahoma," *Washington Post*, January 22, 1935, 3.

34. "Nudity and News," *Washington Post*, April 11, 1934, 8.

35. "And Unashamed," *Washington Post*, April 12, 1935, 8.

6. Moola and Ooh-la-la

1. "Women Extend Fight against Risqué Show," *Chicago Tribune*, September 9, 1916, 3; "The Campaign to Curb the Moving Picture Evil in New York," *New York Times*, July 2, 1911, SM15; "Women's Work, Women's Clubs," *Los Angeles Times*, March 8, 1911, I7; "Moving Picture Shows Censored by Committee," *Atlanta Constitution*, November 13, 1910, B1.

2. "Say Picture Shows Corrupt Children," *New York Times*, December 24, 1908, 4; "Ministers in Censor Clash," *Los Angeles Times*, September 27, 1921, II1; "Presbyterians Ask for 'Clean Movies,'" *New York Times*, May 24, 1922, 18; "'Story of the Nun' Denounced by Priest," *Atlanta Constitution*, July 10, 1911, 2; Erens, *The Jew in American Cinema*, 39; Nelson, "Propaganda for God," 231.

3. "Movies for Catholic Churches," *New York Times*, August 29, 1914, 9.

4. "Committee to Censor Cheap Amusements," *New York Times*, February 24, 1909, 6; "Law to Purify Stage," *Washington Post*, May 5, 1909, 3; "Moving Picture Shows Censored by Committee," *Atlanta Constitution*, November 13, 1910, B1.

5. Whitlock, "The White Slave," 193–216.

6. "Police Ban on Shakespeare," *Chicago Tribune*, June 2 1908, 1.

7. "That Miserable Photo-Play," *Cleveland Gazette*, April 10, 1915, 2; "Race Film Bill Passes House on Negro's Plea," *Chicago Tribune*, May 19, 1915, 7. The law, ultimately enacted in 1917, prohibited other offensive depictions as well. It was never enforced in regard to depictions of African Americans, Native Americans, or Chinese. For bans on the film, see "Birth of Nation Kicked Out of Ohio," *Chicago Defender*, October 2, 1915, 1; "Kansas Rejects the 'Birth of Nation,'" *Chicago Defender*, January 29, 1916, 1; "Thompson Bars Griffith

Film," *Chicago Tribune*, May 15, 1915, 17; "Denver's City Council Prohibits Prejudice Breeding Pictures," *Chicago Defender*, October 23, 1915, 1; "Oakland Puts Ban on Birth of a Nation," *Chicago Defender*, August 14, 1915, 1.

8. Sylvester Russell, "Annual Review of American Colored Actors," *Freeman* (Indianapolis), December 23, 1911, 12.

9. Chief Red Fox, *The Memoirs of Chief Red Fox*, 156–57, cited in Rosenthal, "Representing Indians," 328–52.

10. Hodges, *Anna May Wong*, 62, 181; "MGM Plans Russian Tie-Up . . . Anna May Wong Goes to Europe for Ufa," *Los Angeles Times*, May 17, 1928, A9.

11. Mutual Film Corporation v. Industrial Commission of Ohio, 236 U.S. 230 (1915), no. 456.

12. "Censoring the Movie," *New York Times*, December 28, 1919, XX11; Harris, "Movie Censorship," 122–38.

13. "To Police Their Own Plays," *New York Times*, January 20, 1917, 9.

14. Hollywood too, amidst the dust-up over the kinds of films it continued to produce, was rocked by a scandal. One of its leading comedians, Fatty Arbuckle, was accused of rape in 1921. Despite the fact that Arbuckle, after two trials ending in deadlocked juries, was found not guilty in his third trial, Hollywood knew it had been found guilty by the jury of public opinion.

15. "Film Censorship Bill Revived by Randall," *Los Angeles Times*, February 24, 1919, 13. Among the many arrests for sending obscene material through the mail during Will Hays's watch as postmaster general were indictments reported in "Car Which Killed Child Had Been Here," *Saratogian* (Saratoga NY), April 27, 1921, 5; "Charge Murphy Sent Obscene Cards by Mail," *Buffalo (NY) Courier*, June 8, 1921, 6; "Negro Fractures Leg Attempting to Escape," *Atlanta Constitution*, September 22, 1921, 8; "Pina Confesses He Mailed Bad Letter," *Weekly Journal-Miner* (Prescott AZ), October 12, 1921, 5; "Man under Charges Thought to Be Unsound," *Mt. Sterling (KY) Advocate*, October 18, 1921, 6.

16. "Crafts Rages, Rants, Howls at Films Again," *Los Angeles Times*, January 19, 1922, I1. With Crafts's income and overhead covered by a number of Protestant churches and wealthy contributors, he worked full-time on behalf of Sunday blue laws, the return of Bible study in public schools, enactment of Prohibition, tougher drug laws, restrictions on divorce, and censorship of films. See Foster, "Conservative Social Christianity," 799–819.

17. "Hays Flouts Idea of Public Censors," *Washington Post*, July 25, 1922, 3.

18. "Picking on the Movies," *Los Angeles Times*, February 24, 1924, A4; "Education Department, Censor Bills Rejected," *Washington Post*, May 5, 1926, 1; "Federal Censorship of Pictures Urged," *Washington Post*, April 15, 1926, 2.

19. Black, "Hollywood Censored," 167–89; Rausch, *Turning Points in Film History*, 65.

20. Though repeatedly revised in the years to come, the Motion Picture Code remains in place to this day. In its current form we know it as the ratings system used to label films: G ("general audiences"), PG ("parental guidance suggested"), PG-13 ("parents strongly cautioned"), R ("restricted"), and NC-17 ("no one 17 and under admitted"). Unchanged, however, is that these ratings are the same vice device, in that the power to assign them is in the hands of the film industry itself, not outside censors.

21. "A Code to Govern the Making of Talking, Synchronized and Silent Motion Pictures," reprinted in Belton, *Movies and Mass Culture*, 138–49.

22. Black, "Hollywood Censored," 174.

23. Balio, *Grand Design*, 405.

24. "List of 'Don't' and 'Be Carefuls,'" in *Motion Picture Production Code* (Motion Picture Producers and Distributors Association, 1930); later incorporated into the 1933 updated code, reprinted in Gardner, *The Censorship Papers*, 214.

25. Gardner, *The Censorship Papers*, 163.

26. "Theater News and Views," *Brooklyn Eagle*, April 2, 1911, theater section, 8.

27. "The Nude Drama," *Dubuque (IA) Herald*, July 1, 1869, 2.

28. The basis for the Hollywood film was a 1960 book by the same name—but subtitled *A Fanciful Expedition to the Lost Atlantis of Show Business*. Fanciful because the source material for the book came from Morton Minsky, and author Rowland Barber wanted readers to know that claims made by any of the four Minsky brothers should be regarded in the same way as claims made by any show biz flack.

29. "Fifi, 85, Says She Didn't Bump Minsky's Off Map," *Los Angeles Times*, December 29, 1975, 1.

30. Friedman, "'The Habits of Sex-Crazed Perverts,'" 203–38; "Court Bars Artists at Carroll's Trial," *New York Times*, October 17, 1924, 23.

31. Koch, "The Body's Shadow Realm," 3–29.

32. "Hires Nude Women to Dance," *Evening Gazette* (Burlington IA), December 22, 1896, 1; "Sons of Presidents," *Brooklyn Eagle*, January 13, 1897, 7; "Raided a Dance a la Seeley," *Brooklyn Eagle*, February 4, 1897, 14.

33. "The Sherry Raid," *Brooklyn Eagle*, January 9, 1897, 6.

34. "First Nights of Variety," *New York Times*, August 21, 1894, 5.

35. Karsten, *Encyclopedia of War and American Society*, 554; "'Follies of 1917' Is a Fine Spectacle," *New York Times*, June 13, 1917, 11; "Ziegfeld Follies Opened Last Night," *Brooklyn Eagle*, June 13, 1917, 7.

36. Baker spent virtually her entire career in Paris and on tour in Europe. Through her African- and Latin American–themed dances, often performed topless, she became an international sensation and every bit as wealthy as Sally Rand and her colleagues. "Josephine Baker," *Chicago Defender*, July

31, 1926, 7; "Josephine Baker Signs $10,000 Dance Contract," *Chicago Defender*, February 18, 1928, 10.

37. Paul Harrison, "In New York," syndicated column in *Bluefield (WV) Daily Telegraph*, July 21, 1935, 6.

38. James E. Alsbrook, "Extenuation," in column Line's O' Type, *Plaindealer* (Kansas City KS), September 13, 1935, 5.

39. Dandridge, "Zalka Peetruza," 112.

40. McKay, "The Harlem Dancer," 169.

41. Sandburg, "Vaudeville Dancer," 223.

42. Views of consent are more than skin deep. One of that era's most widely lauded African American poets, Langston Hughes, did posit blame on black strippers in his closing lines of his poem from the 1920s "Nude Young Dancer": "What jungle tree have you slept under, / Night-dark girl of the swaying hips? / What star-white moon has been your mother? / To what clean boy have you offered your lips?" (Hughes, *The Collected Works of Langston Hughes*, 1:29).

43. "Chicago Night Life Unfolded," *Savannah (GA) Tribune*, January 26, 1922, 4; "News Summary-Local," *Chicago Tribune*, January 29, 1922, 1. For white ownership of the Entertainers' Café, see Kennedy, *Chicago Jazz*, 149; "Chorus Must Wear More," *New York Times*, March 1, 1924, 13.

44. "Police Take Actors in Raid on Theatre," *New York Times*, March 12, 1926, 21; "Act, Then Pay Fines—Burlesque Troupe Convinces Judges Performance Was Indecent," *New York Times*, May 11, 1926, 12; "Police Put Censors on Broadway Plays," *New York Times*, September 26, 1924, 22; "Carroll Refuses Bond and Is Jailed," *New York Times*, October 31, 1924, 1; "Earl Carroll Freed," *New York Times*, November 11, 1924, 6.

45. "Church Federation Formed," *New York Times*, December 10, 1920, 31; "Cardinal Condemns Indecency on Stage," *New York Times*, March 16, 1925, 21; "To Boycott Profane Plays," *New York Times*, March 16, 1925, 21.

46. "Cardinal Condemns Indecency on Stage," *New York Times*, March 16, 1925, 21; "To Boycott Profane Plays," *New York Times*, March 16, 1925, 21; "Priest Opens Fire on Modern Writers," *New York Times*, April 19, 1926, 22; "McKee Closes Two Burlesques in 42d St.," *New York Times*, September 20, 1932, 1; "Burlesque," *New York Times*, September 21, 1932, 20.

7. A New Power

1. "Bathing Suits Causes Crisis in Milwaukee," *Post* (Ellicottville NY), July 28, 1950, 3.

2. "Timidly Worn Bikini Catches County's Eye," *Los Angeles Times*, June 16, 1960, D1.

3. "The Inquiring Photographer," *Long Island Star-Journal*, August 1, 1952, 4.

4. "Italian Archbishop Raps New Swim Suits," *Journal-Standard* (Freeport IL), July 26, 1949, 18; "Writer Discusses How Women Should Be Dressed in Public," *Alamogordo (NM) Daily News*, May 2, 1957, 4.

5. "Inquiring Camera Girl," *Chicago Tribune*, May 21, 1959, D11; "Decent or Indecent?," *East Hampton Star*, August 19, 1954, 2; "Bathing Suit Semantics," *Citizen Advertiser* (Auburn NY), August 28, 1954, 4. Bikinis were prohibited during these years in Spain, Portugal, Australia, and elsewhere. See "Bikini Ruled Unlawful by Spain's Police," *Chicago Tribune*, August 9, 1959, 22; "A Beach for Every Tourist Taste in Portugal," *New York Times*, February 24, 1957, 137; Alac, *Bikini Story*, 52.

6. "Uticans Have Mixed Reaction to Topless Suits," *Daily Press* (Utica NY), June 18, 1964, 11; "What to Do about the Topless Problem," *Los Angeles Times*, February 14, 1965, G1; "Red View of Topless Bathing Suit," *Herald Statesman* (Yonkers NY), August 28, 1964, 12; "No Ruling to Cover Situation—Courts Look Other Way at Topless Swimsuits," *Los Angeles Times*, July 27, 1972, SF1; Hoffmann and Bailey, *Sports & Recreation Fads*, 364; "Thong War Breaks Out on Round Lake," *Chicago Tribune*, June 27, 1991, 3; "County Board Rules Out Thong Bikinis at Beach," *Cedar Rapids (IA) Gazette*, July 23, 1994, 2B; "Woman Arrested over Thong at Myrtle Beach," *New Bern (NC) Sun Journal*, May 26, 2013, 18.

7. "Describes Lili's Strip Act to Jury" and "Mom Defends Lilli," *Independent* (Long Beach CA), December 6, 1951, 16A; "Jury Rules Stripping's Art, Frees Lili St. Cyr," *Los Angeles Times*, December 12, 1951, 5.

8. "Convict Two after Vice Squad Raid," *Evening Capital* (Annapolis MD), February 17, 1951, 1; "270 Face Trial in Big Raid on Club," *Oshkosh (WI) Northwestern*, February 8, 1954, 5; "Judge: Exposure Is Not Always Indecent," *Beatrice (NE) Sun*, November 14, 1954, 13.

9. "Pastor Condemns Times Square 'Nudity,'" *New York Times*, February 1, 1954, 25; "Book Censorship Licenses Urged," *New York Times*, February 14, 1934, 21.

10. United States v. O'Brien, 391 U.S. 367 (1968).

11. "Appeals Court Says Nude Dancing Can Be Legal," *Kokomo (IN) Tribune*, May 27, 1990, 12; Barnes v. Glen Theatre, Inc., 501 U.S. 560 (1991).

12. *Barnes v. Glen Theatre, Inc.*, 575, 595.

13. City of Erie v. Pap's A.M., 529 U.S. 277 (2000).

14. St. Louis Municipal Ordinance 62,940 (enacted July 9, 1993), https://www.stlouis-mo.gov/government/city-laws/ordinances/ordinance.cfm?ord=62940 (accessed August 2016).

15. "L.A. Council Retreating on Lap-Dance Ban," *Los Angeles Times*, November 19, 2003, A1.

16. "Strip Club's BYOB Policy under Fire from Official," *Chicago Daily Herald*, January 9, 2008, 4.

17. "Making the On-Line Community Safe for Decency—and Democracy," *Washington Post*, May 29, 1995, 17; "Judge Blocks On-Line Smut Law Enforcement; Order Sparks Confusion over Definition," *Washington Post*, February 16, 1996, B1; Reno v. American Civil Liberties Union, 521 U.S. 844 (1997).

18. Lutz and Collins, *Reading "National Geographic"*; Steet, *Veils and Daggers*. The first photos of unclothed white people in *National Geographic* was in 1989, though their sexual organs were occluded by the local flora.

19. "Magazine Challenges Post Office Authority," Associated Press report in *Corpus Christi Times*, November 18, 1955, 12; HMH Publishing Company v. Summerfield, Civ. Action No. 2745-58, USDC, Washington DC, November 7, 1958; "U.S. Court Upsets Ban on 'Playboy,'" *New York Times*, October 31, 1958, 22; "Proceedings in Playboy Case Dropped," *Chicago Tribune*, November 6, 1958, C2.

20. "Meese Says Playboy, Penthouse Pass His Obscenity Inspection," *Chicago Tribune*, January 30, 1987, 16.

21. "U.S. Tries to Settle Suit with Playboy," *Chicago Tribune*, November 8, 1986, 4.

22. "Exposure Charge Called Foolish," *Chicago Tribune*, May 30, 1969, 3; "Playboy Foes Who Stripped Are Fined $200," *Chicago Tribune*, June 21, 1969, N5.

23. "Sailors Must Ask for Playboy," *Wisconsin State Journal* (Madison), October 18, 1971, section 2, 5; "Drugstores Drop Playboy," *New York Times*, July 27, 1969, 67.

24. Miller v. California, 413 U.S. 15 (1973).

25. Olson, "The G.I. Bill and Higher Education," 596–610.

26. An expurgated version of *Lady Chatterley's Lover* had been published in the United States in 1934, despite an unexpurgated, albeit pirated, edition that had appeared here three years earlier, published under the imprint of William Faro, a.k.a. (take a guess) Samuel Roth. See Roberts and Poplawski, *A Bibliography of D. H. Lawrence*, 151, 753. For a more detailed account of the mercurial Samuel Roth, see Gertzman, *Bookleggers and Smuthounds*.

27. "'Chatterley' Film Banned by State," *New York Times*, September 29, 1956, 12. The film was *The Miracle*, which had been banned on the basis of having been deemed blasphemous. See "Rossellini Film Is Halted by City; 'The Miracle' Held 'Blasphemous,'" *New York Times*, December 24, 1950, 1; Burstyn v. Wilson, 353 U.S. 495 (1952).

28. Mae Tinee, "Why the Big Fuss about 'Chatterley' Film?," *Chicago Tribune*, August 21, 1959, B14; Bosley Crowther, "'Controversial' Movie Has Premiere Here," *New York Times*, July 11, 1959, 11.

29. Daniel A. Poling, "It's Time for a New Crusade," cited and quoted in "Dr. Poling Supports Post Office in Its Ban on 'Lady Chatterley,'" *New York Times*, July 26, 1959, 47.

30. Grove Press, Inc. v. Christenberry, U.S. District Court for the Southern District of New York, 175 F. Supp. 488 (S.D.N.Y. 1959), July 21, 1959. The judge's phrase, "this major English novel," and its influence on his decision revealed another group acquiring greater power in that era. That group consisted of those who determined what is or is not a major English novel: the intellectuals who educated the rising group of Middle Americans. For a while at least, they rode on the coattails (or, better metaphor, shirt tails) of the blue-collar veterans who were now their students.

31. "State Authority to Censor Backed," *New York Times*, July 3, 1959, 6.

32. "Touchiest of All CR Issues Faces Court," *Kingsport (TN) Times*, November 10, 1964, 16.

33. Not all religious authorities shared the judge's view. Roman Catholic cardinal Lawrence Sheehan was among numerous Catholic, Protestant, Jewish, and other clergy in the United States who at the time expressed opposition to laws prohibiting interracial marriage. See "Clergymen Attack Miscegenation Laws," *Lubbock (TX) Avalanche-Journal*, February 17, 1967, 6B.

34. "Virginia Case Broke Marital Color Barrier," *Daily News Record* (Harrisonburg VA), June 11, 2007, A1, A3; "Miscegenation Law Upheld by Virginia Court," *Port Arthur (TX) News*, March 7, 1966, 11.

35. "White Man Marries Negro Woman, Both Held in Alabama," *Daily Herald* (Biloxi MS), April 22, 1937, 2; "Rules Inter-racial Marriage Invalid," *El Paso (TX) Herald-Post*, December 23, 1939, 1; "Marriage Ban Battle Won in Virginia Case," *Southwest Times* (Pulaski VA), February 26, 1968, 2.

36. Dean, *Imperial Brotherhood*, 225.

37. "Who's Going to Bell the Homosexual Cats?," *Raleigh Register* (Beckley WV), October 19, 1964, 4; "'Y' Closes Its Public Rest Room," *Washington Post*, October 18, 1964, A8.

38. Charles, "From Subversion to Obscenity," 262–87; Powers, *Secrecy and Power*, 171–73, 185, 315, 321.

39. "Neighbors Offer Services, Gifts to Assist Walter Jenkins Family," *Washington Post*, October 25, 1964, A8.

40. "Kinsey Report Sex Charges Based on Incomplete Sample," *Austin Daily Texan*, February 22, 1948, 5; Laidlaw, "Marriage Counseling," 39–46.

41. George Crane, "The Worry Clinic," syndicated column cited from *Post-Register* (Idaho Falls IA), January 11, 1949, 4; "George W. Crane Dies at 94; Advised with 'Horse Sense,'" *New York Times*, July 19, 1995, D20.

42. "Solons Debate 'Sex' Ordinance," *Van Nuys (CA) News*, March 10, 1949, part 2, 1.

43. Maude Robinson, "Books," *Salt Lake Tribune*, June 26, 1949, 4M.

44. "Homosexuality Discussion Set," *Daily Review* (Walnut Creek CA), December 25, 1958, 23.

45. George Sokolsky, "Twentieth Century Morals," syndicated column cited from *Sandusky (OH) Register*, August 3, 1962, 4.

46. "4 Policemen Hurt in 'Village' Raid," *New York Times*, June 29, 1969, 33; "Police Again Rout 'Village' Youths," *New York Times*, June 30, 1969, 22; "Hostile Crowd Dispersed near Sheridan Square," *New York Times*, July 3, 1969, 19; "4 Homosexuals Sue to Curb D.C. Police," *Washington Post*, September 10, 1971, C2.

47. "Homosexual Rights Laws Show Progress in Some Cities but Drive Arouses Considerable Opposition," *New York Times*, May 13, 1974, 17.

48. "Homosexuals March for Equal Rights," *New York Times*, June 18, 1977, 55.

49. Bowers v. Hardwick, 478 U.S. 186 (1986); Lawrence v. Texas, 539 U.S. 558 (2003).

50. Previously, the only congressmen known or suspected to be gay were ones who had been arrested for it and another who died of AIDS. See "'Compulsions' Admitted by Rep. Bauman," *Washington Post*, October 9, 1980, A1; "McKinney Dies of Illness Tied to AIDS," *New York Times*, May 8, 1987, B1.

51. In another decision of critical importance to the nation, the Supreme Court also interpreted the Constitution differently from previous justices in order to endorse the views of the prevailing powers-that-be. That decision was *Brown v. Board of Education* (1954), which overturned *Plessy v. Ferguson* (1896). *Plessy* upheld the constitutionality of segregation, including segregated public schools. No legislation had been enacted in the intervening years to provide a legal basis for a different interpretation of the constitutionality of such laws. What had intervened was six decades in which African Americans had struggled to organize themselves into a political force. Among the 3,697 words in the 1954 ruling, here are the 20 words that account for the justices overturning the ostensibly constitutional view of 1896: "Many Negroes have achieved outstanding success in the arts and sciences, as well as in the business and professional world." Those words acknowledged just the socially accepted tip of the iceberg of African Americans' efforts for equal rights, but enough was underneath that tip to alter the way the justices interpreted the Constitution.

52. "Crusade against Teen Pregnancy Creating Tempest," *Huntingdon (PA) Daily News*, July 15, 1996, 2.

53. McDowell, *Magdalen Facts*.

54. "Children Who Are Their Brothers' Keepers," 716–21; "The Unwed Father," 741–42.

55. Males, "Schools, Society, and 'Teen' Pregnancy," 566–68.

56. "Methods of Sex Education Hit at Family Conference," *Washington Post*, March 15, 1950, 13.

57. "Protestants Dispute Stand on Sex Education," *Lowell (MA) Sun*, November 20, 1950, 21.

58. "Foes Fail to End Sex Education Spread," *Washington Post*, June 3, 1969, C1; "Sex Education Foes Show Film on Hill," *Washington Post*, September 17, 1969, C2; Todes, "Pavlov and the Bolsheviks," 379–418.

59. Hyles, *Sex Education in Our Public Schools*. Sermon reprinted in booklet at http://www.jesus-is-savior.com/Books,%20Tracts%20&%20Preaching /Printed%20Sermons/Dr%20Jack%20Hyles/sex_education_in_public _schools.htm (accessed August 2016).

60. Hyles, *Sex Education in Our Public Schools*.

61. "Interview with Our Unofficial 'Censor,'" *New York Times*, October 20, 1946, SM13.

62. Trenholm et al., *Impacts*.

63. Cockburn and St. Clair, *Whiteout*, 73.

64. Alexander, "The War on Drugs," 75–77.

65. Meierhoefer, *The General Effect*, 4; Meier, "The Politics of Drug Abuse," 41–69.

66. "Stamping Out the Drug Habit," *Los Angeles Times*, November 21, 1926, B5; "Doctor Shows How Dope Evil Step by Step Wrecks Victims," *Atlanta Constitution*, January 22, 1923, 2.

67. "Senators Given Sordid Story by Dope Users," Associated Press report cited from the *Los Angeles Times*, June 27, 1951, 19.

68. "Reagan Vows War on Dope Trade," *Washington Post*, October 3, 1982, A3; "Big War on Drugs Is Vowed," *Chicago Tribune*, September 19, 1972, A13; "President Opens War on Drugs," *New York Times*, November 28, 1954, 1; "Veterans Group to War on Drugs," *Washington Post*, March 4, 1935, 3; "Chats with Visitors—Nations Cooperate in War on Drugs," *Washington Post*, October 17, 1921, 6.

69. *Public Papers of the Presidents of the United States*, 1181.

70. "Crack: It's No Longer Just for the Rich," AP report cited from the *Daily Intelligencer / Montgomery County (PA) Record*, July 16, 1986, 6; "'Crack' Puts New Pop in Cocaine Market," *Chicago Tribune*, May 21, 1986, 1.

71. Malcolm, "The Case for the Smarter Sentencing Act," 298–301; Meierhoefer, *The General Effect*, 3–6; Danielle Kurtzleben, "Data Show Racial Disparity in Crack Sentencing," *US News and World Report*, August 3, 2010, http://www.usnews.com/news/articles/2010/08/03/data-show-racial -disparity-in-crack-sentencing; Beaver, "Getting a Fix," 2531–75.

72. Letter from judges in "1997 Statement on Powder and Crack Cocaine," 194–95; Malcolm Gladwell, "N.Y. Crack Epidemic Appears to Wane," *Washington Post*, May 31, 1993, A1; Hamid, "The Development Cycle of a Drug Epidemic," 337–48; Bowling, "The Rise and Fall of New York Murder," 531–54.

73. "Touting Tough Sentencing Laws," *News Herald* (Panama City FL), May 19, 2004, 11A; "Jeb Bush Op-Ed: A Father's View of Drug Addiction," *Chicago Tribune*, January 6, 2016, 19.

74. Conor Friedersdorf, "A Heartbreaking Drug Sentence of Staggering Idiocy," *Atlantic*, April 3, 2013, http://www.theatlantic.com/politics /archive/2013/04/a-heartbreaking-drug-sentence-of-staggering-idiocy /274607/.

75. "GOP Tack on Heroin Crisis Underlines Racial Divide," *Washington Post*, November 29, 2015, A1. Evidence of the spike in heroin use among whites in Cicero et al., "The Changing Face of Heroin Use," 821–26.

76. Reihan Salam, "Gov. Chris Christie: No Life Is Disposable," *National Review*, January 19, 2012, www.nationalreview.com/agenda/288600/gov -chris-christie-no-life-disposable-reihan-salam.

77. "The Bill Clinton Scandal Machine Revs Back Up and Takes Aim at His Wife," *Washington Post*, January 6, 2016, https://www.washingtonpost.com /politics/the-bill-clinton-scandal-machine-revs-up-and-takes-aim-at-his -wife/2016/01/06/a08cf550-b4be-11e5-a76a-0b5145e8679a_story.html.

78. "After President Testifies, First Lady Decompresses," *Washington Post*, January 20, 1998, A4; "Disputing Lewinsky's Taped Claims," *Washington Post*, January 31, 1998, A1; "Hillary Clinton Admits Error in Bringing Up Bush Rumor," Associated Press report in *Cedar Rapids (IA) Gazette*, April 5, 1992, 3A.

79. "The Walters-Clinton Interview," *Washington Post*, June 9, 2003, C1.

80. Colbert King, "Danger Comes Right Over the Counter," *Washington Post*, May 5, 2012, A15.

81. "A White Flag in the War on Drugs," *Washington Post*, April 13, 2012, A17.

82. A similar synthesized drug has more recently surfaced known as "bath salts." Not to be confused with traditional bath salts (though some naive users have, resulting in a profound laxative effect but no high), the drug that has co-opted that name is a crystalized form of substances that are derived from the khat plant or are synthesized to mimic them. Until 2012 those substances also eluded the law by not yet having been specifically banned. The 2012 law also banned analogous substances, but computer-generated molecular models have enabled drug traffickers to synthesize substances that sidestep "analogous." In all likelihood, its use too will decline—albeit after causing considerable damage and heartbreak—for reasons other than such laws, since, as with crack and meth, its effects have proven so dangerous and, due

to rapid changes in what constitutes its active ingredient(s), so unpredictable. See "Synthetic Drugs Known as 'Bath Salts' Strike Families and Communities with Alarming Speed and Savagery," *Elyria (OH) Chronicle*, October 2, 2011, F1. For youths who tried to get high on traditional bath salts, see "Lima Considers Bath Salt Ban," *Lima (OH) News*, June 14, 2011, A1, A7.

83. "Methamphetamine," National Institute of Drug Abuse & Addiction, www .drugabuse.gov/drugs-abuse/methamphetamine (accessed August 14, 2015); "Violent Crime in U.S. Continues to Surge; Homicide Increase Largest in Big Cities," *Washington Post*, December 19, 2006, A1; "Homicides Up 20% in District This Year," *Washington Post*, June 26, 2015, B1; "Police Say Synthetic Marijuana Leading to Increase in Overdoses, Crime," *Las Vegas Review-Journal*, August 16, 2015, http://www.reviewjournal.com/news/ nation-and -world/police-say-synthetic-marijuana-leading-increase-overdoses-crime; Weisheit and White, *Methamphetamine*, 84–94.

8. Think Twice about Vice

1. Dick Armey, "Void the Blank Check for Offensive Art," *Journal Tribune* (Biddeford ME), August 1, 1989, 8.

2. Moyers and Beckett, *Sister Wendy in Conversation with Bill Moyers*.

3. "It Happens Again: 15 Die in Rampage," *Walla Walla Union-Bulletin*, April 21, 1999, 1; Tom Maurstad, "Violent Streak," *Dallas Morning News*, reprinted in *Syracuse Herald-Journal*, April 22, 1999, A12.

4. "Decapitate Your Enemy for 50 Cents," *Wisconsin State Journal* (Madison), January 3, 1993, 1A, 7A.

5. Anderson, "Unintended Negative Consequence," 3–13; Carnagey and Anderson, "The Effects of Reward," 882–89; Anderson and Ford, "Affect of the Game Player," 390–402.

6. Anderson et al., "Early Childhood Television Viewing," i–viii, 1–154; "Judges Lay Crime to Improper Films," *New York Times*, January 18, 1925, 3.

7. "Potpourri," 224; "Text Book Fairy Tales Condemned," *Trenton Evening Times*, August 6, 1908, 7; Brooke Peters Church, "Talks to Parents," syndicated column cited from *Abilene (TX) Morning News*, July 6, 1935, 6.

8. Brown v. Entertainment Merchants Association, 564 U.S. 08-1448, June 27, 2011.

9. Krista Goerte, "Fact Is, There's Nothing Wrong with Video Games," *Paris (TX) News*, February 8, 2013, A4.

10. Wertham, *Seduction of the Innocent*, 90–91.

11. Calvin A. Byers, "Farmer's Diary—the Comic Book Menace," syndicated column cited from the *Mansfield (OH) News-Journal*, June 15, 1948, 4; "Spen-

cer School Pupils Wage War on Comic Books," *Charleston (wv) Daily Mail*, October 27, 1948, 2.

12. "Comic Book Curb Urged by PTA," *Binghamton (NY) Press*, November 17, 1948, 12; "Students to Dramatize Boycott with Bonfire of Comic Books," *Binghamton Press*, December 2, 1948, 5; Twomey, "The Citizens' Committee," 621–29.

13. Hoskins, "Delinquency," 512–37.

14. Katzev v. County of Los Angeles, 341 P.2d 310 (Cal. 1959).

15. Bettelheim, "Review of *Seduction of the Innocent*," 129–30.

16. Long before violent video games, Americans were periodically shocked by killing sprees of random victims. Using as a debut point for such video games the 1992 release of *Mortal Kombat* (in which the victor tears off the head of his—or her—vanquished foe and pulls out the opponent's heart), the most widely reported random killing sprees pre-*Mortal Kombat* were John Patrick Purdy opening fire in a Stockton, California, elementary school in 1989; Laurie Dann doing likewise in a Winnetka, Illinois, elementary school the year before; and Charles Whitman firing on students in a 1966 massacre at the University of Texas. On the other hand, whether or not violent video games contributed, such random killing sprees began to occur more frequently after 1992. On May 21, 1998, Kip Kinkel opened fire on students at Thurston High School in Springfield, Oregon. Three days later, Mitchell Scott Johnson and Andrew Douglas Golden gunned down students at Westside Middle School. The massacre at Columbine occurred the following year, and to date, the list has continued unabated.

17. Tilley, "Seducing the Innocent," 383–413.

18. "The Use of Narcotic Drugs in the South," 127–28; Bowers, "Why Not Government Hospitals," 60–61; Lewitus, "Marihuana," 677–78; "Lung Cancer Rise Laid to Cigarettes," *New York Times*, October 26, 1940, 17; J. K. Finnegan et al., "The Role of Nicotine in the Cigarette Habit," *Science*, July 27, 1945, 94–96; Cutler, "A Review of the Statistical Evidence," 267–82; "Legality of Marijuana Laws Tested in Mass. Court Battle," *Washington Post*, September 26, 1967, A3; *The Cigarette Controversy*, [pamphlet]; Dell and Snyder, "Marijuana," 630–35; Koop, *The Health Consequences of Smoking*, i–iii.

19. In 2011 Anderson and two associates did publish "The General Aggression Model: Theoretical Extensions to Violence," the key word being "theoretical." The article contained no data. See DeWall, Anderson, and Bushman, "The General Aggression Model."

20. Barry, Hiilamo, and Glantz, "Waiting for the Opportune Moment," 207–42.

21. Hanchi et al., "Impairment of Antimicrobial Activity," 700-704; Bluhm, Daniels, Pollock, and Olshan, "Maternal Use of Recreational Drugs," 663-69.

22. "National Health Interview Survey," Centers for Disease Control, www.cdc.gov/nchs/nhis.htm.

23. *Smoking and Health: Surgeon General*, A-9; *Smoking and Health: Advisory Committee*, 25.

24. Shew, *Tobacco Diseases*, 2-3.

25. Faye Marley, "Tobacco—Health Issue," *Science News-Letter*, December 14, 1963, 373; *United States Census of Manufactures*, 2:21A-5.

26. While the tobacco industry could not snuff out the views of those scientists they were unable to employ, it could flick most of their publishing butts out of the country. Bearing in mind that correlation does not prove causation, it remains startling that, among the 322 English-language research articles that included both the words "tobacco" and "cancer" and appeared in scholarly journals in the years 1950 through 1963, all but 47 were published in British or Canadian publications. While not exactly the proverbial place where the sun don't shine, the industry nevertheless couldn't reach the place where tobacco don't grow.

27. "S.C. Leaf Men See Little Effect," *Florence (SC) Morning News*, January 12, 1964, 1.

28. Gilpin and Pierce, "Trends in Adolescent Smoking," 122-27; Pollay and Lavack, "The Targeting of Youth," 266-71; "News of the Week," *Freeman* (Indianapolis IN), January 25, 1890, 2.

29. Teel, Teel, and Bearden, "Lessons Learned," 45-50.

30. The prohibition contingent also succeeded in getting Congress to pass a law in 2009 banning the sale of candy-flavored cigarettes, another effort by the tobacco industry to lure kids in. This success, however, reflected failure. To whatever extent that the ban succeeded in preventing kids from smoking, it revealed the extent to which laws banning the sale of cigarettes to kids were ineffective.

31. See "Victim of Cancer Sues Tobacco Co.," *Washington Post*, October 31, 1954, M3; "Cancer Tied to Tobacco in Lawsuit," *Washington Post*, March 23, 1958, B7; Teel, Teel, and Bearden, "Lessons Learned," 46; Banzhaf et al. v. Federal Communications Commission et al., 405 F.2d 1082, United States Court of Appeals District of Columbia Circuit (1968).

32. Dank et al., *Estimating the Size and Structure*, 219.

33. See "Morals Court Called Vicious by War Board," *Chicago Tribune*, January 6, 1919, 7; "Police Padlock 27 Saloons," *New York Times*, January 9, 1924, 4; "Referee Assails Vice Case Lawyers," *New York Times*, July 22, 1931, 17.

34. See McMurdy, "The Use of the Injunction," 513–17; Hass, "Sin in Wisconsin," 138–51; *Repression of Prostitution in the District of Columbia—Hearings before the Committee on the District of Columbia, United States Senate*, 77th Cong., 1st sess. (Washington DC: Government Printing Office, 1921).

35. "Propose Science to Suppress Vice," *Chicago Tribune*, June 5, 1914, 3; Treadway, "Psychiatric Studies of Delinquents," 1575–92.

36. Davis, "The Sociology of Prostitution," 746, 749.

37. Davis, "The Sociology of Prostitution," 747.

38. Jenness, "From Sex as Sin to Sex as Work," 403; Kalishman, "Prostitution," 4; Weitzer, "Prostitutes' Rights in the United States," 23–41; "Judge Calls Prostitution Law Invalid," *Washington Post*, November 4, 1972, B5; "D.C. Reduced Punishment for Pot—Could Prostitution Come Next?," *Washington Post*, August 12, 2015, https://www.washingtonpost.com/local/first-pot-now -prostitution-a-new-decriminalization-front-opens-in-dc/2015/08/12 /58d861de-4134-11e5-846d-02792f854297_story.html.

39. See Lewis, *The Biology of Desire*.

40. Maule, *She Strives to Conquer*, 159; Sangree, "Title VII Prohibitions," 461–561; "Finding Meager Help in a Sex-Complaint System," *New York Times*, November 27, 1992, D18.

41. Pearl Lemon, "Wife Slavery," *Maine Farmer*, July 2, 1885, 1.

42. Lawson, *Rights, Remedies, and Practice*, 2:1311n5. Among the films with spanking of women were *The Naughty Flirt* (1931); *Flying Down to Rio* (1933); *The Meanest Gal in Town* (1934); *Taming the Wild* (1936); *Bunker Bean* (1936); *The Footloose Heiress* (1937); *Love, Honor and Behave* (1938); *Stronger than Desire* (1939); *Our Wife* (1941); *The Thin Man Goes Home* (1944); *Frontier Gal* (1945); *She Wrote the Book* (1946); *Beauty and the Bandit* (1946); *June Bride* (1948); *Rustlers* (1949); *Stagecoach Kid* (1949); *Look for the Silver Lining* (1949); *On Moonlight Bay* (1951); *Kiss Me Kate* (1953); *Captain Lightfoot* (1955); *Holiday for Lovers* (1959); *Blue Hawaii* (1961); *The Steel Claw* (1961); *Mclintock* (1963); *Donovan's Reef* (1963); "Ricky Loses His Temper," *I Love Lucy*, season 3, episode 19 (Desilu Productions, CBS), broadcast February 22, 1954.

43. "Wife Beating: Major Social Ill?," *Beckley (WV) Post-Herald*, July 21, 1975, 5.

44. "Protection from Abuse Act" described in "Lobbyists Face State Guidelines," *New Castle (DE) News*, October 8, 1976, 1; "It Hurts at Home," *Sandusky (OH) Register*, May 30, 1981, A1, A3. For shortcomings of assault laws, see Fields, "Does This Vow Include Wife Beating?," 40–45, 55–56.

45. Joan Arehart-Treichel, "America's Teen Pregnancy Epidemic," *Science News*, May 6, 1978. For data indicating there was no "epidemic," see Males, "Adult Liaison," 525–45.

46. Bickel, Weaver, Williams, and Lange, "Opportunity, Community, and Teen Pregnancy," 75–181.

47. Vincent and Dod, "Community and School," 191–97.

48. Barbara Goldberg, principal consultant, Barbara Goldberg & Associates, interview with the author, April 6, 2015.

49. Goldberg et al., "Successful Community Engagement," 65–86. See also *Best Practices for Community Engagement*; and Clay et al., "Building Relationships," 274–302.

50. Stephen L. Pevar, Dana L. Hanna, and Robert Doody, attorneys for plaintiffs, Oglala Sioux Tribe and Rosebud Sioux Tribe v. Luann Van Hunnik, Mark Vargo, Hon. Jeff Davis, and Kim Malsam-Rysdon, United States District Court for the District of South Dakota, Class Action Complaint for Declaratory and Injunctive Relief, Case 5:13-cv-05020-JLV, Document 69, filed January 28, 2014.

51. Laura Sullivan and Amy Walters, "Incentives and Cultural Bias Fuel Foster System," National Public Radio, air date October 25, 2011, http://www.npr .org/2011/10/25/141662357/incentives-and-cultural-bias-fuel-foster -system (accessed April 1, 2015).

Bibliography

Abbink, Jon G. "Violence, Ritual, and Reproduction: Culture and Context in Surma Dueling." *Ethnology* 38, no. 3 (Summer 1999): 227–42.

Acts and Laws of the State of Connecticut. Hartford: Hudson and Goodwin, 1805.

The Acts of the Assembly of the Province of Pennsylvania. Philadelphia: Hall and Sellers, 1775.

Advisory Commission on Intergovernmental Relations. *State-Federal Overlapping in Cigarette Taxes*. Washington DC: By the Commission, 1964. www .library.unt.edu/gpo.

Alac, Frank. *Bikini Story*. New York: Parkstone Press, 2013.

Alexander, Michelle. *The New Jim Crow: Mass Incarceration in the Age of Colorblindness*. Rev. ed. New York: New Press, 2012.

——. "The War on Drugs and the New Jim Crow." *Race, Poverty, and the Environment* 17 (2010): 75–77.

Allestreet, Richard. *The Whole Duty of Man*. London: R. Norton, 1716. Reprint, Williamsburg VA: W. Parks, 1747.

American State Papers: Documents—Legislative and Executive of the Congress of the United States from the First Session of the Fourteenth to the Second Session of the Nineteenth Congress, Inclusive. Washington DC: Gales and Seaton, 1834.

Anderson, Craig A. "The Unintended Negative Consequence of Exposure to Violent Video Games." *Cognitive Technology* 12, no. 1 (Spring 2007): 3–13.

Anderson, Craig A., and Catherine M. Ford. "Affect of the Game Player: Short-Term Effects of Highly and Mildly Aggressive Video Games." *Personality and Social Psychology Bulletin* 12, no. 4 (December 1986): 390–402.

Anderson, Daniel R., et al. "Early Childhood Television Viewing and Adolescent Behavior: The Recontact Study." *Monographs of the Society for Research in Child Development* 66, no. 1 (2001): i–viii, 1–154.

Anderson, Jack. "The Right to a Fair Fight: Sporting Lessons on Consensual Harm." *New Criminal Law Review* 17, no. 1 (Winter 2014): 55–75.

Arbor, Edward. "On the Introduction and Early Use of Tobacco in England." *English Reprints* 5, no. 19 (December 10, 1869).

Bailey, Abigail Abbot. *Religion and Domestic Violence in Early New England: The Memoirs of Abigail Abbot Bailey*. Edited by Ann Taves. Bloomington: Indiana University Press, 1989.

Balio, Tino. *Grand Design: Hollywood as a Modern Business Enterprise, 1930–1939*. Berkeley: University of California Press, 1995.

Barry, Rachel Ann, Heikki Hiilamo, and Stanton A. Glantz. "Waiting for the Opportune Moment: The Tobacco Industry and Marijuana Legalization." *Milbank Quarterly* 92, no. 2 (2014): 207–42.

Bates, Anna Louise. *Weeder in the Garden of the Lord: Anthony Comstock's Life and Career*. Lanham MD: University Press of America, 1995.

Baumgarten, Nikola. "Margaret Sanger." In *Reader's Guide to American History*, edited by Peter Parish. Chicago: Fitzroy Dearborn Publishers, 1997.

Beauchamp, Dan E. "Morality and the Health of the Body Politic." *Hastings Center Report* 16, no. 6 (December 1986): 30–36.

Beaver, Alyssa L. "Getting a Fix on Cocaine Sentencing Policy: Reforming the Sentencing Scheme of the Anti–Drug Abuse Act of 1986." *Fordham Law Review* 78, no. 5 (April 2010): 2531–75.

Belton, John, ed. *Movies and Mass Culture*. New Brunswick NJ: Rutgers University Press.

Bennett, A. Hughes. "Hygiene in the Higher Education of Women." *Popular Science* 16 (February 1880).

Bernard, Joel. "Between Religion and Reform: American Moral Societies, 1811–1821." *Proceedings of the Massachusetts Historical Society*, 3rd ser., 105 (1993): 1–38.

Best, Joel. "Economic Interests and the Vindication of Deviance: Tobacco in Seventeenth-Century Europe." *Sociological Quarterly* 20 (Spring 1979): 171–82.

Best Practices for Community Engagement: Tip Sheet. Washington DC: Office of Adolescent Health, U.S. Department of Health and Human Service, 2011.

Bettelheim, Bruno. "Review of *Seduction of the Innocent*." *Library Quarterly* 25, no. 1 (January 1955): 129–30.

———. *The Uses of Enchantment: The Meaning and Importance of Fairy Tales*. New York: Vintage Books, 1976.

Bickel, Robert, Susan Weaver, Tony Williams, and Linda Lange. "Opportunity, Community, and Teen Pregnancy in an Appalachian State." *Journal of Educational Research* 90, no. 3 (January–February 1997): 75–181.

Black, Gregory D. "Hollywood Censored: The Production Code Administration and the Hollywood Film Industry." *Film History* 3, no. 3 (1989): 167–89.

Bluhm, Elizabeth C., Julie Daniels, Brad H. Pollock, and Andrew F. Olshan. "Maternal Use of Recreational Drugs and Neuroblastoma in Offspring: A Report from the Children's Oncology Group." *Cancer Causes & Control* 17, no. 5 (June 2006): 663–69.

Bofman, William. *A New and Accurate Description of the Coast of Guinea*. London: James Knapton, 1705.

The Book of the General Lauues and Libertyes Concerning the Inhabitants of the Massachusetts. Cambridge MA: Printed according to order of the General Court, 1660.

Booth, Martin. *The Doctor and the Detective: A Biography of Sir Arthur Conan Doyle*. New York: Thomas Dunne Books, 2000.

Borell, Merrily. "Biologists and the Promotion of Birth Control Research, 1918–1938." *Journal of the History of Biology* 20, no. 1 (Spring 1987): 51–87.

Bowers, Edwin F., MD. "Why Not Government Hospitals for the Treatment of Drug, Alcohol, and Nicotine Addiction?" *Medical Summary* 41, no. 3 (May 1919).

Bowling, Benjamin. "The Rise and Fall of New York Murder: Zero Tolerance or Crack's Decline?" *British Journal of Criminology* 39, no. 4 (1999): 531–54.

Bradford, William. *History of Plymouth Plantation, 1620–1647*. 1856. Reprint, Boston: Massachusetts Historical Society, 1912.

Bragdon, Kathleen Joan. "Crime and Punishment among the Indians of Massachusetts, 1675–1750." *Ethnohistory* 28, no. 1 (Winter 1981): 23–32.

Brickhouse, Thomas. "Does Aristotle Have a Consistent Account of Vice?" *Review of Metaphysics* 57, no. 1 (September 2003): 3–23.

Brown, L. Ames. "Suffrage and Prohibition." *North American Review* 203, no. 722 (January 1916): 93–100.

Browne, Irving. "The Lawyer's Easy Chair." *Green Bag, an Entertaining Magazine for Lawyers* 9, no. 68 (1897).

Brownson, Orestes. "The Laboring Classes." *Boston Quarterly Review* 3, no. 12 (July 1840): 358–95.

Broyles, William. "Behind the Lines." *Texas Monthly* 3, no. 4 (April 1975).

Bullard, F. Lauriston. "Abraham Lincoln and the Statehood of Nevada." *American Bar Association Journal* 26, no. 3 (March 1940).

Bureau of the Census. *Prisoners and Juvenile Delinquents in the United States, 1910*. Washington DC: Government Printing Office, 1918.

Burnap, George W. *Lectures to Young Men on the Cultivation of the Mind, the Formation of Character, and the Conduct of Life*. Baltimore: John Murphy, 1840.

Burns, Eric. *The Smoke of the God: A Social History of Tobacco*. Philadelphia: Temple University Press, 2007.

Burns, Richard. *The History of the Poor Laws: With Observations*. London: A. Millar, 1764.

Callender, Charles, et al. "The North American Berdache" [and comments and reply]. *Current Anthropology* 24, no. 4 (August–October 1983): 443–70.

Capp, Charles S. *The Church and Chinese Immigration*. San Francisco: Self-published, 1890.

Carnagey, Nicholas L., and Craig A. Anderson. "The Effects of Reward and Punishment in Violent Video Games on Aggressive Affect, Cognition, and Behavior." *Psychological Science* 16, no. 11 (November 2005): 882–89.

Cary, Virginia. *Letters on Female Character Addressed to a Young Lady*. Richmond VA: Ariel Works, 1830.

Charles, Douglas M. "From Subversion to Obscenity: The FBI's Investigations of the Early Homophile Movement in the United States, 1953–1958." *Journal of the History of Sexuality* 19, no. 2 (May 2010): 262–87.

Charlton, Anne. "Tobacco or Health 1602: An Elizabethan Doctor Speaks." *Health Education Research* 20, no. 1 (2005): 101–11.

The Charter Granted by their Majesties King William and Queen Mary. Boston: S. Kneeland, 1759.

Chester, John. *Knowledge and Holiness, the Sources of Morality*. Sermon delivered before the Albany Moral Society, October 5, 1821. Albany: E. and E. Hosford, 1821.

Chief Red Fox. *The Memoirs of Chief Red Fox*. New York: McGraw-Hill, 1971.

"Children Who Are Their Brothers' Keepers: The Little Mothers' Association of New York City." *Kindergarten Magazine* 8, no. 10 (June 1896): 716–21.

Cicero, Theodore J., et al. "The Changing Face of Heroin Use in the United States." *JAMA Psychiatry* 71, no. 7 (2014): 821–26.

The Cigarette Controversy. Washington DC: Tobacco Institute, 1971.

Clay, Joy A., et al. "Building Relationships to Strategically Impact Community Initiatives to Reduce Teen Pregnancy." *Journal of Health and Human Services Administration* 35, no. 3 (Winter 2012): 274–302.

Clemmer, Richard O. "'A Carnival of Promiscuous Carnal Indulgence': Bureaucrats' Ambivalence in Reconciling Capitalist Production with Native American 'Habitus.'" *Dialectical Anthropology* 33, no. 1 (March 2009).

Cockburn, Alexander, and Jeffrey St. Clair. *Whiteout: The CIA, Drugs, and the Press*. New York: Verso, 1998.

Collins, Joseph. "Sex in Literature." *Bookman* 59, no. 2 (April 1924): 129–33.

Collins, Wilkie. *The Moonstone*. New York: Harper & Brothers, 1868.

The Compiled Laws of Nevada in Force from 1861 to 1900. Carson City NV: Andrew Maute, Supt. of State Printing, 1900.

Conant, Charles A. *Alexander Hamilton*. Boston: Houghton, Mifflin and Company, 1901.

The Consolidated Laws of New York, Annotated. New York: Edward Thompson Co., 1916.

Cotton, John. *Abstract of the Lawes of New England*. London: W. Ley, 1641.

Courtwright, David T. "The Hidden Epidemic: Opiate Addiction and Cocaine Use in the South, 1860–1920." *Journal of Southern History* 49, no. 1 (February 1983): 57–72.

Couvares, Francis G., ed. *Movie Censorship and American Culture.* 2nd ed. Amherst: University of Massachusetts Press, 2006.

Craig, John M. "'The Sex Side of Life': The Obscenity Case of Mary Ware Dennett." *Frontiers: A Journal of Women Studies* 15, no. 3 (1995): 145–66.

Crothers, T. D. [Thomas Davison]. *Morphinism and Narcomanias from Other Drugs.* Philadelphia: W. B. Saunders, 1902.

Cunningham, T. [Timothy]. *A New and Complete Law-Dictionary.* London: Law Printers to the King, 1765.

Cutler, Sidney J. "A Review of the Statistical Evidence on the Association between Smoking and Lung Cancer." *Journal of the American Statistical Association* 50, no. 270 (June 1955): 267–82.

Dailey, R. C. "The Role of Alcohol among North American Indian Tribes as Reported in the Jesuit Relations." *Anthropologica*, n.s., 10, no. 1 (1968).

Dandridge, Ray G. "Zalka Peetruza." In *The Book of American Negro Poetry*, edited by James Weldon Johnson. New York: Harcourt, Brace and Co., 1922.

Dank, Meredith, et al. *Estimating the Size and Structure of the Underground Commercial Sex Economy in the Eight Major U.S. Cities.* Washington DC: Urban Institute, 2014.

Davis, Kingsley. "The Sociology of Prostitution." *American Sociological Review* 2, no. 5 (October 1937).

Dean, Robert D. *Imperial Brotherhood: Gender and the Making of Cold War Foreign Policy.* Amherst: University of Massachusetts Press, 2001.

DeBruyne, Nese F., and Anne Leland. "American War and Military Operations Casualties: Lists and Statistics." Washington DC: Congressional Research Service, January 2, 2015.

De Cunzo, Lu Ann. "Reform, Respite, Ritual: An Archaeology of Institutions; the Magdalen Society of Philadelphia, 1800–1850." *Historical Archaeology* 29, no. 3 (1995): 1–168.

Dell, Deena D., and Judith A. Snyder. "Marijuana: Pro and Con." *American Journal of Nursing* 77, no. 4 (April 1977): 630–35.

D'Emilio, John, and Estelle B. Freedman. *Intimate Matters: A History of Sexuality in America.* 2nd ed. Chicago: University of Chicago Press, 1988.

DeMontravel, Peter R. "General Nelson A. Miles and the Wounded Knee Controversy." *Arizona and the West* 28, no. 1 (Spring 1986): 23–44.

DeWall, C. Nathan, Craig A. Anderson, and Brad J. Bushman. "The General Aggression Model: Theoretical Extensions to Violence." *Psychology of Violence* 1, no. 3 (2011): 245–58.

Dow, Neal, and Dio Lewis. "Prohibition and Persuasion." *North American Review* 139, no. 333 (August 1884): 179–98.

Du Bois, W. E. B. "Review of *Race Traits and Tendencies of the American Negro.*" *Annals of the American Academy of Political and Social Science* 9, no. 1 (January 1897): 127–33.

———. *The Souls of Black Folk.* Chicago: A. C. McClurg & Co., 1903.

———. "The Superior Race." *Smart Set* 70, no. 4 (April 1923): 55–60.

Duesenberg, Richard W. "Crime Comic Books: Government Control and Their Impact on Juvenile Conduct." *Mercer Law Review* 7 (1956): 331–51.

Elliot, Russell R., with the assistance of William D. Rowley. *History of Nevada.* 2nd ed. Lincoln: University of Nebraska Press, 1897.

Ellis, Clyde. "'There is No Doubt . . . the Dances Should Be Curtailed': Indian Dances and Federal Policy on the Southern Plains, 1880–1930." *Pacific Historical Review* 70, no. 4 (November 2001): 543–69.

"The Emancipation of Woman." *Herald of Health* 1, no. 2 (February 1866).

Erens, Patricia. *The Jew in American Cinema.* Bloomington: Indiana University Press, 1984.

Eskridge, William. *Gaylaw: Challenging the Apartheid of the Closet.* Cambridge MA: Harvard University Press, 1997.

Evarts, Jeremiah [under pseud. William Penn]. *Essays on the Present Crisis in the Condition of the American Indians.* Boston: Perkins & Marvin, 1829.

Ezell, John. "The Lottery in Colonial America." *William and Mary Quarterly*, 3rd ser., 5, no. 2 (April 1948): 185–200.

Ezell, John S. "When Massachusetts Played the Lottery." *New England Quarterly* 22, no. 3 (September 1949): 316–35.

Falk, Cynthia G. "Forts, Rum, Slaves, and the Herkimers' Rise to Power in the Mohawk Valley." *New York History* 89, no. 3 (Summer 2008).

Faroqhi, Suraiya. *Subjects of the Sultan: Culture and Daily Life in the Ottoman Empire.* Munich: C. H. Beck, 1995. Reprint, London: I. B. Tauris, 2007.

Felt, Joseph B. "Collections Relating to Fashions and Dress in New England." *Supplement to the Connecticut Courant.* Hartford: John L. Boswell, 1838.

Fields, Margery. "Does This Vow Include Wife Beating?" *Human Rights* 7, no. 2 (Summer 1978).

Flaherty, Donald. "Law and the Enforcement of Morals in Early America." In *Perspectives in American History*, vol. 5, edited by Donald Fleming and Bernard Bailyn. Cambridge MA: Harvard University, Charles Warren Center for Studies in American History, 1971.

Foote, Edward B., MD. *Plain Home Talk: Medical Common Sense.* New York: Wells and Coffin, 1870.

Forgey, Donald G. "The Institution of Berdache among the North American Plains Indians." *Journal of Sex Research* 11, no. 1 (February 1975): 1–15.

Ford, Worthington Chauncey. "Mather-Calef Paper on Witchcraft." In *Proceedings of the Massachusetts Historical Society*. Boston: By the Society, 1914.

Fordyce, James. *Sermons to Young Women*. 2 vols. 1766. Reprint, London: Cadwell and Davies, 1814.

Foster, Gaines M. "Conservative Social Christianity, the Law, and Personal Morality: Wilbur F. Crafts in Washington." *Church History* 71, no. 4 (December 2002): 799–819.

Foster, Thomas A. "Deficient Husbands: Manhood, Sexual Incapacity, and Male Marital Sexuality in Seventeenth-Century New England." *William and Mary Quarterly*, 3rd ser., 56, no. 4 (October 1999).

Fowler, Orson, and Lorenzo Fowler. *Phrenology: Proved, Illustrated, and Applied*. New York: W. H. Coyler, 1836.

Freeman, Joanne B. "Dueling as Politics: Reinterpreting the Burr-Hamilton Duel." *William and Mary Quarterly* 53, no. 2 (April 1996): 289–318.

Friedman, Andrea. "'The Habits of Sex-Crazed Perverts': Campaigns against Burlesque in Depression-Era New York City." *Journal of the History of Sexuality* 7, no. 2 (October 1996): 203–38.

Gardner, Gerald. *The Censorship Papers: Movie Censorship Letters from the Hays Office, 1934 to 1968*. New York: Dodd, Mead & Co., 1987.

Garvey, Stephen P. "Can Shaming Punishments Educate?" *University of Chicago Law Review* 65, no. 3 (Summer 1998): 733–94.

Gaskins, Richard. "Changes in the Criminal Law in Eighteenth-Century Connecticut." *American Journal of Legal History* 25, no. 4 (October 1981): 309–42.

Gaudet, Frederick J., George S. Harris, and Charles W. St. John. "Individual Differences in Sentencing Tendencies of Judges." *Journal of Criminal Law and Criminology* 23, no. 5 (January–February 1933): 811–18.

The General Laws and Liberties of New Plimoth Colony. Plymouth: General Court, 1671.

Gertzman, Jay A. *Bookleggers and Smuthounds: The Trade in Erotica, 1920–1940*. Philadelphia: University of Pennsylvania Press, 1999.

Gilfoyle, Timothy J. "Strumpets and Misogynists: Brothel 'Riots' and the Transformation of Prostitution in Antebellum New York City." *New York History* 68, no. 1 (January 1987): 44–65.

Gillingham, Harrold E. "Lotteries in Philadelphia prior to 1776." *Pennsylvania History* 5, no. 2 (April 1938): 77–100.

Gilmore, J. M. "Does Prohibition Prohibit?" *North American Review* 201, no. 712 (March 1915): 463–65.

Gilpin, Elizabeth A., and John P. Pierce. "Trends in Adolescent Smoking Initiation in the United States: Is Tobacco Marketing an Influence?" *Tobacco Control* 6, no. 2 (Summer 1997): 122-27.

Glanvil, Joesph. *Saddicismus Triumphatus: Or, A Full and Plain Evidence Concerning Witches and Apparitions*. 1681. Reprint, London: Bettesworth and J. Barley, 1726.

Goldberg, Barbara, et al. "Successful Community Engagement: Laying the Foundation for Effective Teen Pregnancy Prevention." *Journal of Children and Poverty* 17, no. 1 (March 2011): 65-86.

Goodman, Leon. "Blue Laws, Old and New." *Virginia Law Register*, n.s., 12, no. 11 (March 1927): 663-73.

Gouge, William. *Of Domesticall Duties: Eight Treatises*. 1622. Reprint, Norwood NJ: W. J. Johnson, 1976.

Gould, Josiah. *A Digest of the Statutes of Arkansas*. Little Rock: Johnson and Yerkes, State Printers, 1858.

Graham-White, Anthony. "Ritual and Drama in Africa." *Educational Theatre Journal* 22, no. 4 (December 1970): 339-49.

Grayson, P. W. *Vice Unmasked*. New York: G. H. Evans, 1830.

Greenberg, Douglas. *Crime and Law Enforcement in the Colony of New York, 1691-1776*. Ithaca NY: Cornell University Press, 1974.

Hamid, Ansley. "The Development Cycle of a Drug Epidemic: The Cocaine Smoking Epidemic of 1981-1991." *Journal of Psychoactive Drugs* 24, no. 4 (October 1992): 337-48.

Hamilton, Alexander. *The Works of Alexander Hamilton*. Edited by John C. Hamilton. New York: John F. Trow, 1850.

Hammond, M. B. [Matthew B.] "The Cotton Industry: An Essay in American Economic History, Part 1." *Publications of the American Economic Association* 1 (December 1897): 3-382.

Hanchi, Angela, et al. "Impairment of Antimicrobial Activity and Nitric Oxide Production in Alveolar Macrophages for Smokers of Marijuana and Cocaine." *Journal of Infectious Diseases* 187, no. 4 (February 15, 2003): 700-704.

Harrington, John S. "The Evolution of Obscenity Control Statutes." *William & Mary Law Review* 3, no. 2 (1962): 302-10.

Harris, Albert W., Jr. "Movie Censorship and the Supreme Court: What Next." *California Law Review* 42, no. 1 (March 1954): 122-38.

Hart, H. L. A. "Social Solidarity and the Enforcement of Morality." *University of Chicago Law Review* 35, no. 1 (Autumn 1967): 1-13.

Hass, Paul H. "Sin in Wisconsin: The Teasdale Committee of 1913." *Wisconsin Magazine of History* 49, no. 2 (Winter 1965-66): 138-51.

Hauptman, Laurence M., and Richard G. Knapp. "Dutch-Aboriginal Interaction in New Netherlands and Formosa: An Historical Geography of Empire." *Proceedings of the American Philosophical Society* 121, no. 2 (April 29, 1977).

Hauser, Raymond E. "The Berdache and the Illinois Indian Tribe during the Last Half of the Seventeenth Century." *Ethnohistory* 37, no. 1 (Winter 1990): 45–65.

Hawthorne, Nathaniel. *The Works of Nathaniel Hawthorne.* Boston: Houghton, Osgood and Company, 1879.

Hays, George Edmund, PhD. *The Trend of the Races.* New York: Council of Women for Home Missions and Missionary Education Movement of the United States and Canada, 1922.

Heath, William. "Thomas Morton: From Merry Old England to New England." *Journal of American Studies* 41, no. 1 (April 2007): 135–68.

Henning, Alexandra, et al. "Do Stereotypic Images in Video Games Affect Attitudes and Adolescent Perspectives?" *Children, Youth and Environments* 19, no. 1 (2009): 170–96.

Hentz, Caroline Lee. *The Planter's Northern Bride.* Philadelphia: A. Hart, 1854.

Herzog, Alfred W. "Homosexuality and the Law." *Medico-Legal Journal* 34, nos. 5–6 (August–September 1917).

Hobbs, A. H. "Criminality in Philadelphia." *American Sociological Review* 8, no. 2 (April 1943): 198–202.

Hodges, Graham Russell Gao. *Anna May Wong: From Laundryman's Daughter to Hollywood Legend.* 2nd ed. Hong Kong: Hong Kong University Press, 2012.

Hoffman, Frederick L. *Race Traits and Tendencies of the American Negro.* New York: Macmillan, 1896.

Holmes, Malcolm D., and Judith A. Antell. "The Social Construction of American Drinking: Perceptions of American Indian and White Officials." *Sociological Quarterly* 42, no. 2 (Spring 2001): 151–73.

Hoffmann, Frank, and William G. Bailey. *Sports & Recreation Fads.* New York: Haworth Press, 1991.

Horowitz, Helen Lefkowitz. "Victoria Woodhull, Anthony Comstock, and the Conflict over Sex in the United States in the 1870s." *Journal of American History* 87, no. 2 (September 2009): 403–34.

Hoskins, John A. "Delinquency, Comic Books, and the Law." *Ohio State Law Journal* 18, no. 4 (August 1947): 512–37.

Howe, Daniel Wait. *The Puritan Republic of Massachusetts Bay.* Indianapolis: Bowen-Merrill Company, 1879.

Hughes, Langston. *The Collected Works of Langston Hughes.* Columbia: University of Missouri Press, 2001.

Hunter, Charles E. "The Delaware Nativist Revival of the Mid-Eighteenth Century." *Ethnohistory* 18, no. 1 (Winter 1971): 39–49.

Hutchinson, Thomas. *History of the Colony of Massachuset's [sic] Bay.* 2nd ed. London: M. Richardson, 1765.

Hwang, Jessica. "From Spectacle to Speech: The First Amendment and Film Censorship from 1915–1952." *Hastings Constitutional Law Quarterly* 42, no. 2 (Winter 2014): 381–420.

Hyles, Jack. *Sex Education in Our Public Schools: What Is Behind It?* Murfreesboro TN: Sword of the Lord Publishers, 1969.

Ishii, Izumi. "Alcohol and Politics in the Cherokee Nation before Removal." *Ethnohistory* 10, no. 4 (Fall 2003): 671–95.

James, Bartlett B., and J. Franklin Jameson, eds. *Journal of Jasper Danckaerts, 1679–1680.* New York: Barnes and Noble, 1913.

James I, King of England. *A Counter-Blaste to Tobacco.* 1604. Reprint, Edinburgh: E. & G. Goldsmid, 1885.

Jelliffe, Smith Ely. "Homosexuality and the Law." *Journal of the American Institute of Criminal Law and Criminology* 3, no. 1 (May 1912).

Jeffries, B. Joy, MD. "Leprosy of the Bible, and Its Present Existence in North America." In *Good Health.* Boston: Alexander Moore, 1871.

Jeffrey, Edith. "Reform, Renewal, and Vindication: Irish Immigrants and the Catholic Total Abstinence Movement in Antebellum Philadelphia." *Pennsylvania Magazine of History and Biography* 112, no. 3 (July 1988): 407–31.

Jenness, Valerie. "From Sex as Sin to Sex as Work: COYOTE and the Reorganization of Prostitution as a Society Problem." *Social Problems* 37, no. 3 (August 1990).

Johansen, Bruce Elliott, ed. *The Encyclopedia of Native American Legal Tradition.* Westport CT: Greenwood Press, 1988.

Joyce, James. *Ulysses.* New York: Vintage Books, 1986.

Kahn, Samuel. *Mentality and Homosexuality.* Boston: Meador Publishing Co., 1937.

Kalishman, Pam. "Prostitution." *Off Our Backs* 3, no. 5 (January 1973).

Karsten, Peter, ed. *Encyclopedia of War and American Society.* New York: MTM Publishing, 2006.

Kendrick, William. *Observations Civil and Canonical on the Marriage Contract.* London: S. Hooper, 1775.

Kennedy, William Holland. *Chicago Jazz: A Cultural History, 1904–1930.* New York: Oxford University Press, 1993.

Keverne, Eric B. "Understanding Well-Being in the Evolutionary Context of Brain Development." *Philosophical Transactions: Biological Sciences* 359, no. 1,449 (September 29, 2004): 1349–58.

Kinsey, Alfred C., et al. *Sexual Behavior in the Human Male*. Philadelphia: W. B. Saunders Co., 1948.

Kinshasa, Kwando Mbiassi. *The Man from Scottsboro: Clarence Norris and the Infamous 1931 Alabama Rape Trial*. Jefferson NC: McFarland & Co., 1997.

Koch, Gertrud. "The Body's Shadow Realm." Translated by Jan-Christopher Horak and Joyce Rheuban. *October* 50 (Autumn 1989): 3–29.

Kolb, Lawrence, and A. G. Du Mez. "The Prevalence and Trend of Drug Addiction in the United States and Factors Influencing It." *Public Health Reports* 39, no. 21 (May 23, 1924): 161–73.

Koop, C. Everett, MD. *The Health Consequences of Smoking—Nicotine Addiction: A Report of the Surgeon General*. Washington DC: Government Printing Office, 1988.

Kuhn, Deanna. "Do Cognitive Changes Accompany Developments in the Adolescent Brain?" *Perspectives on Psychological Science* 1, no. 1 (March 2006): 59–67.

Lachance, Paul F. "The Formation of a Three-Caste Society: Evidence from Wills in Antebellum New Orleans." *Social Science History* 18, no. 2 (Summer 1994): 211–42.

Lader, Lawrence. *The Margaret Sanger Story and the Fight for Birth Control*. Westport CT: Greenwood Press, 1975.

LaHood, Marvin I. "Huck Finn's Search for Identity." *Mark Twain Journal* 13, no. 3 (Winter 1966–67): 11–24.

Laidlaw, Robert W. "Marriage Counseling: A Clinical Approach to Homosexuality." *Marriage and Family Living* 14, no. 1 (February 1952): 39–46.

Laird, Pamela Walker. "Consuming Smoke: Cigarettes in American Culture." *Reviews in American History* 28, no. 1 (March 2000): 96–104.

Laws of the State of New York. 2nd ed. Albany: Webster and Skinner, 1807.

Lawson, John D. *Rights, Remedies, and Practice, at Law, in Equity, and under the Codes: A Treatise on American Law*. San Francisco: Bancroft-Whitney, 1889.

Lefever, Harry G. "'Playing the Dozens': A Mechanism for Social Control." *Phylon* 42, no. 1 (1981): 73–85.

Lenroot, Rhoshel K., and Jay N. Giedd. "Brain Development in Children and Adolescents: Insights from Anatomical Magnetic Resonance Imaging." *Neuroscience & Biobehavioral Reviews* 30, no. 6 (2006): 718–29.

Lewis, Marc. *The Biology of Desire: Why Addiction Is Not a Disease*. New York: Public Affairs Publishing, 2015.

Lewitus, Victor. "Marihuana." *American Journal of Nursing* 36, no. 7 (July 1936): 677–78.

Lockington, W. J. "Prohibition in the State of Maine." *Studies: An Irish Quarterly Review* 4, no. 14 (June 1915): 286–94.

Lofaro, Michael A. "The Many Lives of Daniel Boone." *Register of the Kentucky Historical Society* 102, no. 4 (Autumn 2004): 488–511.

Long, Carolyn Morrow. "Perceptions of New Orleans Voodoo: Sin, Fraud, Entertainment, and Religion." *Nova Religio: The Journal of Alternative and Emergent Religions* 6, no. 1 (October 2002): 86–101.

Long, Clarence D., ed. *Wages and Earning in the United States, 1860–1890.* Princeton NJ: Princeton University Press, 1960.

Lookingbill, Brad D. "The Killing Fields of Wounded Knee." *Reviews in American History* 33, no. 3 (September 2005): 379–86.

Lurie, Nancy Oestreich. "Winnebago Berdache." *American Anthropologist*, n.s., 55, no. 5, pt. 1 (December 1953): 708–12.

Lutz, Catherine, and Jane Collins. *Reading "National Geographic."* Chicago: University of Chicago Press, 1993.

MacDonald, William, ed. *Documentary Source Book of American History, 1606–1913.* New York: Macmillan, 1920.

Major, Minor Wallace. "William Bradford versus Thomas Morton." *Early American Literature* 5, no. 2 (Fall 1970): 1–13.

Malcolm, Elizabeth. "The Catholic Church and the Irish Temperance Movement, 1838–1901." *Irish Historical Studies* 23, no. 89 (January 1982): 1–16.

Malcolm, John G. "The Case for the Smarter Sentencing Act." *Federal Sentencing Reporter* 26, no. 5 (June 2014): 298–301.

Males, Mike. "Adult Liaison in the 'Epidemic' of 'Teenage' Birth, Pregnancy, and Venereal Disease." *Journal of Sex Research* 29, no. 4 (November 1992): 525–45.

———. "Schools, Society, and 'Teen' Pregnancy." *Phi Delta Kappan* 74, no. 7 (March 1993): 566–68.

Mather, Cotton. *Diary of Cotton Mather, 1709–1724.* 7th series. Boston: Massachusetts Historical Society, 1912.

———. *Magnalia Christi Americana.* 1702. Reprint, Hartford: Silas Andrus & Son, 1853.

Mather, Increase [uncredited]. *An Arrow against Profane and Promiscuous Dancing.* Boston: Samuel Green, 1684.

Maule, Frances. *She Strives to Conquer: Business Behavior, Opportunities and Job Requirements for Women.* New York: Funk & Wagnalls, 1935.

May, Philip A. "Explanations of Native American Drinking: A Literature Review." *Plains Anthropologist* 22, no. 77 (August 1977): 223–32.

McDowell, J. R. [John Robert]. *Magdalen Facts.* New York: Printed for the author, 1832.

McKay, C. L. "Alcoholic Drink and the Immigrant." *Scientific Temperance Journal* 24, no. 9 (June 1915).

McKay, Claude. "The Harlem Dancer." In *The Book of American Negro Poetry*, edited by James Weldon Johnson. New York: Harcourt, Brace and Co., 1922.

McManus, Edgar J. *Law and Liberty in Early New England: Criminal Justice and Due Process, 1620–1692*. Amherst: University of Massachusetts Press, 1933.

McMurdy, Robert. "The Use of the Injunction to Destroy Commercialized Prostitution." *Journal of the American Institute of Criminal Law and Criminology* 19, no. 4 (February 1929): 513–17.

McNamara, Joseph. "The History of United States Anti-opium Policy." *Federal Probation* 37, no. 15 (1973): 15–21.

Meier, Kenneth J. "The Politics of Drug Abuse: Laws, Implementation, and Consequences." *Western Political Quarterly* 45, no. 1 (March 1992): 41–69.

Meierhoefer, B. *The General Effect of Mandatory Minimum Prison Terms: A Longitudinal Study of Federal Sentences Imposed*. Washington DC: Federal Judicial Center, 1992.

"The Methodist Church in New Orleans." In *A General Digest of the Acts of the Legislature of Louisiana: Passed from the Year 1804 to 1827 Inclusive*. New Orleans: Benjamin Levy, 1828.

Miller, Robert J., and Maril Hazlett. "The 'Drunken Indian': Myth Distilled into Reality through Federal Indian Alcohol Policy." *Arizona State Law Journal* 28 (1996): 223–98.

Million, Elmer M. "Enforceability of Prize Fight Statutes." *Kentucky Law Journal* 27, no. 2 (January 1939): 152–68.

Millward, Jessica. "'The Relics of Slavery': Interracial Sex and Manumission in the American South." *Frontiers: A Journal of Women Studies* 31, no. 3 (2010): 22–30.

Moberg, Dennis J. "On Employee Vice." *Business Ethics Quarterly* 7, no. 4 (October 1997): 41–60.

Mooney, James. *The Ghost Dance*. North Dighton MA: JG Press, 1996.

———. "The Ghost Dance Religion and the Sioux Outbreak of 1890." In *Fourteenth Annual Report of the Bureau of Ethnology to the Secretary of the Smithsonian Institution, 1892–93*. Washington DC: Government Printing Office, 1896.

Morawski, Stefan. "Art and Obscenity." *Journal of Aesthetics and Art Criticism* 26, no. 2 (Winter 1967): 193–207.

Morton, Thomas. *New English Canaan*. Amsterdam, Holland: Jacob Frederick Stam, 1637. Reprint, Boston: Prince Society, 1883.

Moyers, Bill D., and Wendy Beckett. *Sister Wendy in Conversation with Bill Moyers: The Complete Conversation*. Edited by Karen Johnson. Boston: WGBH Publications, 1987. https://www.youtube.com/watch?v=L9pAKdkJh-Y.

Munson, Gorham. "Our Post-War Novel." *Bookman* 74, no. 2 (October 1931).

Nation, Carry [*sic*]. *The Use and Need of the Life of Carry A. Nation.* Topeka: F. M. Steves & Sons, 1909.

Nelson, Richard Alan. "Propaganda for God: Pastor Charles Taze Russell and the Multi-media 'Photo-Drama of Creation' (1914)." In *Invention of the Devil? Religion and Early Cinema*, edited by Roland Cosandey, André Gaudreault, and Tom Gunning. Quebec: University of Laval Press, 1992.

Nevitt, Peter K. "The Legal Aspects of Nudism." *Journal of Criminal Law and Criminology* 41, no. 1 (May–June 1950): 57–61.

New Hampshire, Assembly of. *Acts and Laws Passed by the General Court or Assembly of His Majesty's Province of New-Hampshire in New-England.* Portsmouth: B. Green, 1716.

New Jersey, Province of. *Acts of the General Assembly of the Province of New-Jersey.* Philadelphia: William Bradford, 1736.

New York, Assembly of. *Laws of New-York from the Year 1691 to 1751, Inclusive.* New York: James Parker, 1752.

The New York Society for the Suppression of Vice: Thirty-Eighth Annual Report. New York: By the Society, 1912.

Nichols, Mary Gove. *Mary Lyndon.* New York: Stringer and Townsend, 1855. Reprint, Charleston SC: BiblioBazaar, 2009.

"1997 Statement on Powder and Crack Cocaine to the Senate and House Judiciary Committees." *Federal Sentencing Reporter* 10, no. 4 (January–February 1998): 194–95.

Noble, John. *Records of the Court of Assistants of the Colony of the Massachusetts Bay, 1630–1692.* Boston: County of Suffolk, 1904.

Noble, Marianne. *The Masochistic Pleasures of Sentimental Literature.* Princeton NJ: Princeton University Press, 2000.

Nott, Henry Junius, and David James M'Cord. *Cases Determined in the Constitutional Court of South Carolina.* Columbia SC: Daniel Faust, State Printer, 1821.

Olson, Keith. "The G.I. Bill and Higher Education: Success and Surprise." *American Quarterly* 25, no. 5 (December 1973): 596–610.

O'Reilly, John Boyle. *Ethics of Boxing and Manly Sport.* Boston: Ticknor and Co., 1888.

Oxford English Dictionary. 27th printing. Oxford: Oxford University Press, 1988.

Parmelee, Maurice. *Nudism in Modern Life: The New Gymnosophy.* New York: A. A. Knopf, 1931.

Pennsylvania, Governor and Assembly of. *Laws of the Province of Pennsylvania.* Philadelphia: Andrew Bradford, 1714.

Philips, John Edwards. "African Smoking and Pipes." *Journal of African History* 24, no. 3 (1983): 303–19.

Pickett, Deets, ed. *The Cyclopedia of Temperance, Prohibition, and Public Morals (1917 Edition)*. New York: Methodist Book Concern, 1917.

Platizky, Roger S. "'Like Dull Narcotics Numbing Pain': Speculations on Tennyson and Opium." *Victorian Poetry* 40, no. 2 (September 2002).

Pollay, Richard W., and Anne M. Lavack. "The Targeting of Youth by Cigarette Marketers: Archival Evidence on Trial." *Advances in Consumer Research* 20 (1993): 266–71.

"Potpourri." *Kindergarten* 1, no. 7 (November 1888).

Powers, Richard Gid. *Secrecy and Power: The Life of J. Edgar Hoover*. New York: Free Press, 1987.

Preyer, Kathryn. "Penal Measures in the American Colonies: An Overview." *American Journal of Legal History* 26, no. 4 (October 1982): 326–53.

Public Papers of the Presidents of the United States—Ronald Reagan: June 28 to December 31, 1986. Washington DC: Government Printing Office, 1982–91.

The Public Statute Laws of the State of Connecticut. Hartford: H. Huntington Jr., 1824.

"Purity and Pornography: A Doctor's Reflections on Sex and Obsession in Current Novels." *Current Opinion* 77 (July–December 1924).

Randolph, Thomas Jefferson, ed. *Memoirs, Correspondence, and Private Papers of Thomas Jefferson*. London: Henry Colburn and Richard Bentley, 1829.

Rausch, Andrew J. *Turning Points in Film History*. New York: Citadel Press, 2004.

Reasons, Charles. "The Politics of Drugs: An Inquiry in the Sociology of Social Problems." *Sociological Quarterly* 15, no. 3 (Summer 1974): 381–404.

"Records of the Company of the Massachusetts Bay." In *Transactions and Collections of the American Antiquarian Society*. Cambridge: By the Society, 1857.

Records of the Court of Assistants of the Colony of the Massachusetts Bay: 1630–1692, vol. 2. Boston: County of Suffolk, 1904.

"Records of the Suffolk County Court, 1671–1680." In *Publications of the Colonial Society of Massachusetts*, vols. 29–30, edited by Samuel E. Morrison. Boston: By the Society, 1933.

Remarks of the Hon. Stephen A. Douglas on Kansas, Utah, and the Dred Scott Decision. Chicago: Daily Times Books and Job Office, 1857.

"Report of the Secretary of the Interior." In *Message from the President of the United States to the Two Houses of Congress at the Commencement of the First Session of the Forty Eighth Congress*. Washington DC: Government Printing Office, 1883.

Roberts, Warren, and Paul Poplawski. *A Bibliography of D. H. Lawrence*. 3rd ed. New York: Cambridge University Press, 2001.

Rosenthal, Nicholas G. "Representing Indians: Native American Actors on Hollywood's Frontier." *Western Quarterly Review* 36, no. 3 (Autumn 2005): 328–52.

Sandburg, Carl. "Vaudeville Dancer." In *Smoke and Steel*. New York: Harcourt, Brace and Co., 1920.

Sanger, Margaret. *The Case for Birth Control*. New York: Modern Art Printing Co., 1917.

———. "National Security and Birth Control." *Forum and Century* 93, no. 3 (March 1935).

———. "The Woman Spirit and the Better Day." *Birth Control Review* 3, no. 3 (March 1919).

Sanger, William, MD. *The History of Prostitution: Its Extent, Causes, and Effects throughout the World*. New York: Harper and Brothers, 1858.

Sangree, Suzanne. "Title VII Prohibitions against Hostile Environment Sexual Harassment and the First Amendment: No Collision in Sight." *Rutgers Law Review* 47, no. 2 (Winter 1995): 461–561.

Sawyer, Jeffrey K. "'Benefit of Clergy' in Maryland and Virginia." *American Journal of Legal History* 34, no. 1 (January 1990).

Schnarch, Brian. "Neither Man nor Woman: Berdache—a Case for Non-dichotomous Gender Construction." *Anthropologica* 34, no. 1 (1992): 105–21.

Scott, Arthur P. *Criminal Law in Colonial Virginia*. Chicago: University of Chicago Press, 1930.

Shew, Joel, MD. *Tobacco Diseases with a Remedy for the Habit*. New York: Fowler and Wells, 1855.

Shoemaker, John V., MD. "The Abuse of Drugs." *Journal of the American Medical Association* 42, no. 5 (May 28, 1904): 1405–8.

Shurlock, Geoffrey. "The Motion Picture Code." *Annals of the American Academy of Political and Social Science* 254 (November 1947): 140–46.

Sigel, Lisa Z. "Name Your Pleasure: The Transformation of Sexual Language in Nineteenth-Century British Pornography." *Journal of the History of Sexuality* 9, no. 4 (October 2000): 395–419.

Singer, David. "Hawthorne and the 'Wild Irish': A Note." *New England Quarterly* 42, no. 3 (September 1969): 425–32.

Smith, Daniel Scott, and Michael S. Hindus. "Premarital Pregnancy in America 1640–1971: An Overview and Interpretation." In *Marriage and Fertility*, edited by Robert I. Rotberg and Theodore K. Rabb. Princeton NJ: Princeton University Press, 1980.

Smith, Jerome Van Crowninshield. *The Ways of Women in Their Physical, Moral and Intellectual Relations, by a Medical Man*. New York: J. P. Jewett & Co., 1873.

Smith, Lisa Herb. "'Some Perilous Stuff': What the Religious Reviewers Really Said about 'The Scarlet Letter.'" *American Periodicals* 6 (1966): 135–43.

Smoking and Health: A Report of the Surgeon General. Washington DC: U.S. Public Health Service, 1979.

Smoking and Health: Report of the Advisory Committee to the Surgeon General of the Public Health Service. Washington DC: U.S. Public Health Service, 1964.

Snow, Eliza Roxcy. *The Personal Writings of Eliza Roxcy Snow.* Edited by Maureen Ursenbach Beecher. Logan: Utah State University Press, 2000.

Southwick, Solomon. *Acts and Laws of the English Colony of Rhode-Island and Providence-Plantations in New-England in America.* Newport: Solomon Southwick, 1772.

Spurlock, John. "The Free Love Network in America, 1850 to 1860." *Journal of Social History* 21, no. 4 (Summer 1988): 765–79.

The Statutes at Large and Treaties of the United States of America from December 1, 1845 to March 3, 1851. Edited by George Minot. Boston: Little, Brown and Company, 1862.

Statutes of California, 33rd Session of the Legislature, 1899. San Francisco: Bancroft-Whitney Co., 1899.

Steet, Linda. *Veils and Daggers: A Century of "National Geographic's" Representation of the Arab World.* Philadelphia: Temple University Press, 2000.

Stoddard, Cora Frances., "The Drink Curve and the Immigration Curve." *Scientific Temperance Journal* 24, no. 9 (June 1915).

Stowe, Harriet Beecher. *Uncle Tom's Cabin, or Negro Life in the Slave States of America.* 3rd ed. London: C. H. Clarke and Company, 1852.

Straub, Jacques. *Straub's Manual of Mixed Drinks.* Chicago: R. Francis Welsh Publishing, 1913.

Tanner, John. *A Narrative of the Captivity and Adventures of John Tanner.* London: Baldwin & Cradock, 1830.

Taylor, Irwin. *Kansas Criminal Law and Practice.* Topeka: George W. Crane & Co., 1891.

Teel, Sandra J., Jesse E. Teel, and William O. Bearden. "Lessons Learned from the Broadcast Cigarette Advertising Ban." *Journal of Marketing* 43, no. 1 (January 1979): 45–50.

Thayer, James Steel. "The Berdache of the Northern Plains: A Socioreligious Perspective." *Journal of Anthropological Research* 36, no. 3 (Autumn 1980): 287–93.

Tilley, Carol L. "Seducing the Innocent: Frederic Wertham and the Falsifications That Helped Condemn Comics." *Information & Culture* 47, no. 4 (2012): 383–413.

Tobin-Schlesinger, Kathleen. "The Changing American City: Chicago Catholics as Outsiders in the Birth Control Movement." *U.S. Catholic Historian* 15, no. 2 (Spring 1997): 67–85.

Todes, Daniel P. "Pavlov and the Bolsheviks." *History and Philosophy of the Life Sciences* 17, no. 3 (1995): 379–418.

"To the Editors." *Connecticut Evangelical Magazine* 7, no. 8 (August 1814).

Treadway, Walter L. "Psychiatric Studies of Delinquents, Part IV, Some Constitutional Factors in Prostitution." *Public Health Reports* 35, no. 27 (July 2, 1920): 1575–92.

Trenholm, Christopher, et al. *Impacts of Four Title V, Section 510 Abstinence Education Programs*. Princeton NJ: Mathematica Policy Research, 2007.

Treadway, W. L. "Dedication and Opening of the Lexington Narcotic Farm." *Public Health Reports* 50, no. 31 (August 2, 1935): 996–1000.

Trenk, Marin. "Religious Uses of Alcohol among the Woodland Indians of North America." *Anthropos* 96, no. 1 (2001): 73–86.

Trexler, Richard. "Making the American Berdache: Choice or Constraint?" *Journal of Social History* 35, no. 3 (Spring 2002): 613–36.

———. *Sex and Conquest: Gendered Violence, Political Order, and the European Conquest of the Americas*. Ithaca NY: Cornell University Press, 1995.

Trice, Harrison M. "Alcoholics Anonymous." *Annals of the American Academy of Political and Social Science* 315 (January 1958): 108–16.

Turner, Richard Brent. "Mardi Gras Indians and Second Lines / Sequin Artists and Rara Bands: Street Festivals and Performances in New Orleans and Haiti." *Journal of Haitian Studies* 9, no. 1 (Spring 2003): 124–56.

Tuttle, Sarah. *Letters and Conversations on the Cherokee Mission*. 2nd ed. Boston: Massachusetts Sabbath School Society, 1837.

Twomey, John E. "The Citizens' Committee and Comic Book Control: A Study of Extragovernmental Restraint." *Law and Contemporary Problems* 20, no. 4 (Autumn 1955): 621–29.

Tyrrell, Ian. "Temperance, Feminism, and the WCTU: New Interpretations and New Directions." *Australasian Journal of American Studies* 5, no. 2 (December 1986): 27–36.

United States Census of Manufactures: 1958. Washington DC: Bureau of the Census, 1961.

"The Unwed Father." *American Medicine* 22, no. 11 (November 1916): 741–42.

U.S. Department of Justice. *Attorney General's Commission on Pornography: Final Report*. Washington DC: U.S. Department of Justice, July 1986.

"The Use of Narcotic Drugs in the South." *Medical Standard* 37, no. 4 (April 1914).

U.S. Government, Internal Revenue Regulations No. 35. Washington DC: Government Printing Office, 1915. http://www.druglibrary.org/schaffer/history/e1910/harrisonact.htm.

Verduin, Kathleen. "'Our Cursed Natures': Sexuality and the Puritan Conscience." *New England Quarterly* 56, no. 2 (June 1983): 220–37.

Viereck, George Sylvester. "An Object Lesson in Prohibition." *International* 8, no. 3 (March 1914).

Vincent, Murray, and Patricia S. Dod. "Community and School Based Intervention in Teen Pregnancy Prevention." *Theory into Practice* 28, no. 3 (Summer 1989): 191–97.

Virginia, Assembly of. *Acts of the Assembly Passed in the Colony of Virginia, from 1662 to 1715*. London, 1727.

Walker, Anders. "Legislating Virtue: How Segregationists Disguised Racial Discrimination as Moral Reform Following Brown v. Board of Education." *Duke Law Journal* 47, no. 2 (November 1997): 399–424.

Walker, Edwin. *Who Is the Enemy; Anthony Comstock or You?* New York: Edwin C. Walker, 1903.

Watson, Alan D. "The Lottery in Early North Carolina." *North Carolina Historical Review* 69, no. 4 (October 1992): 365–87.

Webb, George. *The Office and Authority of a Justice of the Peace . . . Collected from the Common and Statute Laws of England and Acts of the Assembly, now in Force; and Adapted to the Constitution and Practice of Virginia*. Williamsburg: William Parks, 1736.

Weber, Henriette. "Silk Stockings and Sedition." *North American Review* 225, no. 839 (January 1928).

Weisheit, Ralph, and William White. *Methamphetamine: Its History, Pharmacology and Treatment*. Center City MN: Hazelden, 2009.

Weitzer, Ronald. "Prostitutes' Rights in the United States: The Failure of a Movement." *Sociological Quarterly* 32, no. 1 (Spring 1991): 23–41.

Wertham, Frederic. *Seduction of the Innocent*. New York: Rinehart, 1954.

White, James C., MD. "Leprosy in America." *New York Medical Journal* 29, no. 2 (February 1879): 196–200.

Whitlock, Brand. "The White Slave." *Forum* 51 (February 1914): 193–216.

Wiedman, Dennis. "Upholding Indigenous Freedoms and Medicine: Peyotists at the 1906–1908 Oklahoma Constitutional Convention and First Legislature." *American Indian Quarterly* 36, no. 2 (Spring 2012): 215–46.

Williams, Alfred Mason. *Sam Houston and the War of Independence in Texas*. Boston: Houghton, Mifflin and Co., 1895.

Williams, Edward Huntington, MD. *The Question of Alcohol*. New York: Goodhue Company, 1914.

Williams, John Hoyt. *Sam Houston: Life and Times of Liberator of Texas an Authentic American Hero*. New York: Touchstone, 1994.

Wilson, Clarence True. "Alcohol the Barrier to Patriotism." *Scientific Temperance Journal* 24, no. 9 (June 1915).

Wollstonecraft, Mary. *A Vindication of the Rights of Woman*. 1792. Reprint, London: T. Fisher Unwin, 1891.

Wood, Janice. "Prescription for a Periodical: Medicine, Sex, and Obscenity in the Nineteenth Century, as Told in 'Dr. Foote's Health Monthly.'" *American Periodicals* 18, no. 1 (2008): 26–44.

———. *The Struggle for Free Speech in the United States, 1872–1915: Edward Bliss Foote, Edward Bond Foote, and Anti-Comstock Operations*. New York: Routledge, 2008.

Woodhull, Victoria. *Victoria Woodhull's Complete and Detailed Version of the Beecher-Tilton Affair*. Washington DC: J. Bradley Adams, 1872.

Woodsum, Jo Ann. "Gender and Sexuality in Native American Societies: A Bibliography." *American Indian Quarterly* 19, no. 4 (Autumn 1995): 527–54.

Workingmen's Party of California. *Chinatown Declared a Nuisance!* San Francisco: Workingmen's Party of California, 1880.

Yarbrough, Fay. "Legislating Women's Sexuality: Cherokee Marriage Laws in the Nineteenth Century." *Journal of Social History* 38, no. 3 (Winter 2004): 385–406.

Young, Ann Eliza. *Wife No. 19, or The True Story of a Life in Bondage, Being a Complete Exposé of Mormonism*. Hartford CT: Dustin, Gilman & Co., 1876.

Zollmann, Carl. "Moving Picture Abuses and Their Correction in the United

States." *Marquette Law Review* 21, no. 3 (April 1937): 105–15.

Index

carriage tax, 32, 220n3

Carroll, Earl, 140, 143-45, 151

cartoon violence, 3-4

Cary, Virginia, 48-49, 52, 55

castration, 31

Catholic Film Society, 125

Catholic Holy Name Society, 145

Catholics: and bikinis, 148; and birth control, 89-90, 94; and drug abuse, 111; and homosexuality, 170; and interracial sex and marriage, 237n33; and pornography, 189; and Prohibition, 96; and teen pregnancy and sex education, 172-73; and temperance movement, 56-57, 223n75; and tobacco smoking, 10; and vice in movies and theatrical performances, 124-25, 132-36, 144-45; and violent comic books, 194

CAT scans, 199

censorship, 81-87, 101, 123-26, 129-35, 161, 231n7, 232nn15-16

Cerf, Bennett, 86

Chester, John, 39

Child Online Protection Act of 1998, 156

child pornography, 156

Chinese Americans, 59, 62-66, 127-29, 136, 178, 186, 204, 211-12

Chinese Exclusion Act of 1882, 63

Christian Coalition, 155

Christian Crusade, 173

Christiansen, Richard, 4

Christie, Chris, 182-83

Church, Brooke Peters, 192

Church Federation, 143-44, 150-51

cigarettes, 1, 6, 10, 102-4, 197-204, 243n30. See also tobacco smoking

Civil Rights Act of 1964, 177, 208

civil rights movement, 179

Civil War, 57-58

The Clansman, 127

Clinton, Bill, 156, 170, 183-84

Clinton, Hillary, 183-84

Coca Cola, 185

cocaine, 2, 65-67, 112, 178-82, 185-86, 197

cock fights, 99

Cohan, George M., 151

Colbert, Stephen, 200

Coleridge, Samuel Taylor, 65

Colgate, Samuel, 79

Collins, Joseph, 85-86

Collins, Wilkie, 65

Columbine High School, 190-91, 242n16

comic books, 193-95

Commission on Pornography, 158

Communications Decency Act of 1996, 156

Communism, 173-74

The Compleat Sportsman (Jacob), 99

Comprehensive Drug Abuse Prevention and Control Act of 1970, 177-78

Comstock, Anthony, 77-83, 87-88, 144, 175

Comstock Act of 1873, 80-84, 88-90, 131, 155-57

Confessions of an English Opium-Eater (De Quincey), 65

Connecticut Society for the Promotion of Good Morals, 38

consensual violence, 20, 53, 100

consent: and adultery, 23; and alcohol drinking and drunkenness, 96, 108-9; and boxing, 100; and child pornography, 156; and drug abuse, 187; and Hamilton-Burr duel, 21;

consent (*continued*)

    and homosexuality, 98, 165; and movies, 125; power of, 23, 214; and striptease, 154; and theatrical performances, 143, 234n42; and tobacco smoking, 202–3; and violent entertainment, 99–100

contraception. *See* birth control

Controlled Substances Act of 1970, 185

Corio, Ann, 140–41

cosmetics, 106

A Counter-Blaste to Tobacco (James I), 9–10

COYOTE (Call Off Your Old Tired Ethics), 207

crack cocaine, 179–82, 187, 241n82

Crafts, Wilbur, 131, 232n16

Crane, George, 167

Crawford, Joan, 134

cross-dressing, 97

Crothers, Thomas, 69

cursing, 20, 28

The Cyclopedia of Temperance, Prohibition, and Public Morals, 95

dancing, 107–8

Dandridge, Ray G., 141–42

darts, 18

Davis, Kingsley, 206–7

Dawson, Jonas, 217n28

death penalty, 22, 31

debtor's prison, 15

Democratic Party, 90, 183

Dennett, Mary Ware, 5, 90, 101

De Quincey, Thomas, 65

designer drugs, 184–87

dice, 18

Diggs, Rebecca, 115

Dilley, Hannah, 25

dipsomania, 109

divorce, 25, 218n42, 232n16

Dixon, Thomas F., Jr., 127

The Doctor Looks at Literature (Collins), 85–86

dog fighting, 100

domestic violence, 5–6, 209–10, 244n42

Donnerstein, Ed, 190

Douglas, Stephen A., 74

Dow, Neal, 96–97

drug abuse, 63–69, 111, 176–83, 197–99, 204, 207–13, 240n82. *See also specific drugs*

drug paraphernalia, 91

Drums Along the Mohawk, 129

drunkenness. *See* alcohol drinking and drunkenness

Du Bois, W. E. B., 60–61, 107–8

dueling, 20–22, 217n30, 218n32

Durante, Jimmy, 120

Eastland, James, 162

Eckerd Drug Stores, 185

Edmunds Act of 1882, 74

Edwin Meese Center for Legal and Judicial Studies, 181

Eisenhower, Dwight D., 165

Elkins, Tice, 148

emotional growth, five sexual stages of, 167

empowerment of women, 208–12

Equal Employment Opportunity Commission, 209

Essays on Sex, 90

eugenics, 89

Evans, John, 40

Evans, Polly, 40

Evarts, Jeremiah, 45

excise taxes, 32, 220n3

Ku Klux Klan, 127

Ladova, Rosalie, 117
Lady Chatterley's Lover (Lawrence), 160–62, 236n26, 237n30
Laidlaw, Robert W., 166–67
Lane, H. E., 119
lap dancing, 154
laudanum, 65, 68–69, 203–4, 211–12
Lausche, Frank, 162
Lawrence, D. H., 160, 236n26
Lawrence v. Texas, 169–70
Lebensreform (Life Reform), 118
A Lecture on Heads, 37–38
Lectures to Young Men (Burnap), 48
Lee, Gypsy Rose, 140–41
Legion of Decency, 135, 161
leprosy, 62
Leslie, Lew, 140, 151
Letournel, Joanne, 141
Letters on Female Character (Cary), 48
levity, 33
Lewis, Dio, 97
LGBTQ, 170–71
Librium, 204–5
licentiousness, 5, 26, 34, 46
Life Reform (Lebensreform), 118
Lincoln, Abraham, 75–76
liquor. *See* alcohol drinking and drunkenness
literature, obscene, 83–87
Little Caesar, 135
Little Mothers' Association, 172
Little Review, 83
living pictures, 139–40
Lord, Daniel, 134–35
lotteries, 29
Louisiana Purchase, 33–34
Love Rights of Women, 90

Loving, Mildred Jeter, 164
Loving, Richard, 164
Loving v. Virginia, 164
Loy, Myrna, 136
LSD, 178
Lucky Strikes, 103
Lyerly, D. K., 67

MacLaine, Shirley, 151
MADD (Mothers Against Drunk Driving), 194
Magdalen Facts, 171–72
mandatory minimum sentences, 177–82
Mann Act of 1910, 82–83
Manousos, Demetrius, 172
Manslaughter, 132
Marbury v. Madison, 220n3
marijuana, 2, 111–13, 178, 182, 184–86, 189, 197–200
Mary Lyndon (Nichols), 50–51, 134–35
Mason, Perry, 5
Massachusetts Society for the Prevention of Vice, 38
Mather, Cotton, 12, 14, 16, 26
Mather, Increase, 24
Mathew, Theobald, 57
Mattachine Society, 166
Maule, Frances, 208
Maurstad, Tom, 190
May-pole dancing and drinking, 26
McCaffrey, Joseph, 151
McCarthy, J. J., 69
McCool, Mike, 100
McDonald, William, 99
McKay, Claude, 142–43
McLaughlin, Dewey, 163
Meese, Edwin, 157–58
Memoirs of a Woman of Pleasure, 39